CRAZY SISTA
Cooking

Cuisine &
Conversation

With

LUCY ANNE BUFFETT

LULU'S™

by **LUCY ANNE BUFFETT** and
ANASTASIA ARNOLD

Foreword by JIMMY BUFFETT

Jennifer
Hope you have
a ball
crazy cooking!
Gumbo
Love
Lulu Buffett
March '16
Birmingham

CRAZY SISTA *Cooking*

Cuisine & Conversation

With

Lucy Anne Buffett

Foreword by JIMMY BUFFETT

Copyright © 2007
by Lucy Anne Buffett and Anastasia Arnold

ISBN: 978-0-9799699-1-1

Already Done, LLC
200 East 25th Avenue
Gulf Shores, AL 36542
251-967-LULU (5858)
www.crazysistacooking.com

Food Photography by: Sara Essex
Location Photography by: Stephen Savage
Design by: Wimmer Cookbooks

Manufactured in the United States of America
First Printing: December, 2007 10,000 copies
Second Printing: January, 2008 10,000 copies
Third Printing: April, 2008 15,000 copies
Fourth Printing: September, 2008 40,000 copies

A portion of the proceeds from the sale of this book benefits LuLu's Love Fund.

WIMMER
COOKBOOKS

A CONSOLIDATED GRAPHICS COMPANY

800.548.2537 wimmerco.com

This book is dedicated to

Mara and Melanie

For your entire lives, you have had
to share me with the pursuit
of my dreams. You were my reason
for never giving up.
Thank you.

"Above all, have a good time."

~Julia Child

FELLOW EATERS,

If you don't think that food is important in the Buffett family, let me tell you a little story. In the early fall of 1979, our father, J.D. Buffett, was in Boston on a business trip that was suddenly cut short by the arrival of Hurricane Frederic in the Gulf of Mexico. By all opinions, Frederic was headed toward Mobile Bay. For a short period at the beginning of World War II, my dad had been stationed in Fort Kent, Maine, where, despite being a Creole boy from the Gulf Coast, he developed a devotion to Maine lobsters. He loved them, and every time he went anywhere in New England for business, he came back with cardboard boxes of lobsters. So even though he was rushing like mad through the crowded corridors of Logan Airport to get back on hurricane patrol at his home in Daphne, Alabama, he could not resist stopping at a lobster pound in the airport and grabbing a couple of crustaceans to go.

To many, a box of lobsters might not seem to be a top-priority item in the way of hurricane preparations, but to my dad it was as important as the duct tape, extension cords, generator, chain saw, and numerous other items he stored in his arsenal to combat the ever-present hurricanes he had grown up preparing for and living through. When he arrived home, he became a whirling dervish, clearing the pier of summer fun gear, securing the hurricane shutters on the house, and lashing down anything that could be turned into deadly projectiles by hundred-mile-an-hour wind gusts. The last item of business was securing his most prized possession, THE GRILL. This was the grill on which he cooked to perfection his famous tenderloin or grilled fish. It had been constructed out of titanium plates designed as armor for warships and smuggled in pieces from the welding shop to the pier at Homeport. It was built to last forever. When he was finished with all his storm preparations, all that was left to do was eat those lobsters.

Our dad was, to say the least, "old school." He was the son of a sea captain and took his first steps on the deck of a rolling ship. He was becalmed and nearly starved on the Sargasso Sea at age 3. He flew through World War II from Maine to Africa to the heights of the Himalayas. J.D. Buffett did not run from life or hurricanes. He rode them out, and on the night of September 12, 1979, when the most devastating hurricane ever to hit Mobile roared up the bay and bore down on the bluffs of his beloved Homeport, he was boiling lobsters in an iron pot over a gas flame and sipping a Cutty Sark on the rocks. His words to me on the phone that night before the splintered pine trees and oak branches snapped the lines of communications to Alabama were, "No goddamn hurricane is going to keep me from my lobsters. We're all battened down, and the bugs are almost ready. If it gets us, it gets us, but at least we go out dining in style."

Frederic did not get "The Grill," but it was lost at sea briefly in a subsequent storm, salvaged and returned to service on the re-built pier. After my dad passed away, J.D's grill was inherited by my sister Lucy and became part of the kitchen gear for her new life as restaurateur at her own little waterfront spot. The grill had been passed, and LuLu's Sunset Grill was born.

It has now been a decade since LuLu left Hollywood for Fairhope to pursue her lifelong love of food. I had been one of the lucky early observers and tasters as LuLu made her journey from cooking at home to becoming a chef on a great yacht, to her years in New Orleans as a food advisor, and finally to trading the sounds of sirens and traffic in Los Angeles for the sounds of crickets and bullfrogs along the shores of Weeks Bay. There she found the perfect place to launch her own spot. After several successful years on Weeks Bay, navigating the floodwaters of Fish River and the politics of South Alabama, LuLu's and J.D's grill moved on to Gulf Shores where both became landmarks along the Intracoastal Waterway.

We Buffetts are used to moving around, and I travel from South Florida to Southern California a lot. Because LuLu's lies directly on that flight path, now I can stop not only for fuel but for a lunch of my sister's cooking. Somehow that stopover meal served along the banks of the Intracoastal Waterway does more than just satisfy the food fetish that began with my grandmother, was nurtured by my dad, and polished up like a shiny ship's bell by my baby (and some say crazy) sister. Those moments spent at LuLu's keep me connected to where I came from. I can drop my anchor in a booth by the water and savor a bowl of gumbo; for me there is more than fresh crabmeat, oysters, okra, shrimp, and filé powder in that bowl. It also contains the faces and memories of friends, family, and events that remind me of the child of the coast that I was and hope to always be.

In this book, LuLu has gotten it all down on paper, with great recipes for food that comes with history. It is a guide to turning your own kitchen into a coastal watering hole for an evening, whether you're in Gulf Shores or Gloucester, Pensacola or Portland. It's all about making a good meal with great

friends in a beautiful setting of your choice, where for an hour or two you too can forget the troubles of the day and be a child of the coast. Bon Appétit.

Jimmy Buffett
Sag Harbor, New York
August '07

Photo by Pamela Jones Photography

DEAR FRIENDS,

This is not your basic "how to" cookbook. I like to think of it more as a visit to my kitchen. You're sitting at the counter as I vigorously chop vegetables and loudly tell stories with a sometimes annoying drawl. We're drinking some iced tea or something stronger, in which case, I tend to get louder and my drawl gets crazy lazy. Good music is playing in the background, and I mean good songs with melodies and lyrics that rip out your heart or make you feel like a princess, like Frank Sinatra, Jackson Brown, or Seal (not that devil music that sounds like a lot of scratchy screaming and sometimes passes for a song). There is plenty of laughter bouncing off the walls as tree frogs squirm across a picture window overlooking the bucolic river. Pick any random day; that is where you can find me, cooking up a storm and talking up a blue streak with family and friends around the stove.

Cooking has been a main character in my personal story since I was a ten-year-old child frying my own French fries for an afternoon snack. At that time, I was also making consistent C's in conduct due to too much "visiting with my neighbor" (as the nuns used to call it). My love of cooking and talking both came naturally, as did my inclination toward rebellion. When everybody else was trying to fit in, I gravitated toward anything different or anything I wasn't supposed to be doing. It was more fun when I didn't get caught, but when I did, I wasn't deterred from doing it again. That's where the crazy part comes in.

Ah, the crazy sister or *sista,* as we say in our neck of the woods. You either are one, have one, or know one. You can trace the gene pool of any Southern family and find one. Sometimes she may seem a bit daft, but her brilliance is in how she makes you think she is crazy because of the simple, peaceful way she views this complicated world. Other times she's the hell-on-wheels wild child, living life out loud, sneaking out of her bedroom window into the deep purple darkness of midnight to meet friends at the bowling alley. That was me. For as long as I can remember, I have prayed to be a simple woman. To date, that prayer has been unanswered. I used to think it was a curse. I have come to accept it as a backward blessing.

I came by it honestly. The people in my family have never been very good at coloring inside the lines. We don't seem to think the way normal people do. My mother blamed it on chance. My father blamed it on the tides. My sister blames it on my brother. And my brother blames it on my grandfather, but, as you may have heard in the song, he has no one but himself to blame.

My mother used to say that she wondered who had kidnapped her "good little girl" when I hit my teens. Once I grew up, I told her all my early wildness must have been the creative part of me exercising self expression. When she laughingly agreed, it was all the absolution I needed for causing my father and her so much grief. I could move on and embrace the new notion that "crazy" wasn't the same as bad and "different" was a badge of courage instead of a demerit.

These days most of my conversations with friends and strangers gravitate toward the subject of my restaurant, LuLu's. If my life were a movie, LuLu's would be the part where the superhero flies into the picture and rescues the desperate heroine from the clutches of disaster. Then they sail into a blazing sunset, eating happily every after. Well, that's my fairytale.

It was never my dream to own a restaurant. For as long as I can remember, I've wanted to write a book. I've tried over the years and postponed it for both frivolous and heart-breaking reasons. Every time my life began a new chapter, the dream would shift a little, but it always persisted.

I vividly remember the day I gave up the dream. I was walking across the weathered grey deck at the old LuLu's; it was filled with people at picnic tables covered with baskets laden with food I'd grown up loving on the Gulf Coast of Alabama: fried shrimp and oysters, gumbo, grilled grouper, and fried green tomatoes. I had been in business for two years and enjoyed the status of resident big shot, which in the restaurant business meant I was the owner, dishwasher, and every other position in between. That day, someone had not shown up for work, and I was filling in on the floor. There was a happy buzz in the air, and the waterfront view was postcard perfect. A local band was pounding out rocking beach favorites. The smell of burgers on the grill made it feel like your own backyard. Locals were two deep at the gazebo bar that had a spectacular view of Fish River overrun with pleasure boats filled with pleasure seekers.

People were enjoying my food and my hospitality, and that felt amazingly rewarding. Things seemed to be working, but a persistent little voice of discontent still gnawed away deep inside of me because the restaurant required all of my energy. Not having the time to write my book had become an anthem that I not-so-quietly suffered in silence; it was simply a great excuse. I was terrified. There's a lot of fear involved in getting what you want.

I had a good thing going, and this was not my first ride on the turnip truck of life. Some of the wisdom and Southern stoicism that blessed my mother and grandmothers had actually rubbed off on me. It became very clear that all of my time would be required if LuLu's was to become "the little dive that could." I made a commitment to seeing it through, no matter what, and no matter where it took me. Unlike the other times I had stopped work on my cookbook, this time I did so without resentment or resignation. I understood that an incredible opportunity was in front of me and it had been put there for a reason. I didn't need to know why or where it was going; I simply had to say yes and have a little faith. When I did, it eventually led me back to these pages. I'm not saying it happened overnight or that it was easy, but it happened. Besides, I knew I was a better cook than I was a writer, and I loved cooking as much as I loved to read and write. Cooking was a job I already enjoyed, and for the first time in my life, I was working for myself. I never imagined that putting my heart and soul into LuLu's would lead me back to my dream.

LuLu's is my miracle. It has grown from a tiny, dilapidated dive to a national vacation destination. Friends and families flock to our shore for an authentic Gulf Coast experience: waterfront, sand, fabulous food, live music every night, and an ocean of fun. Here they can escape the rigors and demands of their lives for an hour or two, or sometimes ten, when taking a vacation from your vacation is needed. As we say on the back of our menu, "Our job is to make you forget about yours for awhile." This book is my attempt to share the light-hearted magic that makes LuLu's a one-of-a-kind experience.

Most of the recipes in this book are what we serve at LuLu's with a few from my personal repertoire thrown in for extra flavor. You'll find Southern and coastal classics written for ease and simplicity because in the "world of me," I get bored quickly and frustrated with anything complicated.

The introductions to the various chapters are anecdotal essays that will give you a glimpse into the hopefully humorous "behind-the-scenes" life of LuLu's and me. Some of my beloved friends and family, who have been gracious enough to be guinea pigs over the years, have offered a few stories just to keep me honest. I hope you enjoy the mental meanderings, or if you prefer, move directly to the Specialty Drinks section and get this party rolling. Either way, this book is for you. I humbly thank you for holding it in your hands.

Gumbo Love.....

Lucy Anne "LuLu" Buffett
Point Clear, Alabama
August 3, 2007

The story goes something like this: "Once upon a time, a Gulf Coast darling born and raised in one L.A. (Lower Alabama) found herself living and dying in another L.A. (Los Angeles, California). She was born of a clan of adventurous spirits, thriving on life in the sun and life on the run. Still, LuLu knew she'd had just about enough of the plastic pace of Hollywood and yearned for the sweet comfort of home and a way of life that is about living.

"With many failures in her pocket and many triumphs in her heart, she packed her bags and her cats, Jazz and Whisper, and headed back to parts known, back to the place where her roots had grown. The memories of a childhood scented by magnolias, crab boils, tire swings, and the glories of Mobile Bay were calling her home.

"LuLu is a passionate entertainer, a natural storyteller, and, not unlike her big brother, Jimmy, can throw a party you will be hard-pressed to forget...or possibly, remember. She moved to a beautiful spot on Weeks Bay, Alabama, and LuLu's Sunset Grill was born – 'Where life is good and lunch lasts forever.'"

That's the story...at least as far as I've been told! My daughter Mara wrote that piece to launch LuLu's website, and I love it. In addition to her lovely prose, however, there is one piece of the story I should add: my parents, J.D. and Loraine "Peets" Buffett, were in failing health and needed me to come home and assist in their care. Family ties have always been strong in the Buffett clan, and I believe Peets and J.D. guided me home at just the right time in my life. I hadn't intended to become a restaurateur, but the stars aligned just so for that inkling of an idea to become a reality. And the rest, as they say, is history.

Starting out in LuLu's original location, I had to work with available materials, which were rough... at best. The existing business, which had pretty much been a glorified bait shop and hangout for a fairly rough crowd, had fallen into disrepair. Just as I was negotiating the lease, Hurricane Georges pounded Weeks Bay, flooding the facility. It turned out to be a blessing; all of the kitchen equipment had to be replaced. Too bad the same was not true of the infrastructure! Rain came through the light fixtures. Equipment would suddenly come on unassisted. Mysterious light switches would turn on nothing! And the plumbing? Fahgettaboutit! It took long weeks of elbow-grease and hard labor to bring the tiny digs to some semblance of order. There were many times, drenched in sweat with a frayed do-rag on my head, that I thought about throwing in the towel. It seemed like every time

I turned around I found rotten wood and burst pipes. I thought, "This is too much — I can't do it." And then after a cleansing breath and a cold beer, I picked myself up off the floor, wiped dirty tears across my face, and got back in the game. My parents had taught all their children to be strong and resourceful; the various chapters of my life had taught me to be self-sufficient. No one else was going to tote this load; it was up to me. This was one of the first hurdles I crossed in my journey to create LuLu's, and I'm grateful for

the lesson. It takes the reality of being the one scrubbing the toilets and mopping the greasy floors to be able to enjoy success with humility.

There are few things that can't be perked up with a coat of sunny yellow, pink, or turquoise paint! I chose Caribbean colors to cover the worn boards and cheer the place up. The palette I picked for my quirky little dive boosted my spirits and went a long way in establishing the basics of the LuLu's lifestyle that would eventually emerge. I did not, however, want to polish away the essence of the waterfront dive bar. There was something genuine and familiar in the layers of history that had accumulated, the flotsam and jetsam of memorabilia that defined it as well-loved. I decided to keep as much of the weathered character as possible, dress up the rest with funky island décor, serve terrific food, showcase great music, and have myself a "high-class dive."

The original restaurant comprised a very small (did I mention it was tiny?) building, a separate gazebo bar, and a short, two-tiered deck connecting the two. At first I had very few tables under roof. Just five small two-tops fit inside the corridor of interior space not consumed by the kitchen, which was miniscule. On the screened porch there were five wooden booths. Outside on the deck

I had something like six picnic tables. The bar was rigged with about a dozen PVC-pipe-and-plastic-strap barstools. That's it. I figured, well, with only enough seats for a couple dozen customers at any given time. I should be able to handle it. I had the crazy idea that running a little waterfront joint wouldn't take up much of my time; I could

LuLu's Weeks Bay at the Sunset Grill

spend lazy afternoons overlooking Weeks Bay from my vantage point on the porch, writing (this very cookbook) and watching sunsets. This restaurant business was going to be a breeze! Well, that's not at all what Fate had in mind.

Word spread like wildfire, and very soon we were overrun. "LuLu's Sunset Grill" had hit the map. We began planting picnic tables on the lawn between the deck and the dock. It was becoming a bona fide tourist destination, and before long another bar was added, the kitchen expanded, decks extended, and pavilions built. My dad's dilapidated old fishing boat was transformed into an oyster bar. If that weren't enough, a pirate shipwreck was brought onto the beach to function as a bandstand. Whoa, Baby! Life moves fast — grab a helmet!

At the beginning, I had some pretty idealistic notions. I wanted to serve only the finest ingredients and even thought we could grow our own vegetables and catch fresh shrimp right out of Mobile Bay. Maybe I could even educate the locals to the continental cuisine I had come to love after ten years on the West Coast. *Surely,* if someone crossed my cosmopolitan path, they'd gladly follow it!

My delusion that this would be easy swiftly melted away in the face of stark reality. Owning and managing a restaurant is a full-time gig; well, only if the term *full-time* is used in this instance to mean consuming every waking moment. I learned quickly that flexibility is essential and practicality trumps idealism almost every time. In other words, my career as a shrimper was over before it began, and the closest I got to a garden was a dilapidated john-boat moored at the restaurant entrance, which I had filled with cricket caca and, literally, a boat-load of fresh herbs that grew as big as elephant ears.

Still, I was determined "homemade" would prevail, by God, even if "home-grown" had to fall by the wayside. I tried to raise the sophistication level of the menu with items such as grilled salmon, rice pilaf, and stir-fried veggies...even if I would be the only one to order them! Also, I insisted that we serve mint from the boat garden in the iced tea. One day a very kind elderly gentleman dressed in overalls stopped a server and said, "Ma'am, excuse me, but there's something in my tea." "Yes, sir. That's mint," she politely replied. "Maybe so," he said, "but there's still a leaf in my tea. Can you get me another one?"

"Light-bulb" moments are astonishing; the truth hits you faster than a sneeze. That day, I learned I am what I am: a Gulf Coast guppy, born and reared on red-clay gullies and warm, brackish bays. I may have lived in New York and Los Angeles, but *I* was L.A., Lower Alabama, from my fake fingernails all the way down to my pretty painted-pink toes. And so was LuLu's. I had to let LuLu's be what it was, *just this side* of a "high-class dive" with the finest food I could muster, served with home-grown love. I accepted this truth, succumbed to popular opinion, and put in a fryer. For folks in L.A., if you're sitting at the water's edge at sunset, it's only right and proper to have Southern-style *fried* seafood with your cold beer. I learned to go with the flow; we pretty much made it up as we went along...we still do.

LuLu's became the local watering hole. It was a hit; it was a vibe. More than anything, it was fun. Regulars emerged, staking claim on tables and barstools. Romances blossomed, soap-opera dramas unfolded, marriages were put asunder, and lifelong friendships were formed. Bail was set and paid. The denizens of Fish River and Magnolia River, the "River Rats," kept the bar busy *every* Sunday. (To *not* be at LuLu's was to be out of the loop.) It was the official unofficial meeting place; there was always a knot of "Rats" stationed at the end of the boat-bar. It was town-hall, community-center, front-porch...for many of the folks along the rivers and bays, it was church.

LuLu's also became a second home for the employees as they adopted each other as brothers and sisters. Many guests and employees were on a first-name basis and often fraternized socially apart from the restaurant. We kept a pretty feisty roster of servers though, and to the day I die I will never forget the stunning discovery that one waitress was running her own triple-X-rated "service" industry in the parking lot after hours! When I confronted her about it, she didn't deny it; rather, she told me, "Well, Miss Lucy, ever since I started working here, I've gone back to my bad ways!" I often called LuLu's the "Second Chance Café" (I've had so many second chances in my life), and I told her I would put

this behind us and give her another chance. She didn't return to LuLu's, but I wish her well (and hope she hasn't gone back to her "bad ways").

I'm a stickler for great customer service, and I've had to be tough sometimes to protect the high standards I expect of my staff; I've been met with some very interesting management challenges. Still, I've always known that the employees are the heartbeat of LuLu's and that it wouldn't exist without their enthusiasm and dedication. I love them, and they know it. It's a famous fact that I can't get through a staff meeting without tears of gratitude. Some of the very

first employees I hired at the "old" LuLu's are still with me all these years and many dramas later.

The kitchen is the soul of LuLu's — but without the employees who seasoned it, none of it would have happened. And that's why I posted bail as often as I did. The sound of unintelligible rap "music" and screeching guitars emanating from the cramped, broiling hot kitchen was as pungent as the aromas of food. Whatever kept the rag-tag band of cooks happy was just fine with me. The kitchen was roughly the size of a Honda Civic and featured a firebrand crew of goateed boys willing to endure the smothering heat, leaking roof, and never-ending food orders. I adored them, despite the fact that, more than once, they nearly drove me to quit LuLu's altogether.

Perhaps the Honda analogy is a bit of an overstatement...but the original kitchen was smaller than the ladies' room! Even after the expansion, no more than six people (including the dishwasher) could fit inside before they would start tripping over each other. Five people handling hundreds of orders for very hungry people...I know, it sounds like a recipe for disaster, but the kitchen crew handled each calamity and kept right on cooking. It was a liability to bring in more hands to help (especially mine); it screwed up their rhythm...best to let the tiny gang handle it on their own. They stuck up for each other like brothers. Once, when a key line cook was in jail, the kitchen manager brought him (and all the other inmates) fried chicken from the restaurant every day for the three weeks of his incarceration. From practical jokes to impromptu swimming parties, the staff found ways to deal with the never-ending stress of a commercial kitchen.

Rain profoundly affected the workings of LuLu's. All the refrigeration equipment had to be stored out the back door, so that any time fresh shrimp or mayonnaise was needed, it was out into the rain you'd go. During the early days, I had almost no seating under-roof, so customers stayed away when a storm was brewing. One day in sweltering heat, a thunderstorm began rumbling across the bay. Stifling hot and with no customers to serve, the entire kitchen staff ran out and leapt into the bay to cool off like puppies, playing and "chilling out." LuLu's wasn't about rules; I thought it was hilarious... but they did have to quit dripping before they were allowed back to work!

An integral part of the LuLu's Lifestyle is music. We started our ongoing practice of highlighting local musicians with live performances. In fact, one of our most beloved concerts was Bubba himself. Jimmy wasn't able to attend my mother's big 80th birthday party, so he decided to make it up to her with a *private* Mother's Day concert. Just a few friends, no big deal...yeah, right. As I mentioned earlier, word travels fast along our kudzu-vine. This double-top-secret info was in the hands of just a couple people. *Somehow,* more than a thousand people showed up for big brother's barefoot tribute to Mama! He welcomed the horde with his trademark grin, saying "Hey, I only told Jimbo Meador, what are all y'all doing here?" It was a fabulous solo concert for Mama; his set consisted exclusively of her favorites, and with Peets sitting right up front, he sang as though she were the only person watching under the stars that night. The family got in on the act with his daughter, Savannah, my daughters, Mara and Melanie, and me jumping up onto the pirate-ship stage to join him for our nostalgic rendition of the Crocodile Song. It was a fantastic night and a once-in-a-lifetime experience for everyone at LuLu's.

By 2003 the restaurant had reached maximum density; we were trying to put five pounds of sugar in a two-pound bag. The infrastructure couldn't handle any more pressure from expansion or development and the customers just kept coming. What a great problem, right? Our lease was due to expire and not to be renewed. So with the bittersweet blessings of our loyal locals, we bade adieu to LuLu's birthplace. But you know I can't just do something the easy way, hell, no! We had to make the move in style. I was moving LuLu's from the waterfront of Weeks Bay to the waterfront of the Intracoastal Waterway.

The ICW, as it's commonly known, is often frequented by barge traffic. I thought, "What could be more perfect?" We held a blow-out farewell party, loaded everything we could onto a barge (including the LuLu's vintage Falcon, palm trees, and the pirate-ship stage complete with a band) and escorted by a flotilla of River Rats, rocked the whole she-bang down Mobile Bay!

KNEAD THE DOUGH

One person's fierce passion, blind perseverance, creativity, and generosity are directly responsible for the sheer existence of LuLu's at Homeport Marina. Mac McAleer's inspiration and ideas shaped LuLu's into the thriving enterprise it is today. He shared his entrepreneurial wisdom with me when things at the old LuLu's reached critical mass. I had just learned that ownership of the property on which LuLu's stood had been transferred from the Weeks Bay Reserve Foundation to the State of Alabama via federal funds and that the state would not renew LuLu's lease. So my options were to find another place for LuLu's to flourish — or quit.

Mac's entrepreneurial spirit was honed in his years at the helm of Krispy Kreme® Doughnuts and later brought to bear in the creation of McAleer Marine boat-design and boat-building company. In his teens, Mac started in his father's Krispy Kreme® franchise at "the Loop" in Mobile and went on to become CEO of the corporation; the iconic "Hot Now" Krispy Kreme® slogan was born in Mac's brain. After he retired, he moved back to the area to do what he loves: live on the waterfront and play with boats. When he discovered LuLu's, he was impressed and saw potential for growth. Despite the fact that he is a successful entrepreneur, I didn't immediately seek out or want to take his advice. I was sad about the whole situation. I didn't want to leave my family of loyal customers and friends — I would have stayed there forever. I didn't want to have to start all over again and that's what it felt like I was going to have to do. I was tired. But in my family, we work. I needed a job, and Mac reminded me I had fifty other jobs to save beyond my own.

Mac persisted in offering his help. (That sounds so genteel. Actually, he nudged me, pulled me along, and eventually dragged me, sometimes kicking and screaming, into the realization of the new LuLu's.) Eventually I relented and listened to what he had to say. Lease problem or not, LuLu's had reached its maximum earning potential in the old location. A legal battle with the State of Alabama could prove not only costly and lengthy, but could ultimately result in failure. Even if I prevailed, I would never own the property and could be forced to move later after sinking money into much-needed repairs. Finally, he had seen what I'd done with this little venue and believed in my ability to recreate that success on a larger scale. He saw possibilities I didn't see. He knew what I didn't know: that I had already proven I could accomplish my goal.

Having Mac declare his confidence in me might be the greatest gift he has ever given me. He knew I could do it, but I didn't know how. And then Mac did what he does — he opened a door.

Mac's a savvy businessman, and he saw the potential in investing in LuLu's. He pitched me his plan. He said, "You just keep on cooking cheeseburgers, and I'll go find you a new location." Mac would find a suitable property based on our mutual specifications, buy it, and contract with LuLu's in a build-to-suit lease. At the end of the day, it was a sound business arrangement and a win-win situation for us both.

It didn't take me long to decide. As much as I loved LuLu's home below the Fish River Bridge, I had finally accepted that it held no future. The hunt was on for an appropriate site. Mac soon bird-dogged a spot in Gulf Shores, Alabama.

He had decided to aim for Gulf Shores based on his highly scientific research method of demographic targeting: checking out license plates in the parking lot. Mac wandered the LuLu's parking lot and noticed that tag after tag was from out-of-town. Where were they coming from? All over the country. That meant they had to be vacationing in Gulf Shores and Orange Beach. Mac understood something else in that parking lot: if you want a lot of customers, you've got to give them a place to park. His criteria were clear; he wanted to replicate the original location, complete with a river, a bridge, a marina, and a nice, big parking lot.

He found an old seafood market next to a bridge on the waterfront of the Intracoastal Waterway at the entrance to Gulf Shores. Mac took me to see it. I looked at the dilapidated building and thought, "You've got to be kidding." He wandered around the huge, deserted parking lot and declared, "This is perfect!" Mac is a visionary; he can literally picture a project's completion, and he saw something I did not see that day: the wildly successful LuLu's of today.

Groundbreaking began immediately, and the massive undertaking of renovating the six-thousand-square-foot market into a restaurant was underway. Mac put all his efforts into building LuLu's, putting off construction of the marina, which he named "Homeport" in honor of my parents' home. We weren't allowed to increase the existing footprint, so the structure was stripped down to its studs and trusses and completely redone. The number of people who transformed the derelict compound into LuLu-land is just shy of an army — a very busy army. LuLu's was completed just nine months after Mac closed on the property, a veritable miracle.

After some unforeseeable snags, LuLu's was ready to reopen on Mardi Gras...a fitting birthday, don't you think? We had intended to open a week earlier, but the incessant torrential rains of that early spring dampened our plan, so we decided to open "softly" as they say in the business. No ads.

No fanfare. Just unlock the doors on Mardi Gras Day. Our new staff was in place and ready to greet the public. The restaurant sparkled. We were ready. Or so we thought. That day, more than three hundred people were lined up outside the doors awaiting entry. The typical wait for a table was between three and four hours, and still they waited, God bless them. From the moment the doors opened until the exhausted and overwhelmed crew locked up, LuLu's was filled to capacity with old locals, new locals, Parrotheads, snowbirds, vacationers, grandparents, and children laughing and playing. People sent flowers of congratulations, grieved a little for the old place, praised the new place, danced to the music, and forgave our many opening-day jitters and hiccups. I was filled with gratitude and joy. He was right! It was going to work!

Thank you, Mac, for believing in me and giving me the opportunity to shine. Without your ideas and assistance, this new-and-improved dream wouldn't have come true; I am so very grateful. Thank you for fanning my spark into a brightly-burning flame. I love you.

NuLuLu's — Destination Fun

Of all the many chapters of my life, I can fairly easily break down the most recent ones into "old" LuLu's and "new" LuLu's. One day while we were building the new restaurant and LuLu's was still open on Weeks Bay, to clarify where the supplies were supposed to be delivered amid the confusion, we created the designations LuLu's or the new LuLu's which quickly became abbreviated to "NuLu's."

Anyone who knows me knows that I am rarely rendered speechless. But that is what happens, at least for a couple of moments, when I walk into "NuLu's." It is mind-boggling to wander into this beautiful bustling restaurant brimming with fun, food, and festivity. When I think of how all this started on Weeks Bay and how far it's come, I am awed. What began as my little "high-class" dive has become a massive enterprise celebrating a lifestyle that embodies working hard, playing hard, living well, and being happy. It humbles me into a moment of silence and gratitude to watch it in action.

For a while after we opened the new restaurant, I would occasionally be approached by an "old" patron commiserating with my eviction from the "old" place and lamenting how they "sure did like the 'old' place better." I would agree to how great it had been. I saw no need to share that during the last week before I closed the "old" restaurant, the point-of-sale system's computer brain collapsed, the soft-drinks gun exploded because rats (the rodent kind) had chewed the piping to pieces underneath the "quaint" gazebo bar, the sewage pumps became more temperamental than usual, all of the t-shirts in storage had mildewed, and both the freezer and ice machine went down. By the time we closed the door on Weeks Bay, I had done my grieving; I was excited to be moving on.

Though "NuLu's" kept the footprint of the existing building, every inch of the structure was torn down except the metal frame and trusses. Over a quarter mile of pipe was pulled out from what had been an ice plant over fifty years earlier. We were building a brand-spanking new restaurant from the floor up. It was thrilling to know I would have a facility that captured the spirit of the old LuLu's, but one that was built for business! I remember for the first month, every time I walked into the place I would muse to myself, "Damn, this is a *REAL* restaurant," as if what I had been doing for the last five years had been a hobby!

The current incarnation of LuLu's is mind-boggling. Through the efforts of hundreds of laborers, contractors, managers, advisors, friends, and family, LuLu's now employs more than 250 people, serving over a million customers a year! While LuLu's is still my baby, she's grown into needing a lot of nannies. An army (servers, bartenders, bussers, and bar-backs; business staff, finance managers, merchandisers, and website wizards; the security team, hostess brigade, dock tenders, and maintenance folks; the invisible kitchen crew, "Official Cheerful Sweeper," and fine management team) makes sure this baby's cradle keeps on rockin'.

As you cross the bridge from Pleasure Island onto mainland Gulf Shores, Alabama, look for LuLu's yellow flag flying over the bright pink restaurant with its vast turquoise roof at the entrance to Homeport Marina. You can't miss it. The first hint that you're about to encounter something out of the ordinary is the hundred or so enormous palms lining the road leading to the restaurant. Immediately they mentally transport you someplace else, someplace tropical, someplace FUN. Usually every space of the huge parking lot is filled, lively beach music is playing through unseen speakers, and there are folks everywhere — wandering around the gleaming Homeport Marina and checking out the yachts, idling in the merchandise shop, checking out the funny t-shirts, and playing volleyball and dancing on the beach. Throngs of people wait at the front door lounging in Adirondack lawn chairs and on teak benches, willing to enjoy the view for the two hours it sometimes takes to get a table.

Probably the most popular while-you-wait hang-out at LuLu's is the beach; it extends around fully half of the building from the bulkhead at the ICW to the parking lot. It is massive, dotted with dozens of picnic tables, and showcases the Bama Breeze bar, which is named after the song on my brother's *Take the Weather with You* CD. I was lucky enough to do a cameo in his video of the same name.

I played "the bar owner LuLu" who jumps up on the stage and sings "Freebird" with the band. It wasn't much of a stretch for me — more like typecasting, as they say in Hollywood — and it was loads of fun.

The LuLu's team does a terrific job of keeping the mood upbeat and lively. We show Sixties-era surf movies on a huge blow-up movie screen on the beach every Monday night in the summer...how fun is that? We have huge Mardi Gras and New Year's Eve parties. The annual Parrothead gathering, "Stars Fell on Alabama," and our "LuLupalooza" music festival are big time, joyful events. But I have to tell you, as fun as these events are, I would wager good money that the staff would vote the Annual Employee Party as their favorite!

"Gatemouth" Brown and Melanie Buffett

Naturally, music still plays an important part of LuLu's identity. You'll hear fun and familiar Buffett tunes on Radio Margaritaville most of the time, and live music every night. Our musicians range in influence and style, so there's always something fresh to experience. We've had some great names on the LuLu's stage including the late, great Clarence "Gatemouth" Brown. Whatever the genre, you can count on an energetic live set every time you visit LuLu's.

And then there are the children...everywhere you look! We could probably populate a medium-sized grammar school on any given Saturday. Without question, the beach is their domain, with our famous pirate-shipwreck stage, sand-mountains, volleyball courts, Fountain For Youth, ring-toss games, and snow-cone stand. The beach games are covered with kids playing happily together. They scale the sand-mountains, build sandcastles, and make sand-angels on the beach. We host annual events for them such as Noon Year's Eve, a special midday treat just for children. And they love the annual arrival, via seaplane, of Billy Claus (Santa's little brother from the tropics) at Christmastime.

Truly, LuLu's blows me away. Everywhere people are smiling, dancing, playing...just like old times, except now you could fill a concert hall with them. It's constant, relentless activity and movement-all-go-no-quit, all the time. It's alive with color and character — quirky tropical artifacts, nautical accessories, and tikis in every corner. Even the bathroom murals are a marvel. Footage from our many different LuLu's events is constantly looping on a jumbo-screen television. The walls are adorned with photos of my brother, sister, and me as children; black & white shots of my family; and magazine features too numerous to count. Even the dolphins get in on the act, showing off for the deck patrons with their regular displays.

The scale of LuLu's has grown beyond my wildest dreams. Our merchandising has gone from a few t-shirts and hats sold out of the bar to its own division handling the volume of LuLu's gear that is sold through our store pavilion and website. I can't tell you how much I love being out of town somewhere and unexpectedly seeing someone sporting a LuLu's t-shirt. I think, "Wow, that is so cool!"

For all the t-shirts and swag we sell, people still come to LuLu's for the food. We tried to "fancy-up" the menu when we re-opened. After just four days of kitchen confusion, we scrapped it and went back to doing what we do best, casual authentic regional cuisine. Translation: lots of fried food. To this day, our Big Fried Seafood basket is our best seller.

When the new LuLu's was under construction, it came as no surprise that the gleaming kitchen was the staff's favorite destination. The new kitchen seems like a vacation paradise in comparison to the old one. Wildfire business needs a kick-ass kitchen to match. We now have a gigantic space tricked-out with all the commercial necessities for smooth sailing. What was a chaotic, if determined, "kitchen-that-could" is now a well-oiled (not greasy!) machine. Once there was room for just six staffers; today's 2000-square-foot "back of the house" comfortably accommodates at least 50 people at any given time. Gone are the woven Rastafarian tams & ratty concert t-shirts... replaced by fresh hats and t-shirts emblazoned with "GALLEY" for the crew and the crisp white jackets and checkered pants of a bona fide kitchen for the supervisors. Only my loyal

Wes Loper, LuLu's favorite "son"

old LuLu's veteran kitchen crew could be so gleeful about shiny new stainless steel walk-in coolers and a 20-gallon gumbo kettle. And the chilly AC? Oh, happy day!

Not long after the new LuLu's opened, I was walking through the kitchen and heard a disembodied voice ordering, "We need more slaw on the line!" Immediately puzzled, I realized just how far my little LuLu's has come...all the way to a kitchen intercom system. So much for nudging your fellow line-cook in the ribs. And the kitchen music? Still awful, still loud, but hey, whatever works.

Great attitude is also what works for the whole restaurant. We hire qualified, upbeat team-players that "get it." I want my employees to be happy working at LuLu's. It has always been more than just a restaurant and bar; LuLu's is a lifestyle of carefree happiness, and my employees orchestrate that. When I'm by myself, sometimes I like to sit at one of my five favorite spots and just watch the symphony play. When they are "fine tuned," it's better than the Allman Brothers Band in the seventies. With so many moving parts, it's inevitable that things go awry from time to time, but the team has become so adept and capable over the years, it's rare that little problems become big ones.

Employees have come and gone...customers, too. Friends and relationships change, always. "In the tropics, they come and they go." But *all* of the people who've populated the LuLu's story have contributed to the fulfillment of our mission to serve authentic Gulf Coast food in a carefree, life-loving environment.

LuLu's continues to be a work in progress. One of the things Mac taught me is that no matter how well something is working, it can always be improved upon. I can't wait to find out what the future has in store for my little "high-class" dive. Whatever it is, we'll enjoy the ride! We'll simply continue to do what we've always done...make it up as we go.

THE HIGH WATER MARK

Six months after we opened LuLu's at Homeport Marina, just as I was getting the hang of feeding several hundred people a day, we were forced into reasoning with hurricane season. This wasn't the now infamous Katrina, which later would postpone future development we had planned around LuLu's, but Ivan, the strong Category 3 storm whose eye swept across Perdido Key, Florida, and Orange Beach, Alabama, mere spitting distance from our *brand new* restaurant in Gulf Shores.

Mac had gone to great lengths to ensure that the new facility embodied the quaintness and friendly ambiance that had endeared the original to thousands, but he also made sure it was constructed with the finest materials available and outfitted with the best equipment. Thus, he insisted on the 140-mph glass used in the retractable garage-door walls. This was our first big storm test. We developed a hurricane evacuation and button-down-the-facility plan. Outside, everything that was movable (and potentially airborne) was brought inside the building including all of the picnic tables, fans, outdoor televisions, volleyball nets, coolers, sand-pile toys, 300-plus teak chairs and bar stools, dozens of large garbage cans, the kids' fish feeder, large potted plants, and even my Mustang convertible.

As the storm approached, Mac and I drove to his house in Perdido Key and closed it down. We headed back to LuLu's on the beach road and were passing by the Flora-Bama® when we noticed a hand-painted sign in the window informing the few folks on the road *"We are still open!"* Joe Gilchrist, the owner, had been a great help and an inspiration in my early days as a saloon keeper. I called him once and cried, "How do I do this?" He chuckled and said, "Just mortgage your house, Baby, and pay it off after each season."

We immediately turned into the famous state-line bar. There were a few brave souls serving the handful of determined locals who refused to leave. After all, they probably hadn't been home in several days anyway. It was a given that the Flora-Bama® wasn't going to close until the last possible minute, and they told us that we could still get food. We ordered two cheeseburgers to go and had a beer as we waited, watching the Gulf boil with wicked anticipation of the dangerous guest about to arrive. I think we got the last two burgers ever cooked in the old place. There was an eerie feeling in the heavy air, and we left as soon as our food was ready, wishing all the best of luck. As it turned out, they would need it.

We made one final stop before heading back to LuLu's. When I was a youngster, the place where everyone gathered at the beach was called the Hangout. It was where Highway 59 dead ends into the Gulf of Mexico, and while there is no sign of the building remaining, for those of us who spent our coming-of-age summers there, it will live on as the Hangout forever. Now it is public parking that stretches from a municipal beach pavilion to *The Pink Pony Pub,* a holdover from the good ole days.

Mac and I walked out onto the blustery beach. We had both grown up on brackish Mobile Bay, a favorite port for high-category hurricanes, and were well acquainted with the pounding seas that serve as the knock on the door for an approaching storm. Soon, the seas would take on a very different behavior, a condition that coastal people recognize: the slick-as-glass sea that invites recklessness. We know it for what it is — the calm *before.* We're all too familiar with the fury of a terrible storm and its ensuing physical and emotional damage, and as beautiful and dramatic as the beach was that day, we also knew, as coastal dwellers do, it will be what it will be. The only thing we can do is what is in front of us and wait.

Mac and I drove back to the restaurant. Most of the roads had been closed, and a light, steady rain was beginning to fall. We stood for several minutes in complete silence just gazing at our beautiful project. The restaurant had been open a mere six months, and the massive challenge of turning a pristine five-acre inlet into a one-hundred-slip, first-class marina was still in progress. We had done what we could to protect the restaurant. To preserve the contents of the coolers and freezers, Mac's guys hooked up an enormous generator in back of the restaurant to kick on automatically when the inevitable loss of electricity would occur later that night. For some reason, like foals being born, big storms seem only to come ashore in the safety of darkness.

I said a prayer and asked my parents, who were now enjoying calm seas and smooth sailing in Heaven, to keep a watchful eye over my beloved restaurant. Mac sprinkled holy water that his mother had brought him from the Vatican around the beach and marina. Sometimes it takes everything you've got to turn an ill wind another direction. We locked all of the doors and wrote with magic marker on the glass front door, "Ivan Go Away." I literally kissed the ground, and we left to ride out the storm with friends in a safe house on Fish River.

We waited out the storm in the manner to which we had become accustomed. When the status of a hurricane moves from a "watch" to a "warning" and you're not evacuating, the nervous excitement kicks into hurricane survival mode. Collect gasoline, ice, generator, good red wine, liquor, cigarettes; grab a couple of changes of clothes, throw perishables and all the food in the freezer into coolers, and head to high ground. As the rain pelted down and the river rose toward the roof of the boat house, we prepared for the wait as we always do, in true Southern style. We had gathered hundreds of pounds of ice in Igloos and enough libations to intoxicate a small nation. About 20 of us began cooking the abundance of food liberated from our freezers. All local and national television coverage was tracking the storm, and it was headed straight toward Alabama's Gulf Coast — very bad news. The generator was fueled and ready to be fired up as soon as the electric company cut the power. I stayed up all night (I always do), creeping over sleeping bodies stretched out on inflatable mattresses and sofas to check the rise of the river. The most frightening thing about riding out a hurricane is the sound it makes when it passes over you. The roaring of the wind and shrieking of the giant pines bent in stubborn submission are reminiscent of a dying animal. That is what it sounds like. But not when the eye is right overhead. That is when everything becomes eerily quiet. The wind dies to a mere howl. The pounding rain backs off to a heavy drizzle. That is when the husbands in the house take their all-terrain vehicles out to ride around the neighborhood to check out the damage. Believe me, they aren't out there for sport; they are counting down the moments until they can start clearing the highway. It's also when the wives tell them they better be back in 30 minutes before the bands on the west side of the storm, the most damaging bands, will arrive. A waterfront wife with any sense at all makes sure that the life insurance policies are up to date before hurricane season.

As soon as the storm was over, before the highway department and local authorities could get to us, our guys fired up chainsaws and began clearing the driveway and roads of the debris covering them. They were maniacal in their mission. Everyone wanted to check on their homes as soon as possible, and unfortunately many had suffered significant damage. Mac and I were anxious to find out what effect the storm may have had on LuLu's and Homeport Marina.

As soon as the streets were opened up for local business owners late the next morning, we headed to Gulf Shores. The devastation was everywhere, but as we drove down the road to the restaurant, enormous relief swept over us because most of our palm trees were still standing. When we got to the building, all seemed well. No windows were broken. The brilliant turquoise roof was intact and shimmered under a now crystal-clear blue sky and brilliant sun. I tried to open the front door, but it seemed stuck, and my key wouldn't work, so we peered through the glass garage doors and found everything just as we left it. Our prayers had been answered! Not so fast...

We walked around to the deck on the waterway, and that's when we saw the damage: the opposite end of the deck was crumpled beyond recognition. The concrete deck bar had been slammed into the side of the building, which left a gaping hole exposing the dishwashing station in my beautiful new kitchen. The boat dock on that end of the deck was completely ripped away, and jagged pieces of lumber were precariously stacked on top of each other like a fragile house of cards. It was curious because it certainly didn't resemble the damage that we had seen which had been caused by wind or rain. Fortunately, we had witnesses who could tell us what happened.

After Mac completed the restaurant, he had begun building his marina. The fellows digging out the tons of dirt from the inlet to create the marina had stayed on their tugboat during the storm. The captain of the crew was a short, wide man I liked to call Tiny. He told us that around 4 a.m. two gargantuan barges tied together east of us up "the ditch" (our affectionate nickname for the ICW) had apparently broken from their moorings, and the runaway barges, swept down the Intracoastal by the roaring tide, crashed into the restaurant. It was an amazing mess. We would later learn that those barges took out many decks and boat houses along their perilous journey before ending up on dry land three miles inland after the tides subsided.

One of our managers was finally able to get through the roadblocks and brought another set of keys, and we were able to get inside through a backdoor. The large generator was grinding away, and when we walked into the kitchen, all the coolers were humming — a very good sign. We toured the remainder of the restaurant, and all seemed fine with the exception of the awful wreckage in the one corner. I immediately walked behind the big bar, shoved open a cooler, and pulled out several beers, hoisting them up to the heavens and announced, "Well, the beer's still cold!"

It is always a perfectly splendid day after a hurricane, ironically (cruelly?) illuminating all of the wreckage caused by Mother Nature's fury. We sat on the deck sipping the beer, and though we were momentarily crushed by the challenge ahead of us, we realized that we could have suffered far worse consequences. As we would learn in the hours to come, many of our friends and customers had lost both their businesses and homes in the storm.

By sunrise the next morning, Mac had pulled his crews off of the marina, and they were back at LuLu's clearing away the damage to begin rebuilding. The electricity was still off, but the monster generator chugged along as long as it was fed fuel. As the roads opened up, many of our employees returned, eager to assist in the cleanup efforts. I knew we would have to feed ourselves and our employees, so I asked them to fire up my Daddy's old grill out on the beach, and we cooked up a mess of cheeseburgers that day. Most of our food inventory had remained viable since our coolers never went down, and there wasn't another restaurant up and running yet.

The next day at lunch we invited the armies of relief workers to come for lunch. Word swept through the community swiftly that LuLu's had food, ice, and cold beverages. Residents trying to make sense of their devastated lives flocked in to drown their new sorrows and support their friends. LuLu's became a community center again like it had been at the old place, and we happily shifted into the community service business. On the third day we placed a sheet of plywood on Highway 59 painted simply with the following message:

FREE CHEESEBURGERS 12 – 2PM LULU'S

We continued to give away food and soft drinks for five days until other folks were able to get back in business. As always happens in a coastal community after a catastrophe, the part of the human spirit that continues to flicker in the face of desperate darkness began burning brightly. Everyone helped each other get back on their feet. The hole in our kitchen was patched enough to get the Board of Health's blessing, and we were able to get back to business almost as usual. Over the next four months, we served customers inside while Mac rebuilt the dock, deck, and bar, which included a replica of the barge that had hit us during the storm; it was aptly dubbed the "Barge Bar."

Only with the dedication, support, and hard work by so many people were we back in full swing by the time our 2nd anniversary arrived on Mardi Gras Day. We took off and haven't stopped since.

LuLu's General Manager Johnny Fisher and Crew

A Letter "To" LuLu — by Mac McAleer

Dearest Lucy,

Be careful what you ask for... sometimes you just might get it! Here you go: some thoughts from the doughnut man...aka, Mac the business advisor, friend, and occasional sparring partner.

Dates escape me, as you well know, but episodes do stick in this 57 year ol' brain. I had to "Google" Jimmy Buffett to find the date of his benefit concert for the Gulf Coast Hurricane Georges Relief Fund. It was back in December of '98. That was the evening I met your brother backstage, and we ran the name game on the Mobile Catholics. He had graduated from McGill Institute in '64, the same year I arrived. That was also the night he asked if I could help his sister in her new business venture. He thought since I was the Krispy Kreme® guy that maybe I could just deliver doughnuts daily to your bait-shop in this out-of-the-way location in Lower Alabama on Hwy 98 at Fish River. I thought,

Mac McAleer at home on Fish River

"Sell doughnuts in a bait shop? Now there's an appetizing aromatic combination. Are you kidding?" He wasn't. "What the hell," I said, "I'll run over and check it out."

So there I found you, a struggling entrepreneur, gutting it out, selling cheeseburgers and gumbo, something called "L.A. Caviar" (looked a lot like black-eyed peas to me), and cold beer at your "Sunset Grill," and next door, live and "fresh-dead" shrimp in the Bait Shop. What an operation! As they say in the biz, it's all about location...and you were off the map, lost in the swamps (excuse me...estuary), tucked under the bridge, out of sight, and possibly out of your mind! Little did I know.

Opening day of "Bait Shop Breakfast" was a *huge* success...at least a dozen locals showed up. Joe and Penny dropped by.

Joni and JoAnn donned their mink coats for the occasion. The doughnuts-in-the-bait-shop concept came and went, but I grew to respect what you were striving to accomplish in your, as you called it, "high-class dive."

As time moved along, I would occasionally drop by between doughnut shop visits just to check in at the Lu. It was to me a very Southern version of "Cheers." The boaters, the bikers, the drama queens, the plumber always on the prowl...and there you were, your sassy self, strutting around as if you owned the place...which you did. It was your first shot at your dream, and you were giving it all you had and then some.

The food was great, the beer was cold, the music was live and sometimes could be heard up to 2 miles away, or so said the complainer upriver. The word spread...it was a fun place, an escape, and *everybody* wanted to be at LuLu's.

The numbers improved from year to year, and I remember the time you finally didn't have to borrow the money to make it through the off season. I could feel your relief because, as you knew, I was on your side. I was your biggest fan. Still am.

Not many people knew why you left Los Angeles. I did. Your mom Peets' sudden stroke had left her bound to that wheelchair. Your dad J.D. was fading away slowly. Alzheimer's, what a devastating curse! They were both here in Alabama, and you were not. So you packed up your Miata and headed east on the 10 until you hit the 98 exit at Spanish Fort, then south to Daphne and Homeport, the Buffett family retreat on the Eastern Shore of Mobile Bay. And you were home, again.

After a few months of settling back in, with an assist from your brother Bubba (as y'all call him), you cranked up your restaurant and together with your daughters, Mara and Mel, became the caretakers of your folks and half of the folks in and around Baldwin County. Your mom so enjoyed her trips down to LuLu's. Margaret would pick her up in the handy-van, custom built so she could ride shotgun in her wheelchair. She lit up around all the customers and friends, as did they... and, oh, how she enjoyed her oyster loaf and mmm...that gin and tonic. She had a beautiful life right up to the very end. What a sweet, charming Southern lady she was. Peets and J.D. passed within four months of each other. God bless them; they were special gifts.

The letter arrived in February, three weeks before you shared it with me. It was tucked into that rusty old drawer in the "executive suite" of the bait shop. I could tell something was bothering you. You just weren't yourself. As you began to read it aloud, your hands shook and your voice quivered. You made one hell of an attempt to hold back the tears. They came...you read. The State of Alabama, owner of the property which LuLu's was built on, had decided that this establishment did not now meet the criteria of the land use and that you would have to vacate the property by the end of the year.

All I could do was hold you and say, "Everything's gonna be all right."

After the shock subsided a bit and we exhausted all possibilities around the idea of trying to stay, a decision had to be made. "What do you want to do?" I asked. "I don't know," you said, "I don't know." You were exhausted. After years of just making it season to season, the thought of starting over again was overwhelming to you. "Should I go back to California?" you asked. What you had built over those years was an incredible escape experience... not just for the locals, but visitors from all over the country. Remember when we would walk the dirt parking lot just to check out the car tags to see where all of those people came from? Kansas, Minnesota, Michigan, Texas, Mississippi, Louisiana, Kentucky, even New York City... they were all on family vacations at Gulf Shores, 18 miles away. They were seeking you out; LuLu's had become a destination. This "high-class dive" was finally on the map. And now the State of Alabama was kicking you out...along with your 50 employees! I said, "I don't think so. We need a plan!"

So we decided that I would go search for a new site, and you would keep selling cheeseburgers, business as usual. I met with Mike, our friend and a LuLu's regular who was into real estate and also upset about the situation. Many people were. The word had gotten out, and people were pissed! LuLu's had become an institution, and LuLu's was you. Friends and friends of friends volunteered to do anything and everything. Whatever...

We found the site. It grew on you over time. Your brother came by one day for gumbo, and we took him to check it out. His comment: "Ahh...LuLu's on steroids...cool."

We sketched up a plan, which was quickly approved by all of the agencies thanks to the diplomatic team of Ken and Joe, gathered up all of our friends, and dug in. Johnny and Tom became the demolition duo. Jerry was always screaming commands; he's hard of hearing ya' know. Emery was constantly moving "dirty" dirt on our environmentally-challenged site. What a team, reproducing our dream, LuLu's at Homeport Marina.

Fat Tuesday '03, on the new stage and again in tears, you thanked at least 600 of your closest friends and all 100 of your employees for their unwavering support. LuLu's was back. LuLu was back.

We overcame a major hurdle that year, and somewhere along the way I fell for you, Lu, and you for me. On October 12, of 2005, with a few friends from Fairhope and the sweet people of Crooked Island in the Bahamas, we tied the knot at Bird Rock Lighthouse and became two type-A's together on our way. God help us.

All my love, Mac
Fish River, August 10, 2007

LuLu Essentials

ONE HEART MARINADE

SALTY PEPPA FOR EVERYTHING

LULU'S CHIPOTLE TACO SEASONING

LULU'S CRAZY CREOLA SEASONING

LULU'S JERK SEASONING

LULU'S CRAZY FRYING FLOUR

PERFECT FRIED SHRIMP

LULU'S CRAZY FRYING CORNMEAL

PERFECT FRIED OYSTERS

CHICKEN STOCK

SHRIMP STOCK

FISH STOCK

LuLu Food Philosophy

My love affair with cooking began at my grandparents' home in Pascagoula, Mississippi, where my grandmother "Mom" Buffett (that's what the kids called her) playfully complained about my constantly being "underfoot" in her kitchen. She was a terrific Southern cook who prepared large meals every day, even when my grandfather, Captain James (Jimmie) Buffett, was at sea.

Once a month Daddy would load us all up in the old station wagon after church on Sunday, and we would drive the sixty miles from Mobile to his Gulf Coast family home to have dinner; it was nothing short of a celebration feast: fried chicken, roast beef, gumbo leftover from Friday, mashed potatoes, rice and gravy, green beans, stewed squash and onions, speckled butter beans, potato salad, sliced tomatoes, rolls, watermelon iced down in galvanized tubs, pound cake with fresh strawberries, and dewberry pie with vanilla ice cream. It was simple boarding-house food, but what captured my heart was how good everything tasted and how happy everyone was.

There was always beer chilling in the ice under the watermelon and a bottle of rum hidden in the

garage for the men; this was a Buffett gathering after all. The house was filled with lots of noise: adults talking and laughing over rock and roll (shocking!) on the transistor radio while the Saints game blared on the television in the living room and in the den. The passel of cousins and neighborhood kids were always causing a ruckus playing backyard games and running through the house. Those Buffett Sunday gatherings encouraged all of us kids to "live out loud." The festivity stirred up my delight in cooking and my absolute belief that food is not merely sustenance for life but a celebration of life.

I love to eat, and I adore cooking. Over the years I've meandered along a culinary path that has taken me from fish sticks in a tract house in west Mobile to beluga caviar on a yacht in Manhattan and back home to boiled crabs at the end of the pier on the

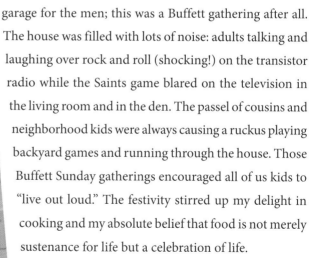

Eastern Shore of Mobile Bay. I've cooked with hand-me-down pots and pans on rusted-out apartment stoves, as well as on the finest commercial equipment available. I read a cookbook like most people read a comic book. I would just as soon have a blue-plate lunch at the "meat-and-three" diner down the road as a Coquille Saint-Jacques at the swankiest French bistro in Paris. Food is my passion; cooking is my art. In hard times it is my meditation. It makes me feel better because I like who I am when I cook.

I am self-taught, so I don't have the credentials or knife skills of a bona fide chef. There are many more proficient and educated professionals who have far more curiosity and imagination around food, but you'd be hard pressed to find anybody who delights in entertaining and feeding people more than I do.

I aspired to create haute cuisine at one point in my life and enjoyed the challenge. I'm quite capable of preparing a beef Wellington or whipping up my own pâte feuilletée (or "puff pastry" as we call it.) I've also been humbled by an impractical creativity that suggested it would be a good idea to use raspberry vinegar in a pasta salad. The pasta developed measles, bright pink splotches. Right about then I decided to rein in my experimentation. As I've grown older, I've given up my complicated ways... at least where cooking is concerned...and have wandered back down the road toward home, preparing the gracious and simple classics of my Gulf Coast childhood. I'm not such a food snob anymore, but I am a stickler for using the best quality and freshest seasonal and regional ingredients available. There's no need to scrimp on quality; spend the extra coin for name-brand instead of generic food. Use real vanilla extract instead of imitation flavoring.

Age has allowed me to laugh at my culinary disasters, which seem always to occur when I'm in a hurry and not paying attention. My more mature brain has clocked enough hours multi-tasking and would prefer more multi-amusement. You simply have to laugh at pulling a charred-to-leather roast out of the oven and ordering pizza for your ten starving and slightly intoxicated dinner guests!

1.   You've gotta really love it to do it really well! Honey, if you don't *like* to cook, I suggest healthy take-out, so you can spend your time doing whatever it is that you do enjoy.

Testing recipes in Key West

2.   Easy does it! Swanky formal dining can be very impressive, but it is also full of pressure. I prefer casual entertaining and so do most guests. Keeping menus and recipes simple will enhance your enjoyment of cooking, especially if you are a novice. (My loved ones will probably guffaw when they read this because I've never done anything simple in my life.) If you use cookbooks to actually cook the recipes instead of collecting them for pleasure, choose the ones at your level of proficiency, but don't be afraid to be adventurous. The worst thing that can happen is that you throw away what didn't work and go out to eat. The more you cook, the better you will become and the more familiar you'll be with culinary language like sauté, chiffonade, braise, and whisk.

3.   There are few original recipes. Food is trendy, like fashion, and borrows from tradition. Any top chef without an ego problem will agree. Talent is knowing what to cook and how to put a dish together, putting your own flair on a classic dish or combining flavors that wouldn't ordinarily be put together. If you are an adventuresome soul who loves a culinary challenge, don't be intimidated by the length of the ingredients list or the difficulty of the instructions because you're just doing what cooks have done for ages, following a recipe.

4.   Fresh, fresh, fresh. Did I say FRESH? Use fresh ingredients if at all possible. It makes anything you cook healthier and better tasting. Frozen is the next best choice and canned is the last resort (unless you "put them up" yourself last summer) because of the massive amount of sodium in canned food. Squeeze lemons for fresh lemon juice. Use cherry tomatoes because they are available all year long. Fresh herbs add so much flavor, especially to salads; I keep a large barrel of herbs growing all the time. When using fresh herbs instead of dried, use twice as much as the recipe calls for and add them in the last ten minutes of cooking.

5. While cooking, listening to your favorite music is a must. It is fundamental to a successful result in the world of LuLu. I'm listening to Elvis as I write these words. When I cook, this is the music I enjoy because basically I'm stuck in the '70's, and in my heart I'm still 28 years old: prep to James Taylor, cook to the Allman Brothers Band in winter and my brother, Jimmy, in summer, serve to Grover Washington, and clean up with Aretha!

6. There is a difference between a dry ingredients measuring cup and a liquid ingredients measuring cup. Or is there? I'm certainly not going to abandon cooking a recipe that calls for ½ cup of sugar, simply because I only have a Pyrex® measuring cup in the house. Improvise. Use what you have, and that goes for ingredients as well as equipment.

7. Never cook shrimp for more than 3 minutes. Period.

8. Feel the food! Handle food with care and reverence; it is life force. Don't be afraid to get messy using your hands to toss a large bowl of cole slaw.

9. Keep it clean. When I say I like "clean food," I mean that dishes should be prepared with no more fat than is germane to the dish and that few or no chemicals are part of the ingredients. I don't like to shop for clothes, but going to the grocery store for me is as exciting as going to Saks Fifth Avenue for some women. As soon as I get home, I fill my large ceramic farm sink with produce and clean it carefully. This is especially necessary today because of the inordinate amount of pesticides and preservatives used to grow and store fresh food.

10. In the movie *Like Water for Chocolate,* there is a scene when all of the guests at a large wedding dinner begin sobbing because the meal was prepared by Tita who is brokenhearted because Pedro, her true love and the groom, has married her older sister, Rosaura. As Tita prepares the wedding feast, her grief and tears fall into the food and the guests begin feeling the same emotions that Tita feels. I take this story to heart because I know that the energy surrounding the way food is prepared transfers into its result. I can walk into the front of my restaurant and know immediately if there is a problem in the kitchen. The kitchen is the heart of any restaurant or home, and if there is discord or confusion in the "back of the house," its energy transfers metaphysically to the front; it becomes tangible and results in problems. I began a ritual several years ago. When I cook a pot of gumbo, I season it with love and meditate on an intention for the quality I'm trying to attract in my life such as peace or patience. It may sound like magic or my own little spooky voodoo, but I've found that it works and doesn't cost a thing except a little crazy faith.

TEN INGREDIENTS FOR A HAPPY LIFE

1. You are what you eat and think.

2. Accept that life is always working for you, not against you.

3. Life is; just live it!

4. Trying to be perfect is a set-up for failure and misery.

5. The sun comes up every morning; even when it's hiding behind a cloud or lost in the fog, it's there.

6. When you don't know what to do: BE STILL.

7. Run toward what you fear; close your eyes and dive into it.

8. Say "thank you" every day, especially to someone else.

9. Say "I'm sorry" every day, especially to yourself.

10. You are the only one who can walk your path, but you are never alone.

HOW TO LULU

There are five mainstays to cooking à la LuLu: stock, prep, season, grill, and fry.

STOCKING THE POT — I cook a lot, and I'm constantly throwing vegetable trimmings into pots of simmering water with scraps of meat, fish carcasses, chicken necks, or shrimp heads. It's one of those things that I do as I'm doing everything else, but having stock on hand is a staple in my house, especially when I'm trying to reduce the amount of fat in a recipe. There are containers and ice trays in my freezer filled with of all kinds of homemade stock. My uses for stocks range from making soup or cooking rice to adding extra liquid to a dish. Conveniently, a variety of good stocks are now commercially available; they are appropriate substitutes for homemade. I will, when necessary, break my cardinal rule of only using "fresh" and use canned chicken broth.

PREP FOR SUCCESS — Be the star of your own cooking show and invest in a set of clear Pyrex® bowls, a quality cutting board, and a comfortable knife. When preparing several dishes at a time, it is imperative that all ingredients are ready before you need them. Timing is everything, and the only way to pull it off is to prep ingredients before you start cooking. I will have dozens of bowls of cut vegetables or meat arranged together according to their sequence in a recipe. Besides being practical, it makes for a pretty display.

Men tend to have fancier knife skills than women, which I envy, but have no desire or intention to emulate. I'm better when I take things slowly, especially when sharp edges are involved. Yes, there are correct methods for using knives in the kitchen. These were developed for safety, efficiency, and to eliminate waste. A generous New York executive chef taught me how to hold the blade of the knife between my thumb and forefinger just above the handle instead of holding the handle with my thumb and middle finger, my index finger teetering precariously on top of the blade. The important thing is to find a knife that you're comfortable using, and when slicing, employ a time-worn sports analogy: keep your eye on the ball — or the onion should that be the case.

Because the LuLu's Lifestyle requires simplicity, I have tried to eliminate confusion in terms of what size and in what manner an ingredient should be prepped. I simply chop my food, finely if it needs to be small and coarsely if it needs to be large and chunky. Otherwise the recipe will simply read "chopped," calling for medium-sized pieces. For sliced ingredients, the instructions will indicate whether it needs to be thin, medium, or thick. When instructions call for a specific cut, it will be clarified, like the onion in the West Indies Salad: "thinly sliced in half-moons." In other words, cut the onion in half and cut it in half again, then slice.

I prefer food with lots of texture, so most of my cooking is done with chunky ingredients unless a recipe requires otherwise. For instance, the parsley in the L.A. Caviar must be finely chopped. I have an idiosyncrasy about keeping the shapes and sizes of the ingredients uniform. I would never put *sliced* onions with *chopped* bell peppers, but I love using contrasting colorful ingredients. I like my food to be beautiful as well as delicious.

FLAVOR MATTERS — I'd simply rather not eat bland and tasteless food. I'm looking for salty, sweet, spicy, and savory. To simplify things, there are two methods I use to give my food flavor: liquid marinade or dry seasoning mix.

In my kitchen, meat or seafood is marinated before it is cooked. It flavors the protein and keeps it moist and tender. My favorite concoction is extremely versatile and can be used with meat, chicken, or seafood, thus its name "One Heart Marinade."

When it comes to seasoning, I turn to the basics: salt and pepper. Salt brings out the flavor in food. I salt food generously for that reason, but I don't like to overdo it. In our neck of the woods, we use Creole seasoning in almost everything, and it's important to remember that Creole seasonings typically have a lot of sodium, so you'll have to adjust salt accordingly. LuLu's Crazy Creola Seasoning™ has less salt than most commercial brands. Of course, if you have a medical condition that requires you to restrict sodium, by all means follow your doctor's orders and modify recipes accordingly. My doctor encourages me to walk the righteous path when it comes to my diet. When he scolds me for not following his orders, I like to remind him that I met him at the gazebo bar at old LuLu's drinking margaritas. Everything is alright in moderation, right, Rick?

I use LuLu's Crazy Creola Seasoning™ for "blackening" purposes. Chef Paul Prudhomme introduced the term into the American lexicon with his famous Blackened Redfish. After a few years, redfish had to be put on the endangered species list; the dish had become popular, and the blackening method spread like a brushfire across the country. It is a distinctive flavor of my childhood, and in our family, LuLu's Crazy Creola Seasoning™ remains a favorite way to prepare not only fish but also shrimp and chicken.

My fascination with all things Caribbean includes "jerk" seasoning, which hails from Jamaica. The two qualifying ingredients are allspice and habanero peppers, which create an exotic sweet and hot flavor. It can be made either as a wet paste-like marinade or a dry rub. The best jerk chicken I have ever had was at a quaint jerk shack on a dirt road that ran along the shore of Montego Bay. This incredible aroma caught my senses as I walked along the beach, and I followed the smoke that was streaming out of a rusted fifty-five-gallon drum filled with smoldering wood. Over the coals was a grill topped with the most scrumptious-looking charred chicken you can imagine. I could tell it had been slow-smoking for a long time. The cook dragged himself out of his hammock to wait on me. He cheerfully put a couple of pieces of chicken on a paper plate and scooped some potato salad out of an ice chest then gave me a plastic fork and napkin. There was no plastic knife offered; it was clearly not needed because this chicken was to be eaten with your fingers. The chicken had been slathered with jerk paste and kept in a cooler overnight before being slow-cooked on the grill. I ate that jerk chicken leisurely, savoring every bite as I sat overlooking the spectacular turquoise waters of the Caribbean Sea. Pure bliss.

I knew I had to include this exotic new flavor in my repertoire. Since habaneros are not always readily available in my neighborhood, I created a dry version using cayenne pepper for the heat: LuLu's Jerk Seasoning. It is versatile enough to use with any protein, including steak. I simply brush whatever I'm cooking with a little olive oil, generously sprinkle with the seasoning, and refrigerate it overnight. At LuLu's we use it to infuse our traditional chicken salad with a little island flavor.

GRILLING WITH GRACE AND GUMPTION — In my neighborhood of ancient live oaks dripping with Spanish moss overlooking a lazy river, the barbecue grill remains a sacred piece of lawn art as well as the designated gathering place for men to weave chest hairs and show off their prowess. The women don't mind being excluded from that domain. We sneak cigarettes, sip cocktails, and whisper among ourselves about who (and what) really rules the world. Grilled food is a Southern institution, so it's no surprise that leisurely entertaining with grilled delicacies is a major element of the LuLu's Lifestyle.

In 1979, my father designed his dream grill and surreptitiously had it fabricated in the machine shop at the shipyard where he worked. It is a massive metal masterpiece heavier than the Titanic. When our pier was blown away in both Hurricanes Frederic and Georges, the weathered boards were strewn for miles along the crumpled shore, but Daddy's grill survived each time. It lay peacefully on the bottom of Mobile Bay exactly where it fell, right where the end of the pier used to be. Technically, it belongs to my brother Jimmy, and I'll send it to him any time he wants as long as he pays the shipping. After making the rounds at both LuLu's, it now resides by the pool at home and is used on special occasions when we're cooking for 100 or more. We also have a gas grill for convenience and, of course, the phenomenal Big Green Egg®, which, by the way, deserves all of its hype. At the restaurant we serve approximately 84,000 burgers and blacken or grill 43,000 pounds of seafood every year. Even in the land of fried, died, and gone to heaven, grilling still enjoys a respectable popularity.

FRY WITH THE FLOW — Fried food has become a cardinal sin in our culture of self-help and self-care. I happen to agree with the health-conscious movement; I'm also a born rebel and have always flirted with the forbidden. So I make this confession right now: I WILL NEVER GIVE UP FRIED FOOD!

At LuLu's our best selling item is the Big Fry Basket. It's piled high with grouper when available or catfish, shrimp, oysters, crab claws, French fries, and hush puppies. I can hear the collective gasp from the AMA's cardiologists; the saving grace is that it feeds two. We have eight fryers with an automatic filtering and supply system pumping out a little over 75,000 pounds of fried seafood and 219,930 pounds of French fries each year! At an average length of 4 inches each, if you

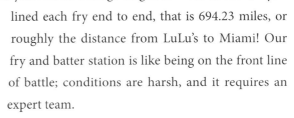

lined each fry end to end, that is 694.23 miles, or roughly the distance from LuLu's to Miami! Our fry and batter station is like being on the front line of battle; conditions are harsh, and it requires an expert team.

I'm not the best fry cook in the world even though my daddy could fry chicken better than "The Colonel." He would shake his chicken pieces in a paper bag with flour, salt, and pepper before carefully dropping them in hot grease. I believe there is an art to cooking beautiful fried food, and over the years I've picked up a few tricks of the trade.

The most important secret to successful frying is getting the oil hot enough and keeping it hot. That's easy to do with electric fryers with thermostats, but before we had those or candy thermometers to monitor temperature, you had to flick a little flour into the oil to see if it would sizzle. When it did, it was hot enough. Truly talented flickers know that it's all in the wrist. Of course, if you get the oil too hot, it fries the crust outside but leaves the inside raw. Generally, the first few pieces of any fried food are sacrificial and thrown away to get the oil just the right temperature, which by the way, is 355 degrees.

Deep-frying requires lots of oil and a skillet with tall sides. At home, I use an old cast iron Dutch oven pitch black with age that belonged to my great-aunt Loraine, but any heavy skillet will do. I have always used peanut oil because it can maintain a high temperature for a long time before it breaks down and begins to burn. Scientists have concocted new versions of frying fat for commercial purposes; we use one at the restaurant that is trans-fat free and engineered to help the food brown, which I find curious but helpful for an operation as large as ours.

The skillet needs to be tall-sided because you have to use plenty of oil when deep-frying. It is important not to crowd the skillet with too many pieces at one time. There must be room for them to roll around if the pieces are small, like okra. If the pieces are large, there needs to be enough room to safely turn them, which you should only do once. Let the hot oil do its magic, and don't interfere too much. For one thing, you'll knock all the breading off, and what's the fun of that?

When you're coating the shrimp or okra or whatever you're frying, make sure the batter or breading covers it completely. At LuLu's we use milk and buttermilk baths and double dip many of our items for an extra-crunchy crust.

When the fried items begin to float to the top, they're done. Gently remove the pieces that are floating and drain well on paper towels or a brown paper bag. Do not, however, I mean NEVER EVER cover food that you've taken out of the fryer. With no place for the heat to escape, it will create steam and make your beautifully fried dish soggy and mushy.

FRY A LITTLE TENDERNESS — If I had to whittle my whole How To LuLu down to one simple message, it would be to cook with love. Cooking with careful preparation and gentle handling, fresh ingredients, and positive intentions adds up to a heartfelt, joyful experience. Bring love into the kitchen, and you will be serving it in the dining room.

I use this marinade

for almost everything, thus the name ONE HEART. It works well with chicken, steak, shrimp, and cold-water fish like salmon and tuna, especially for grilling. Of course, I think that you can never overdo garlic so feel free to add more or as much as your friends and loved ones will tolerate.

One Heart Marinade

MAKES 1 CUP

½ cup teriyaki sauce

2 tablespoons crushed garlic

¼ cup mirin or sake

1 teaspoon coarsely ground black pepper

2 tablespoons extra virgin olive oil

2-3 dashes LuLu's Perfect Pepper Hot Sauce™

1. Whisk all ingredients together.

 LuLu Clue: I just throw all of the ingredients into a shallow baking dish. Then I add whatever I'm cooking. This marinade is dark and salty because teriyaki sauce is basically soy sauce with sugar. I coat the food well and only let it marinate for about 20 to 30 minutes on each side.

 LuLu Clue: White wine or vermouth can be substituted for the mirin, which is a Japanese rice wine. When cooking steak, I sometimes substitute red wine.

Salty Peppa for Everything

MAKES ABOUT ¼ CUP

1 tablespoon salt
1 teaspoon garlic powder
1 teaspoon onion powder
½ teaspoon white pepper
½ teaspoon black pepper
⅛ teaspoon cayenne pepper
½ teaspoon paprika

1. Mix all ingredients together. Store in a small airtight container.

 LuLu Clue: For an exotic Caribbean flavor, add 1 teaspoon ground coriander and ½ teaspoon ground thyme.

LuLu's Chipotle Taco Seasoning

MAKES ¼ CUP

2½ teaspoons chili powder
1 tablespoon taco seasoning
1 teaspoon dried chipotle powder
½ teaspoon salt
½ teaspoon dried cumin

1. Combine all ingredients. Store in an airtight container.

LuLu's Live Maritime Theater

☼ LULU ESSENTIALS

LuLu's Crazy Creola Seasoning

MAKES ½ CUP

1 tablespoon salt
2 tablespoons granulated garlic
4 teaspoons granulated onion
¼ cup paprika
1½ teaspoons black pepper
2 teaspoons cayenne pepper
2 teaspoons white pepper
½ teaspoon dried thyme leaves
½ teaspoon dried oregano leaves

1. Combine all ingredients. Store in an airtight container.

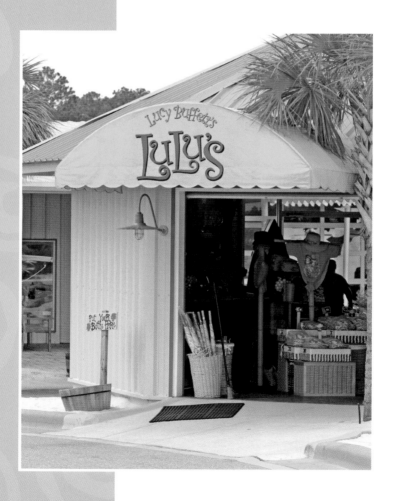

LuLu's Jerk Seasoning

MAKES ABOUT ¼ CUP

1 teaspoon ground white pepper
1 teaspoon dried onion flakes
1 teaspoon granulated onion or
   onion powder
1 teaspoon cayenne pepper
1 teaspoon ground allspice
1 teaspoon black pepper
1 teaspoon ground thyme
½ teaspoon ground cinnamon
1 teaspoon garlic powder
1 teaspoon dried red pepper flakes
2 teaspoons kosher salt
Pinch of orange peel granules
Pinch of lemon peel granules

1. Combine all ingredients. Store in an airtight container.

LuLu Clue: I use cayenne for the heat (staying true to my roots) and just a hint of cinnamon.

LuLu with Guy Harvey

In LuLu-Land,

"Fried, Died, and Gone to Heaven" is gospel. Once upon a time, LuLu's menu items included rice pilaf and steamed vegetables, but we threw away more than we sold. If there is one thing I have learned as a restaurateur, it's to give your customers what they want. Gulf Shores vacationers and locals alike want fried shrimp...or anything else we can throw in our fryers.

Our Crazy Flour uses our own Creola Seasoning, and we spike the mix with extra black pepper to give it that special LuLu's love. In the restaurant we use flour to bread our shrimp, crab claws, okra, and green tomatoes. The key to successful deep frying is to get the oil hot enough and keep it hot; if you don't, that's when your food gets greasy. The "culinarily" correct temperature for frying is 350 degrees, but I prefer a little hotter and have seen some Southern fry masters turn it up to 375 degrees, especially when using a cast iron Dutch oven over a propane cooker in the driveway.

LuLu's Crazy Frying Flour

MAKES 2 CUPS

2 cups all-purpose flour

2 tablespoons LuLu's Crazy Creola Seasoning™ (page 50)

1½ teaspoons salt

1 tablespoon black pepper

1. Combine all ingredients and mix thoroughly.

Perfect Fried Shrimp

MAKES 6 SERVINGS

LuLu's Crazy Frying Flour (recipe above)

2 cups whole milk

2 pounds large headless shrimp, shell on

6 cups peanut or vegetable oil, or enough to fill a skillet about 2 inches deep

Lemon wedges for garnish

1. Place frying flour in a bowl; set aside.
2. Place milk in a separate bowl.
3. Peel shrimp, leaving tails intact. Cut back of shrimp halfway to butterfly and remove vein. Place shrimp in a bowl and set aside.
4. In a cast iron or heavy skillet, heat oil to 355 degrees over medium-high heat. (Use a candy or fry thermometer for accuracy or heat until a little flour flicked into the oil sizzles.)
5. Working with a few shrimp at a time, dredge through flour, dip in milk, then dredge through flour again.
6. Gently drop into hot oil. Fry until golden brown or until shrimp float to the top, about 3 to 4 minutes. Adjust heat as necessary to keep oil temperature around 355 degrees. Drain on paper towels and serve immediately.

As they say in these parts

it's a sin to use flour to fry oysters or mullet. There are a zillion different recipes to bread or batter, but the only ones worth their salt use cornmeal, not cracker meal (whatever that is) and not corn-flour or any other combination of dry ingredients, including, yes, crushed up corn flakes. Please, that's an insult to any self-respecting bi-valve marine mollusk or funny looking ray-finned fish. As with our frying flour, we generously grace it with lots of black pepper and LuLu's Crazy Creola Seasoning™.

LuLu's Crazy Frying Cornmeal

MAKES 2 CUPS

2 cups white all-purpose cornmeal

2 tablespoons LuLu's Crazy Creola Seasoning™ (page 50)

1 tablespoon black pepper

½ tablespoon salt

1. Combine all ingredients.
2. Mix well.

Perfect Fried Oysters

MAKES 4 SERVINGS

LuLu's Crazy Frying Cornmeal (recipe above)

6 cups peanut or vegetable oil, or enough to fill a skillet about 2 inches deep

1 quart oysters, drained

1. Make LuLu's Crazy Frying Cornmeal and set aside.
2. Heat oil in a cast iron skillet to 355 degrees. (Use a candy or fry thermometer for accuracy or heat until a little flour flicked into the oil sizzles.)
3. Taking a few oysters at a time, dredge through cornmeal mixture coating thoroughly.
4. Gently drop into hot oil. Fry until golden brown turning once or until they float to the top. Drain on paper towels and serve immediately.

 LuLu Clue: When frying multiple batches, place cooked seafood in a 200 degree oven to keep warm.

Chicken Stock

MAKES ABOUT 4 QUARTS

1 (4- to 5-pound) whole chicken

6 quarts water

2 onions, chopped into large chunks

2 carrots, chopped into large chunks

6 ribs celery, chopped into large chunks

1 bunch green onions, chopped into large pieces

1 green bell pepper, chopped into large chunks

Handful of parsley with stems, thoroughly washed

1 teaspoon whole black peppercorns

1. Run cold water over and through chicken. Trim off excess skin.

2. Place all ingredients into an 8- to 10-quart stockpot over high heat. Bring to a boil.

3. Reduce heat to medium or until stock is simmering. Skim foam off the top. Cook chicken for 1 hour, continuing to skim as needed.

4. Remove chicken and let cool. Remove meat from bones and reserve for another use. Return bones to stock and continue cooking for 2 hours or until stock is reduced to about 4 quarts.

5. Place uncovered stockpot in an empty sink. Fill sink with water and ice around the stockpot. Stir stock every 15 minutes until completely cooled. Strain stock and refrigerate or freeze immediately.

Making stock

can be an all-day affair, but if you're pressed for time, there are shortcuts to be had with commercial pastes now on the market. When they're available, I always buy shrimp with the heads on and freeze them for use later. The stock will be richer if you use shrimp heads. When you're making a shrimp bisque, authentic stock is a must. Sure, I've used plain old water when I've made gumbo in a hurry and it turned out alright. However, when I'm making the best of a rainy day or have the blues and am making gumbo as therapy, I make it this way and let it simmer for hours while I listen to my 70's music and drink freshly-squeezed grapefruit juice (with just a little bit of vodka).

Shrimp Stock

MAKES ABOUT 4 QUARTS

Heads, tails, and shells from 5 pounds of peeled shrimp, or tails and shells from 4 pounds of shrimp and 1 pound shrimp in the shell

6 quarts water

3 onions, chopped into large chunks

6 ribs celery, chopped into large chunks

1 bunch green onions, chopped into large pieces

Handful of parsley with stems, thoroughly washed

2 lemons, sliced into ¼-inch rounds

1 teaspoon whole black peppercorns

1 whole clove garlic

1. Run cold water over shrimp heads and shells (or shrimp if using them).
2. Place all ingredients into an 8-quart stockpot over high heat. Bring to a boil.
3. Reduce heat to medium or until stock is simmering. Skim foam off the top. Continue to skim as needed.
4. Cook stock for 2 hours or until stock is reduced to about 4 quarts.
5. Place uncovered stockpot in an empty sink. Fill sink with water and ice around the stockpot. Stir stock every 15 minutes until completely cooled. Strain stock and refrigerate or freeze immediately.

LULU ESSENTIALS

Fish Stock

MAKES ABOUT 4 QUARTS

Heads, tails, and bones of 3-4 white fish (about 4-5 pounds), such as snapper or grouper

6 quarts water

1 cup white wine

2 onions, chopped into large chunks

2 leeks, chopped into large chunks

6 ribs celery, chopped into large chunks

1 bunch green onions, chopped into large pieces

Handful of parsley with stems, thoroughly washed

2 lemons, sliced into ¼-inch rounds

1 teaspoon whole black peppercorns

1 whole clove garlic

1. Run cold water over fish heads and carcasses, rinsing well.
2. Place all ingredients into an 8- to 10-quart stockpot over high heat. Bring to a boil.
3. Reduce heat to medium or until stock is simmering. Skim foam off the top. Continue to skim as needed.
4. Cook stock for 2 hours or until stock is reduced to about 4 quarts.
5. Place uncovered stockpot in an empty sink. Fill sink with water and ice around the stockpot. Stir stock every 15 minutes until completely cooled. Strain stock and refrigerate or freeze immediately.

 LuLu Clue: Leeks must be washed thoroughly because they can retain a lot of dirt in the layers. I slice and separate them into rings and soak them in a sink of cold water. Then I rinse them at least twice in a colander.

My Mother Peets' Philosophy

1. *Read often, including the classics*
2. *Accept everyone for who they are, not what they do*
3. *Be well-travelled*
4. *Learn to be a listener*
5. *Live by the sea*
6. *Listen to your spirit and find joy*
7. *Education, like money, doesn't make you happy — but it sure helps*
8. *Love and family are the best things we have*

Specialty Drinks

BAMA BREEZE

LOOPTY-LU

JUICY GINGER COOLER

THE "MO-PERFECT" MARGARITA

THE CADILLAC MARGARITA

THE ROSARITA MARGARITA

LUCY'S FAVORITE MARGARITA

LULU'S RASPBERRY REEF MARGARITA

LULU'S BIG BLUE SHARK MARGARITA

MISS BRENDA'S "POMARITA" MARGARITA

LULU'S RUM PUNCH

THE MIGHTY FINE MOJITO

KEY LIME MARTINI

THE ORIGINAL BOAT DRINK

JET SKI KILLER

THE BEST BLOODY MARY

"NOLA STYLE" HURRICANE

LULU'S WORLD FAMOUS BUSHWACKER

LULU'S PAINKILLER

MARINA MAMA

THE BLOODY BULL

THE KEY LIME FREEZE

THE ICW 155 MUDSLIDE

MOTHER'S MILK

CUBA LIBRE

THE OTHER SIDE OF THE BAR

Bartending ain't easy. Forgive the slang. But it's the truth. Sure, cracking open a couple of tall-boys might be a no-brainer, but if you're behind a bar, any bar, you're *stuck behind the bar.* You can't walk away from war stories, heartbreak tales, rude customers, or even the hairy letch who wants to know what time your shift ends. Each bartending venue is fraught with its own set of perils; at LuLu's our numero uno issue is the sheer number of customers my bartenders have to serve. People will wait an hour for a table if they have to – not so for a cocktail; they want their refreshments when they want them — and right away. Hence the reason we've got three public bars in addition to a service bar. (The "service bar" is the one you don't see; they make *all* the drinks for *all* the tables!)

In the more metropolitan areas of the country, a mixologist enjoys a level of professional respect that has yet to find its way into the back roads and beaches of the South. I am trying to change that with my staff. LuLu's offers the opportunity for professional bartenders to be just that, professional. My bartenders are my ambassadors of the LuLu's Lifestyle...and skilled craftsmen. You need super-human hearing, quick hands, an unerring sense of proportion and flavor, and above all patience. With swift action and team effort, my bar staff has it all.

We want to relax, dance, and sing. We want to have a good time. We want a temporary trip to the tropics without the airline ticket. We want to believe there's a little bit of pirate in each of us. We want to push our toes into the warm sand, sipping a cool adult beverage. It's what LuLu's brings to life every day. Picture it: a tropical libation, frosty and sweet in a sultry, curvaceous glass; pretty paper umbrellas speared through tart pineapple wedges that glisten in the rosy light of sunset; freshly squeezed citrus floating in a highball glass piled high with cracked ice; a slice of lime, a sprig of mint, or an impossibly red cherry. It is two parts island rum and one part joy. It is the palette of celebration, the flavor of fun.

You want to be a bartender? (Or at least a great host?) Here are a few tips: *always shaken, never stirred.* Your shaker should be so cold when mixing a martini that it sticks to your hand. In order to make a variety of drinks well, you should have a good quality strainer. It fits over the top of your shaker, allowing the liquor, but not the ice to flow through. In a pinch, use two glasses, one inverted into the top of the other. "Rimming" has nothing to do with basketball; it's the way you dip the rim of the glass in lime juice (or simple syrup) to make salt or sugar stick to it. "Muddling" is a fancy term for smushing something into the bottom of a glass with a wooden pestle (a spoon will do), such as in an Old-Fashioned or a Mojito. A "floater" is the extra pour of premium liquor on top of the concoction just ordered, provided to give your guest vivid and immediate results: Pour With Caution! And finally, don't skip the garnish! Presentation matters...otherwise, why would women wear pantyhose?

If you're like me, you prefer the other side of the bar! Why not leave it up to my highly skilled team at LuLu's to mix your adult beverages? And please remember to tip them; they work very hard so that you can have a good time. Have you ever been in a bar and heard the bartender ring the brass bell? That's their way of saying thanks for a great tip. Let them ring the bell for you.

My brother Jimmy's recording of "The Bama

Breeze" was his homage to coastal dives, particularly the famous Flora-Bama on the beach at the Alabama-Florida State line. He sent me a little love when he changed the lyrics to call the bar owner "LuLu." And when he asked me if I wanted to play the bar owner in the video. I mused for just a second, thinking...hmmm. A woman who owns a bar, drinking a beer, jumps up on the stage and sings with the band...it wasn't much of a stretch! I had crazy fun shooting the video. But I'm glad I have my day job! Now I enjoy this drink at my own "Bama Breeze" bar on the beach at LuLu's.

Bama Breeze

MAKES 1 DRINK

2 ounces Absolut® Citron vodka
1 ounce coconut rum
Juice of ½ fresh lime
2-3 ounces cranberry juice
½ ounce simple syrup
Lime wedge to garnish

1. Fill a tall glass with crushed ice.
2. Add vodka and rum.
3. Squeeze lime juice into glass.
4. Fill with cranberry juice.
5. Add simple syrup to desired sweetness.
6. Stir.
7. Garnish with fresh lime wedge.

LuLu Clue: To make your own simple syrup: In a small saucepan, bring ½ cup water and ½ cup sugar to a boil. Remove from heat and cool to room temperature, then cool, pour syrup liquid into a storage container. This will keep, refrigerated, for a long time.

Every bar I love

has it own "signature" drink, my favorites being in New Orleans — Snug Harbor's famous "Monsoon" and, of course, Pat O'Brian's potent "Hurricane." (It was a high school rite-of-passage for all my friends, back when the drinking age was 18, to sneak over to New Orleans and return with the tell-tale hurricane glass.)

I wanted LuLu's to have a special drink we could likewise call our own, and this light, pink lemonade-inspired creation makes the perfect refreshment on the hottest days of summer. Of course, it's not required you drink it through a "crazy straw," unless you want to get the full LuLu's "loopty" vibe.

Loopty-Lu

MAKES 1 DRINK

1 ounce Margaritville® Mango tequila

1 ounce Absolut® Citron vodka

2 ounces sour mix

2 ounces pink lemonade

Lemon slice and cherry to garnish

1 crazy straw

1. Fill a shaker with crushed ice.
2. Pour mango tequila, vodka, sour mix, and pink lemonade over ice.
3. Shake vigorously.
4. Pour into a tall glass.
5. Garnish with fresh lemon and cherry.
6. Have fun with a "loopty" (crazy) straw.

Talk about the definition

of "refreshment!" This drink blends the cooling essence of mint with a stimulating hint of ginger. Not too sweet, not too fruity...just right. After watching a Food Network show that featured homemade ginger beverages, our fabulous ginger-lovin' general manager, Johnny Fisher, was moved to create one for LuLu's. He enthusiastically enlisted the help of "princess" and assistant GM, Nancy VanWynen, and together after many, many...um, many test batches at the tiki bar, created this one-of-a-kind, perfectly pleasing, and even a little invigorating, thirst quencher.

Juicy Ginger Cooler

MAKES 1 DRINK

½ ounce ginger-mint simple syrup

2 ounces Bacardi Limon® rum

4 ounces cranberry juice

Splash of Sprite®

Lemon slice and fresh mint to garnish

1. Fill a glass with ice.
2. Add simple syrup and rum.
3. Add cranberry juice and top with a splash of Sprite®.
4. Garnish with a slice of lemon and a sprig of fresh mint.

LuLu Clue: To make **ginger-mint simple syrup:** In a small saucepan, bring ½ cup water and ½ cup sugar to a boil. Add ¼ cup chopped fresh ginger and ½ cup fresh mint leaves. Let steep until cool. Strain liquid into a separate container. This will keep, refrigerated, for a long time.

If the bar at the old LuLu's had held a cocktail popularity contest,

the "JB Perfect Margarita" would have won, hands down. It was so popular, in fact, that we had a hard time keeping the necessary ingredients in supply from the state liquor store. That problem was solved when Jimmy started making his own Margaritaville tequila. So I figured the new and improved version is Mo-Perfect! Yes, the rumors are true: the drink will not freeze (it has so much spirit to it), there is a 4-drink maximum, and...um, did I say all of the rumors are true?

The "Mo-Perfect" Margarita

MAKES 1 DRINK

½ **fresh lime, cut into 4 wedges (absolutely must be fresh), divided**

2 ounces Margaritaville® gold tequila

½ **ounce Margaritaville® silver tequila**

½ **ounce Cointreau® orange liqueur**

¾ **ounce Rose's® lime juice**

1 splash orange Curaçao liqueur (not optional)

Coarse salt to rim glass

Lime wedge to garnish

1. Fill a shaker with ice.
2. Squeeze 3 fresh lime wedges over ice. (Throw the squeezed lime wedges into the shaker...believe me, it adds to the drink!)
3. Pour gold tequila, silver tequila, and orange liqueur into shaker.
4. Add lime juice and a splash of orange Curaçao liqueur.
5. Shake vigorously.
6. Rim the outer edge of a margarita glass with lime wedge and turn glass upside down in a plate of coarse salt (the lime juice helps the salt stick to the glass).
7. Fill salted glass with ice and strain mixture to the top.
8. Garnish with remaining lime wedge.

LuLu Clue: This drink is for the "Margarita Purist," who likes the drink salty, not too sweet, and never ever uses sour mix! It's best if you have a bar shaker handy. If not, stir to satisfaction.

The Cadillac Margarita

MAKES 1 DRINK

1½ ounces Margaritaville® gold tequila

¾ ounce Grand Marnier® orange liqueur

2 ounces sour mix

Juice of ½ fresh lime

1 fresh lime wedge

Coarse salt to rim glass

Lime wedge to garnish

1. Fill a shaker with ice.
2. Pour gold tequila, orange liqueur, sour mix, and fresh lime juice into shaker.
3. Shake vigorously.
4. Rim the outer edge of a margarita glass with a fresh lime wedge and turn glass upside down in a plate of coarse salt. (The lime juice helps the salt stick to the glass.)
5. Fill salted glass with ice and strain mixture to the top.
6. Garnish with fresh lime wedge.

With a splash of pink reminiscent of the sunset, cranberry juice balances the bite of tequila and sour mix in the Rosarita Margarita. It's a refreshing favorite, rimmed with sugar and garnished with lemon instead of lime. Plus, the cranberry helps curb the next-day headache! Gracias.

The Rosarita Margarita

MAKES 1 DRINK

1¼ ounces Sauza® Conmemorativo® anejo tequila

¾ ounce Cointreau® orange liqueur

1 ounce sour mix

1 ounce cranberry juice

1 fresh lemon wedge

Sugar (or coarse salt) to rim glass

Lemon wedge to garnish

1. Fill a shaker with ice.
2. Pour tequila, orange liqueur, sour mix, and cranberry juice into shaker.
3. Shake vigorously.
4. Rim the outer edge of a margarita glass with lemon wedge and turn glass upside down in a plate of sugar. (The lemon juice helps the sugar stick to the glass.)
5. Fill sugared glass with ice and strain mixture to the top.
6. Garnish with a fresh lemon wedge. (If you like it extra sweet, you can coat each side of lemon garnish with sugar, too.)

This one is strictly for the Margarita aficionado...no sweet or sour "juices" to distract from the perfect flavor and the perfect "buzz"...just a little lime and a reeeaaal good time.

Lucy's Favorite Margarita

MAKES 1 DRINK

2 ounces Patron® silver tequila

1 ounce Patron Citronge® orange liqueur

Juice of ½ fresh lime

1 fresh lime wedge

Coarse salt to rim glass

Lime wedge to garnish

1. Fill a shaker with ice.
2. Add tequila, orange liqueur, and lime juice. (Throw the squeezed lime into the shaker...believe me it adds to the drink!)
3. Rim the outer edge of a margarita glass with fresh lime wedge and turn upside down in a plate of coarse salt. (The lime juice helps the salt stick to the glass.)
4. Fill salted glass with ice and strain mixture to the top.
5. Garnish with fresh lime wedge.

LuLu's Raspberry Reef Margarita

MAKES 1 DRINK

1 ounce Margaritaville® gold tequila

1 ounce Margaritaville® silver tequila

½ ounce Chambord® raspberry liqueur

½ ounce Cointreau® orange liqueur

2 ounces sour mix

1 fresh lime wedge

Coarse salt to rim glass, optional

Fresh lime wedge to garnish

1. Fill a shaker with ice.
2. Pour gold tequila, silver tequila, raspberry liqueur, orange liqueur and sour mix into shaker.
3. Shake vigorously.
4. Rim the outer edge of a margarita glass with a lime wedge and turn glass upside down in a plate of coarse salt. (The lime juice helps the salt stick to the glass.)
5. Fill salted glass with ice and strain mixture to the top.
6. Garnish with fresh lime wedge.

SPECIALTY DRINKS

LuLu's Big Blue Shark Margarita

MAKES 1 DRINK

2 ounces Margaritaville® silver tequila

½ ounce blue Curaçao orange liqueur

2 ounces sour mix

1 fresh lime wedge

Coarse salt to rim glass, optional

Fresh lemon and lime wedges to garnish

1. Fill a shaker or glass with ice.
2. Add silver tequila, orange liqueur, and sour mix.
3. Shake vigorously.
4. Rim the outer edge of a margarita glass with a lime wedge and turn glass upside down in a plate of coarse salt. (The lime juice helps the salt stick to the glass.)
5. Fill salted glass with ice and strain mixture to the top.
6. Garnish with fresh lemon and lime wedges.

This cocktail is positively a tribute to one of the most loved, admired, sometimes feared, but most of all, vital members of the LuLu's family... Chief Mama and number cruncher/controller, Brenda Lake. She's not much of a drinker, but after sampling a pomegranate-infused margarita in Key West, she requested a rare second round. She asked our bar manager, a Key West transplant himself, if he could duplicate one for the LuLu's menu. He mentioned that this trendy drink was already on its way "out of style," to which she simply replied, "perfect!" He granted her wish, and it's now on the menu, full of love and antioxidants just for you, Miss Brenda!

Miss Brenda's "Pomarita" Margarita

MAKES 1 DRINK

1 ounce Margaritaville® gold tequila

1 ounce Margaritaville® silver tequila

½ ounce Pama® pomegranate liqueur

½ ounce Cointreau® orange liqueur

2 ounces sour mix

1 fresh lime wedge

Coarse salt to rim glass, optional

Lime wedge to garnish

1. Fill a shaker with ice.
2. Pour gold tequila, silver tequila, pomegranate liqueur, and sour mix into shaker.
3. Shake vigorously.
4. Rim the outer edge of a margarita glass with a lime wedge and turn glass upside down in a plate of coarse salt. (The lime juice helps the salt stick to the glass.)
5. Fill salted glass with ice and strain mixture to the top.
6. Garnish with fresh lime wedge.

A good Rum Punch

is one of those drinks that no matter where you are, no matter what season of the year, can transport you to any tropical paradise you so desire…I close my eyes and am at the Blue Bar at the Pink Sands Hotel in Harbour Island…where would you like to be?

LuLu's Rum Punch

MAKES 1 DRINK

1 ounce Captain Morgan® Original spiced rum

½ ounce Myer's® dark rum

½ ounce coconut rum

2 ounces sour mix

1 ounce pineapple juice

1 ounce cranberry juice

Splash of grenadine, optional

Cherry and fresh tropical fruit to garnish

1. Fill a tall glass with ice.
2. Add spiced rum, dark rum, coconut rum, and sour mix to glass.
3. Add equal portions of pineapple and cranberry juice.
4. Add a splash of grenadine if you like it a little sweeter.
5. Stir well.
6. Garnish with a cherry and fresh tropical fruit, such as orange, lemon or lime slices, or pineapple wedge.

Famous for its exquisite waterfront dining, Louie's Backyard in Key West is just as (if not more) infamous for its "colorful" patrons. It's a loopy cross between Truman Capote and Julia Child with a little Hunter S. Thompson thrown in the mix after hours. On any given day, you can share the bar with a salty old fishing guide spending his last few bucks while he waits for the wind to change. Besides being one of my favorite places in the world, Louie's serves up a mighty fine Mojito. The bartenders hate to make them — all the muddling and they can never make just one. As soon as they serve one, there is the inevitable onslaught of orders from curious first-timers, neophytes to tropical libation. Their secret is to serve it in a short highball glass, with only a touch of simple syrup.

The Mighty Fine Mojito

MAKES 1 DRINK

4-6 fresh mint leaves, loosely packed

3-4 fresh lime slices

1 ounce simple syrup

2 ounces light rum

Soda water

Sprig of fresh mint and lime slice to garnish

1. In a glass, add fresh mint leaves and fresh lime slices.
2. Pour simple syrup just to top of lime and mint.
3. Muddle with a pestle or a wooden spoon.
4. Fill glass with ice.
5. Add rum.
6. Fill almost to top of glass with soda.
7. Pour gently into another glass a couple of times to mix well... be careful that the soda does not get too fizzy.
8. Garnish with a sprig of fresh mint and a lime slice.

Key Lime Martini

MAKES 1 DRINK

1 ounce vanilla vodka

½ ounce Licor 43®

½ ounce Ke Ke Beach Key lime liqueur

¼ ounce Key lime juice

1 fresh lime wedge

Crushed graham cracker cookie, optional

Lime wedge to garnish

1. Fill a shaker with ice.
2. Pour vanilla vodka, both liqueurs, and Key lime juice into shaker.
3. Shake vigorously.
4. Rim the outer edge of a martini glass with a lime wedge and turn glass upside down in a plate of crushed graham cracker cookie. (The lime juice helps the crumbs stick to the glass.)
5. Strain mixture to the top of glass.
6. Garnish with fresh lime wedge.

Such a simple, easy drink

for a simple, easy way of living. A kissin' cousin to the "Rum Punch," it can take you to more sultry climates no matter where you may be. A lovely and refreshing alternative to sweeter, fruitier tropical drinks.

The Original Boat Drink

MAKES 1 DRINK

2 ounces Mount Gay® rum
Splash of tonic water
Fresh lime wedge to garnish

1. Fill a tall glass with ice.
2. Pour rum into glass.
3. Top with a splash of tonic water.
4. Garnish with fresh lime wedge.

Disclaimer: No jet skis

have been harmed in the creation of this powerful cocktail, but the name sure makes our insurance company jumpy! They asked me to take it off the drink menu, but Parrotheads absolutely love them (you know who you are!) and that's reason enough for me to keep this favorite on the list. I'm always deeply suspicious of a blue cocktail, but the amount of rum in this tends to quell my fears. Of course, you should <u>never</u> operate jet skis under the influence, but if you're safely on LuLu's deck, a Jet Ski Killer is just the thing for a zoom-zoom afternoon.

Jet Ski Killer

MAKES 1 DRINK

½ ounce Captain Morgan® spiced rum

½ ounce Cruzan® coconut rum

½ ounce blue Curaçao orange liqueur

½ ounce crème de banana liqueur

4 ounces pineapple juice

Cherry and lemon slice to garnish

1. Fill a shaker with ice.
2. Pour spiced rum, coconut rum, orange liqueur, crème de banana liqueur, and pineapple juice into shaker.
3. Shake vigorously.
4. Pour into a tall glass.
5. Garnish with a cherry and lemon.

LuLu Clue: We serve this drink frozen or on the rocks at LuLu's. Most folks prefer it on the rocks, but if you'd like a sweeter, milkshake version, simply follow the above directions and substitute a frozen piña colada mix and/or vanilla ice cream in place of pineapple juice.

The Best Bloody Mary

MAKES 1 DRINK

1½-2 ounces vodka (my personal favorite is Absolut®)

1 teaspoon Worcestershire sauce

½ teaspoon prepared horseradish

Pinch of black pepper

Dash of celery salt

½ teaspoon Pickapeppa® sauce

2-4 dashes LuLu's Perfect Pepper Hot Sauce™, optional

1 lemon wedge

2 ounces Mott's® clamato juice or V8® 100% vegetable juice

Lemon or lime wedges, celery stalks, olives, pickled beans, pickled okra, or cucumber wedges (or anything else from the garden) to garnish

1. Fill a tall glass with ice.
2. Add vodka.
3. Add Worcestershire, horseradish, black pepper, celery salt, Pickapeppa® sauce, and hot sauce.
4. Squeeze in juice of lemon wedge.
5. Fill to top with clamato or vegetable juice.
6. Toss mixture in a shaker cup.
7. Pour back into glass.
8. Garnish as desired.

LuLu Clue: This tasty beverage is all about options: playing around with the ingredients makes this classic concoction a signature drink. Add more horseradish if you like it spicy and remember to "Live, Love, and Laugh," as this cocktail is a great way to start your weekend.

"NoLa Style" Hurricane

MAKES 1 DRINK

1 ounce Southern Comfort®

1 ounce light rum

½ ounce Chambord® raspberry liqueur

3 ounces orange juice

3 ounces unsweetened pineapple juice

½ ounce grenadine

Splash of Bacardi 151® rum, optional

Orange slice, pineapple wedge, and cherry to garnish

1. Fill a hurricane glass with ice.
2. Add Southern Comfort®, light rum, and raspberry liqueur.
3. Fill glass with equal parts orange juice and pineapple juice.
4. Add grenadine.
5. Shake vigorously..."shake it like a hurricane."
6. Top off drink with a splash of Bacardi 151®.
7. Garnish with your choice of tropical fruits and a cherry.

MY FIRST BLOODY MARY
By Mara Delaney Buffett

Most kids might say the first thing they learned to "fix" in the kitchen was cereal or maybe a peanut butter and jelly sandwich. The first thing I learned to "fix" was a Bloody Mary, honest-to-God-truth.

Mama often threw dinner parties on the weekends at her friend Bob Meriwether's house. She was at the center of an eclectic and creative set of friends, a tight little group of bohemians in Mobile's southern-conservative garden district. These weekly soirees were never the standard dinner-and-drinks affair. If you were invited, you learned to expect the unexpected.

As dinner wound down, there might be games or sing-alongs around Bob's white baby grand piano. My favorite times were when Mama would pass out copies of a "script" she had written for the night's entertainment; the grown-ups would then put on some sort of bizarre one-act play, everyone's part having carefully been written especially for them. The kids, having long been sequestered to a faraway bedroom to watch movies and entertain themselves, would more than likely have fallen asleep by this time. It was not uncommon to be roused from sleep to act as "extras" in the plays. With our drowsy heads cleared of dreams, and the sleep rubbed from our eyes, our appetite for adventure would kick in full-force. Within minutes we'd be squealing with delight, more than game for a little play-acting in the middle of the night with our parents.

Some folks may find this odd, unconventional, or even irresponsible...I would heartily disagree. It was simply fun! Our family never pretended to subscribe to a "Leave it to Beaver" suburban family flawlessness. We were nothing like the saintly Cleavers, all tucked up in our perfect world, the pride of the neighborhood. We were the crazy folks across the street, where there were late nights, a few famous food fights, lots of music, laughter, and of course, much in the way of refreshments.

Some folks may even question a mother's parental scruples on the mornings following such revelry. Propped up on pillows, surrounded by books and newspapers, with one of those chilled blue masks wrapped gently over her eyes, she dictated to me the ingredients of the perfect morning-after cocktail ...I'd get a sweet "Baby, can you go fix Mama a real good Bloody Mary?" and run off to the kitchen as fast as lightning to start experimenting.

> *A tall glass with lots of ice, three fingers of vodka, filled almost to the top with V-8® or Clamato®, a sprinkle of this and that, a large dollop of horseradish, lots of Worcestershire sauce, a squeeze or two of lemon juice, a few dashes of hot sauce (she likes them spicy), and her "secret" ingredient: a few dashes of Pickapeppa® sauce. Shake it well, be careful not to spill, and a pickled bean and a stalk of celery would do to finish nicely.*

After one of these, she would be up in no time, cooking *something*.

I've been making Bloody Marys now for over 30 years, and I have been told by many people that I make one of the best. For the Bloody Mary connoisseurs out there, you know that no two "Bloodys" are alike. There may be a little something in the fridge you decide to add (secretly), to see if anyone notices — a little bit of olive juice or spicy bean juice, even some of the au jus from last night's pot roast. In my opinion, making a good Bloody Mary carries out a valuable service to those in need. It's a healing art...something I learned from one of the best.

What's not to love?

A frosty milkshake of a cocktail drizzled with chocolate syrup, packing a sneak-up-on-you punch...de-lish! Sometimes I'll skip dessert altogether and order this famous LuLu's favorite instead. Let me tell you, sip sensibly (especially if you order it with a rum "floater") or you'll be Bush*wacked!*

LuLu's World Famous Bushwacker

MAKES 1 DRINK

2 ounces coffee liqueur

1 ounce crème de cacao chocolate liqueur

1½ ounces dark rum

2 ounces half-and-half

1 scoop vanilla ice cream, optional

1-2 cups crushed ice

Chocolate syrup

Splash of Myer's® dark rum, optional

Cherry to garnish

1. Pour coffee liqueur, crème de cacao, dark rum, half-and-half, vanilla ice cream, and ice in a blender.
2. Blend well until smooth.
3. Swirl a large glass with chocolate syrup.
4. Pour drink into glass.
5. Top with a splash of Myer's® rum.
6. Garnish with a cherry.

 LuLu Clue: Instead of a "splash" of Myer's® on the top, some folks like to fill the straw with rum, so their first sip is memorable...literally going straight to the head.

Mike Ferrell's oft-repeated remark about making his

sometime indispensable Painkillers is, "I might have a hangover, but it won't be today!" It's a well-known fact that it's a bad idea to try to go drink for drink with Anastasia's husband Michael, unofficial mayor of Fish River, but if you do, make sure he fixes up a batch of this sure-fire cure for you the next day. It's a bit of juice, a bit of coconut, a bit of nutmeg and a bit of hair o' the dog.

LuLu's Painkiller

MAKES 1 DRINK

2 ounces Appleton® Special Jamaican rum

3 ounces orange juice

2 ounces pineapple juice

1 ounce Coco Lopez® cream of coconut

Cherry and freshly grated nutmeg to garnish

1. Fill a tall glass with ice.
2. Pour rum, orange juice, and pineapple juice into glass.
3. Add a "swirl" of cream of coconut.
4. Shake vigorously.
5. Garnish with a cherry and freshly grated nutmeg on top. (Don't skip the nutmeg, it's what makes this drink so good!)

LuLu Clue: The ground nutmeg found in the spice section of the grocery store works fine, but freshly grated takes this interesting drink to another level.

Marina Mama

MAKES 1 DRINK

1 ounce Captain Morgan® spiced rum

¾ ounce coconut rum

¾ ounce crème de banane liqueur

Splash of Coco Lopez® cream of coconut

Equal parts pineapple juice and orange juice

Lime wedge and cherry to garnish

1. Fill a tall glass with ice.
2. Add desired amounts of spiced rum, coconut rum, and crème de banane liqueur.
3. Add a splash of cream of coconut.
4. Top with equal parts unsweetened pineapple juice and orange juice.
5. Shake well.
6. Garnish with fresh lime wedge and a cherry.

The Bloody Bull

MAKES 1 DRINK

2 ounces vodka

Juice of ½ lemon

Juice of ¼ lime

2 pinches celery salt

1 teaspoon Worcestershire sauce

½ teaspoon Pickapeppa® sauce

3-4 splashes LuLu's Perfect Pepper
Hot Sauce™

2 ounces beef stock

3 ounces Mott's® clamato juice or
V8® 100% vegetable juice

Lemon or lime wedges, celery
stalks, olives, pickled beans,
pickled okra, or cucumber
wedges (or anything else from
the garden) to garnish

1. Fill a tall glass with ice.
2. Add vodka.
3. Add lemon and lime juices, celery salt, Worcestershire sauce, Pickapeppa® sauce, hot sauce, and beef stock.
4. Fill with vegetable juice.
5. Toss in a shaker cup.
6. Pour back into glass.
7. Garnish as desired.

 LuLu Clue: Au jus from a pot roast works incredibly well in this drink in place of beef stock. More options: garnish with a large shrimp or bleu cheese-stuffed olives. You can also rim the glass with Old Bay® seasoning.

The Key Lime Freeze

MAKES 1 DRINK

2 ounces light rum

¾ ounce Key lime juice

¼ ounce Rose's® lime juice

2 ounces half-and-half, divided

1 scoop vanilla ice cream, optional

1-2 cups crushed ice

1 fresh lime wedge

Crushed graham cracker cookie,
optional

Lime and cherry to garnish

Ke Ke® Beach Key lime liqueur,
optional

1. Pour the following ingredients into a blender: light rum, Key lime juice, Rose's® lime juice, 1 ounce half-and-half, ice cream, and ice.
2. Blend until smooth, adding remaining 1 ounce half-and-half to desired consistency.
3. Rim the outer edge of a glass with a lime wedge and turn glass upside down in a plate of crushed graham cracker cookie.
4. Pour frozen mixture into glass.
5. Garnish with fresh lime wedge and a cherry.
6. Swirl top with Key lime liqueur, if desired.

The Intracoastal Waterway...

is our front yard. (Anastasia is insisting that I point out here that it's "Intra-" not "Inter" as it is often mispronounced.) Technically, our portion of it is the Gulf Intracoastal Waterway, the canal through which commercial and recreational boats traffic from Carrabelle, Florida, to Brownsville, Texas. Perched along its northern bank in Gulf Shores, LuLu's makes for an exciting dolphin-watching vantage point. Our "address" on the ICW is mile marker #155, so you can easily find LuLu's on a navigational chart.

The ICW 155 Mudslide

MAKES 1 DRINK

1 ounce vodka

1½ ounces coffee liqueur, divided

1 ounce Baileys Original Irish Cream®

2 ounces half-and-half

1 scoop vanilla ice cream

1-2 cups crushed ice

Cherry to garnish

1. Pour vodka, 1 ounce coffee liqueur, Baileys®, half-and-half, vanilla ice cream, and ice in a blender.
2. Blend until smooth.
3. Pour into a glass.
4. Float remaining ½ ounce coffee liqueur on top.
5. Garnish with a cherry

LuLu Clue: Try throwing an Oreo® cookie in the blender with the other ingredients. It will make you smile!

Mother's Milk

MAKES 1 DRINK

2 ounces Mount Gay® or anejo rum
4 ounces club soda
Splash of Coca-Cola®
Lime wedge to garnish

1. Fill a tall glass with ice. Add rum.
2. Pour club soda almost to the top.
3. Add a splash of Coke®.
4. Garnish with fresh lime wedge.

Cuba Libre

MAKES 1 DRINK

2 ounces Bacardi® rum
½ fresh lime
4 ounces Coca-Cola®
Lime wedge to garnish

1. Fill a tall glass with ice. Add rum.
2. Squeeze lime juice into glass.
3. Fill with Coke®.
4. Garnish with a fresh lime wedge.

  SPECIALTY DRINKS

Starters & Snacks

L.A. (LOWER ALABAMA) CAVIAR

ALMOST SMOKED TUNA DIP

LULU'S PERFECT PEEL AND EAT SHRIMP

HEAVENLY FRIED CRAB CLAWS

LULU'S WEST INDIES SALAD

FAMOUS FRIED GREEN TOMATOES

LULU'S JERK CHICKEN QUESADILLAS

CREOLA BLACKENED SHRIMP QUESADILLAS

DEEP FRIED OKRA

JALAPEÑO HUSHPUPPIES

CRAZY CHICKEN FINGERS-GRILLED

CRAZY CHICKEN FINGERS-FRIED

LULU'S MEXI-LOCO PIE

SLOPPY SHRIMP

CRISPY COCONUT FRIED SHRIMP

CRAZY CHEESY QUESO DIP

CARAMELIZED ONION AND SPINACH DIP

LUCY B. GOODE'S CRABCAKES

SWEET AND SASSY ICEBOX PICKLES

SHRIMP BUTTER

PIMENTO PARTY CHEESE

A High-Five for Coconut Shrimp

I am a great believer in beginning a meal with an appetizer. Sure, I would like to think it has something to do with having a discriminating palate or being a sophisticated diner, or perhaps even honoring family tradition...but quite frankly, I just *love* to eat; and when I go out to eat, I want to eat as many good and different things as possible. As far as my "refined" palate is concerned, I am convinced that it is directly related to my acute sense of smell and my prominent nose, which the family affectionately calls the "Buffett Beak" — we all seem to have one!

Starters were not a common practice at our family dinner table, but rather an exclusive treat in which to be indulged when we went out to eat after payday. In fact, my first recollection of an appetizer is crab claws at dinner with my parents. This is a classic, famous Mobile dish. Start with a "mess" of blue crab claws, tail ends, with the shell cracked away to expose the sweet brown meat. The claws are then dredged in seasoned flour and deep-fried to a "golden brown" — just as good Southern cuisine should be.

Even when the time between the first and the fifteenth stretched over three weekends and the coffers were dry, my parents would still pile us into the station wagon after their long day of work at the shipyard and take us to Roussos or the Captain's Table on the Causeway over Mobile Bay. When purse strings were tight, the children ate meatloaf or spaghetti while Peets and J.D. had a couple of gin & tonics. Priorities have always been clear in my family; Buffetts are known to be willing to spend their last five dollars on a shrimp loaf and a cold beer. Good food and libation are simply encoded in our gene pool.

When I throw a dinner party, it is essential I provide something for my guests to nibble on so that they don't fall down before dinner! I can get so entranced in the preparation of the meal and frivolity of the gathering that an invitation for 7:30 p.m. might actually get served closer to 9. A word of caution for the novice Buffett dinner guest: Beware of the "F**k Dinner!" hour — when the wine is flowing and no one cares about dinner anymore and cocktails start tasting better than food!

One of the first lessons I learned as I started LuLu's was that there is a profound difference between being a catering chef and expediting a commercial kitchen. In the beginning it was my intention to be the head cook. After all, the menu was made up of my favorite recipes and being the control freak that I am, surely *only* I could oversee that the dishes were being prepared and plated properly. I may have fed 250 cowboys on my sister's Montana ranch an authentic New Orleans Jambalaya buffet, but calculating how many French fries are needed for the twenty hand-written tickets hanging above my head takes a brain more focused than mine (and one that didn't spend its early twenties in Key West)! I lasted five days in the kitchen before I crumpled onto the greasy brick floor in tears; I fired myself as head cook.

I went on to work about twenty other jobs at the restaurant until one day, someone didn't show up in the kitchen; I decided to pitch in and help. We had run out of prepped Coconut Shrimp, one of the favorite STARTER & SNACKS menu items. Before we had the opportunity to "86 it," restaurant slang for being unavailable or sold out, we had about five orders to be filled. I thought, "No problem, I'll just get back there and *throw some together*."

Unfortunately, one does not just "throw together" Coconut Shrimp. It takes peeling, de-veining, dipping, dredging, dipping again, dredging, and then patting on the coconut. Since my forced retirement as line cook, I had sorely forgotten the rigors and pressure of that position. When I was about halfway through completing the outstanding orders, I erupted, "Who the (blank) put this on the menu?"

"You did." the kitchen staff sang in unison.

"Well, it's off the menu. Permanently!" I shot back.

Restaurant kitchens function like an orchestra pit at a Broadway play, invisible but essential. The last thing you want to do is mess with their rhythm. Our moment of tension could have gone one of two ways...frustration and anger or amusement and levity.

Finally, one of the fry guys lifted his hand to "high five" me and another gave me a big hug. The rest of the shift went very smoothly, especially after I had fired myself again and exited the kitchen. The menu was rewritten and reprinted the next day, and there was never another Coconut Fried Shrimp served at LuLu's! (But the recipe is on page 110!)

This is one of my favorite

LuLu's dishes, and I make it at home all the time. During one memorable chapter of my life, I ran with a group of highly disreputable folks who lived in lavish historic homes on Washington Square in Mobile, Alabama. We had weekly soirees complete with costumed cabaret numbers around a white baby grand and copious amounts of cocktails and hors d'oeuvres. Right before I opened LuLu's, we had a reunion celebrating my friend Suzanne Cleveland's birthday. One of our "partners in crime," John Coleman, arrived with a great black-eyed pea dip. John is a barbecue aficionado, redneck lawyer and rogue gourmand, so it gave me great pleasure to steal his recipe! Because I had just returned from living in Los Angeles, I gave it a little LuLu's twist and the L.A. reference: a perfect fit for my high-class dive. It has been on the menu at LuLu's since day one and is one of the restaurant's signature dishes. Today, we make it in twenty gallon batches.

L.A. (Lower Alabama) Caviar

MAKES 20 TO 25 SERVINGS

DRESSING
¾ cup balsamic vinegar
½ cup extra virgin olive oil
¼ cup sugar
2 teaspoons salt
1 teaspoon black pepper

4 (15-ounce) cans black-eyed peas, rinsed and drained
1 cup chopped green bell pepper
1 cup chopped yellow bell pepper
1 cup chopped red bell pepper
1 cup chopped red onion
1½ cups cherry tomatoes, quartered
1 cup finely chopped fresh parsley

1. Combine all dressing ingredients in a jar; cover tightly, and shake vigorously to dissolve sugar. Set aside.
2. Place peas in a large glass or stainless steel bowl.
3. Add all bell peppers, onions, tomatoes and parsley. Pour dressing over top and toss well. Transfer to a plastic container, cover and refrigerate for at least 2 hours before serving.
4. Serve with tortilla chips or saltine crackers.

This recipe contains one of my favorite ingredients: NO STRESS! Your friends will think you've been standing over a smoker all day when you've actually been getting your nails done. It's quick, easy, scrumptious, and addictive...proven by the astounding number of family, friends, and customers who've not only requested the recipe, but almost begged for it.

We've had LuLu's patrons from as far away as Wisconsin, New Jersey, Alaska, Hawaii, and even the Middle East email the "comments" section of our website saying they would "do anything for the recipe," since no substitute has satisfied their craving. I am grateful to these people who've traveled far and make LuLu's a stop on their journeys; I am more than happy to share the recipe with you all.

Almost Smoked Tuna Dip

MAKES 8-10 SERVINGS

2 pounds fresh or frozen tuna steaks, thawed

1 cup white wine or water

1 tablespoon liquid smoke flavoring

1 medium-size yellow onion, finely chopped

1 tablespoon LuLu's Perfect Pepper Hot Sauce™

1 tablespoon lemon juice, freshly squeezed

2 tablespoons LuLu's Crazy Creola Seasoning™ (page 50)

1½ tablespoons lemon pepper seasoning

¾-1 cup mayonnaise

1. Preheat oven to 350 degrees.
2. Place tuna steaks in a shallow, lightly greased glass baking dish. Add wine or water and liquid smoke. Cover with aluminum foil and bake for 30 to 40 minutes or until fish is thoroughly cooked. Remove fish from baking dish and cool completely.
3. In a large salad bowl, crumble tuna into medium-size chunks. Do not over-crumble the fish — this is a chunky dip, not a spread.
4. Add chopped onion, hot sauce, lemon juice, Creole seasoning, and lemon pepper.
5. Gently fold in *just enough* mayonnaise to hold together.
6. Place dip in a 2-quart plastic container and refrigerate for at least 2 hours or overnight. At LuLu's, we serve it with fresh saltine crackers.

 LuLu Clue: Liquid smoke has tons of salt, which is why you don't have to add any more. Never, ever use "cooking wine." It's filled with sodium and other things I can't pronounce. I always use the wine I'm serving (or drinking, of course); I'm also fond of using sake when a recipe can handle the sweetness. For those preferring a low-calorie version, I have found that using a light or reduced-fat mayo doesn't harm the integrity of the recipe. Never, ever use fat-free mayonnaise; it tastes like paste, and I'm not sure it qualifies as food.

LuLu's Perfect Peel and Eat Shrimp

MAKES 4 SERVINGS

1½-2 gallons water

1 cup LuLu's Perfect Pepper Hot Sauce™

¾ cup freshly squeezed lemon juice

1½ cups liquid Zatarain's® crab and seafood boil

1 (3-ounce) bag Zatarain's® dry crab and seafood boil

5 bay leaves

½ cup LuLu's Crazy Creola Seasoning™ (page 50)

¼ cup salt

2-3 pounds large headless shrimp with shells

1. Combine all ingredients except shrimp in a large stockpot. Bring to a full rolling boil. Be prepared to have the spices "tickle" the back of your throat. Gesundheit!

2. Add shrimp. Cook for 2 minutes.

3. Turn off heat and cover for 1 minute. Drain shrimp in a colander and place a layer of ice on top to stop cooking process.

4. Allow to cool for at least 5 minutes. Drain and refrigerate. Serve with my Red Horseradish Sauce (page 174).

LuLu Clue: Don't be afraid that this dish will be extra spicy; it takes that much seasoning to permeate the shells.

STARTERS & SNACKS

This is the traditional way

to enjoy crab claws along the Gulf Coast. Every beach restaurant from Bay St. Louis to Pensacola offers these delicacies. As a child, this was a "must" first course for our family when we went out to dinner on the Causeway on Mobile Bay. At LuLu's, crab claws have become one of our signature dishes because they are simply heavenly.

Heavenly Fried Crab Claws

MAKES 4 SERVINGS

2 cups LuLu's Crazy Frying Flour (page 52)

2 cups whole milk

1 tablespoon LuLu's Perfect Pepper Hot Sauce™

6 cups peanut or vegetable oil, or enough to fill skillet about 2 inches deep

1 pound fresh blue crab claws, shells removed

Lemon wedges for garnish

1. Place frying flour in a bowl.
2. In a separate bowl, combine milk and hot sauce.
3. In a cast iron or heavy skillet, heat oil to 355 degrees over medium-high heat. (Use a candy or fry thermometer for accuracy or heat until a little flour flicked into the oil sizzles.)
4. Take a few crab claws at a time and dredge through flour. Dip in milk, and then dredge through flour again.
5. Gently drop in hot oil. Fry until crab claws are golden brown. Adjust heat as necessary to keep oil temperature around 355 degrees. Drain on paper towels and serve immediately with lemon wedges.

LuLu Clue: As with any crustacean, the claw meat is the sweetest. Crabmeat becomes stringy when frozen, so I use fresh. When fresh crab claws aren't available, I substitute crawfish tails.

CONFESSIONS OF A SHAMELESS ADDICT
By long-time friend, Bobbo Jetmundsen

Addictions: okay, there are a few to confess. First, way too often I crave a glass (ok, bottle) of red wine; I'm particularly fond of Napa Valley cabernet sauvignon. Down South we mostly treat AA as a two-step program...Alka Seltzer and Advil. Second addiction: Krispy Kreme® doughnuts. I can eat them pretty darn fast and usually do before I can restrain myself to a reasonable limit. When I'm finished, I glance at my belly, convinced that because I ate them so fast, I didn't really just inhale 3350 calories and countless carbs. They are kryptonite to my diet.

Third, crab claws. Fried. You'll never find them anywhere like you do along the coast of Alabama. Mississippi can't do it. New Orleans can cook any other type of crabmeat as well or better, but not a fried crab claw. I'm talking about something that only tastes this way in either Mobile County or Baldwin County, Alabama. The first time I had them growing up, I was hooked. And the claws at LuLu's are the best damned things I've ever had. Fat claws fried and dipped into cocktail sauce one after the other until they are gone. That good. You could absolutely care less that the pile of discarded claws in front of you is bigger than anyone else's. Shameless good. Get yourself in front of a pound or so of them, grab the hard part, dip the fried end into the tub of sauce, slide the damn thing into your mouth sideways and grab the meat between your teeth, pull slowly on the claw and, voilà, the lump of crabmeat lands on your tongue. Chew, swallow, and repeat. Eventually, when you can't breathe too well, chug a bit of whatever you're drinking and say "How you duerring?" to whoever is nearby.

Jimmy once wrote that no one wants to put the time in required to become a legend anymore. Well, let's just say that with the cast of characters that wander into his sister's joint, LuLu's will become legendary on its own. I can't wait to return, walk in, sit at the bar, and sip libations to the live music onstage.

That coconut of Lucy's didn't fall far from the ole palm tree. She's got a "tin cup for a chalice filled up with red wine" and knows all about "fishing the pilings where the fishing is best." And for the sister of a Son of a Son of a Sailor, LuLu's won't be "wasting away again" anytime soon...unless those delectable, succulent, fried Mobile Bay jumbo crab claws run out. I tremble at the very thought of it.

Bobbo on a wine-fueled mission

97

This dish originated in Mobile, Alabama at Bayley's Steak and Seafood Restaurant and has nothing at all to do with the West Indies. It is a mystery as to how this luscious crab dish got its name but it remains the crown jewel of Gulf Coast cuisine. It is a Buffett family favorite. Every Christmas, I overnight-ship two pounds of this coastal delight to both my brother and sister at their Rocky Mountain retreats. West Indies Salad is present at all of my fancy dinner parties, as well as on any given Saturday afternoon at our tiki bar, poolside. Pink champagne is my favorite beverage to drink with this irresistible crab delicacy, but I've also been known to swig ice-cold beer and eat West Indies Salad with my fingers.

LuLu's West Indies Salad

MAKES 4-6 SERVINGS

1 pound fresh jumbo lump blue crabmeat

Salt to taste (about ½ teaspoon)

Freshly ground black pepper to taste (about ¼ teaspoon)

½ medium Vidalia® (or sweet) onion, sliced paper thin, in half moon shape

⅓ cup vegetable oil

⅓ cup white vinegar

⅓ cup ice water (with 4-5 ice cubes)

1. Place half the crabmeat gently in the bottom of a glass bowl or plastic container, carefully picking out any shell. Sprinkle with just a smidgen of salt and pepper.
2. Cover crab with a layer of onion.
3. Repeat steps with remaining crab, salt, pepper, and onion.
4. Pour oil and vinegar over layers.
5. Place ice cubes in a liquid measuring cup. Fill with water until volume reaches ⅓ cup and pour over crab.
6. Cover and marinate for at least 2 hours before serving.
7. When ready to serve, shake bowl gently, or if using a leak-proof plastic container, turn upside down and back upright to gently mix salad.
8. Serve in a shallow bowl with juice.

LuLu Clue: It really is this easy, and the ice cubes are crucial. Don't ask me why, but when I haven't included them, the dish just doesn't taste the same.

LuLu Clue: Jumbo lump is expensive because there are only two pieces of the meat yielded from a single crab, but it's worth it. You can use regular lump crab, but you must carefully and delicately pick through it for shells.

A Long Way from Alabama to Montana

My wife and I are lifelong lovers of the ocean and its provender, but we live at 5000 feet in the Northern Rockies, a condition we relish until the wind blows the snow across the road a month or two too long. Hope then resides in a rich fantasy life fueled by the occasional kindnesses of friends and family in the form of letters and care packages. For many, vitamin D enriched cod liver oil, a light box, obsession with sports teams, bourbon in square bottles, or unnecessary remodeling help them make it through the long low-light period. It is, I have heard remarked, the moon of schnapps and jumper cables. One thing we look forward to with somewhat unhealthy emphasis is the arrival of Lucy's Christmas shipment of West Indies Salad, but it's a long way from Alabama to Montana. Our happiness one Christmas fell into the hands of a famous parcel service, which transferred it from airplane to airplane, then to all the wrong places, then to kindly relatives who tried to forward it on in the hands of holiday-exhausted shipping personnel (extending the delivery time beyond what is deemed safe for seafood), until finally a uniformed driver leaning into whirling snow brought to our door on Christmas Eve, a holy time in the lives of millions, many

pounds of hopelessly spoiled crabmeat bobbing in formerly savory seasoning. If ever we considered sobbing over a missed meal, that was the time. Anyone who has ever eaten Lucy's West Indies Salad will understand.

*~ Thomas McGuane
(rancher, novelist, fisherman,
sailor, brother-in-law)
McLeod, Montana,
August 2007*

Famous Fried Green Tomatoes

MAKES 4 SERVINGS

2 cups LuLu's Crazy Frying Flour (page 52)

2 cups buttermilk

1 tablespoon LuLu's Perfect Pepper Hot Sauce™

4 green tomatoes

6 cups peanut or vegetable oil, or enough to fill a skillet about 2 inches deep

LuLu's WOW Sauce™ (page 173)

1. Preheat oven to 200 degrees.
2. Place frying flour in a bowl.
3. In a separate bowl, combine buttermilk and pepper sauce.
4. Slice green tomatoes ¼-inch thick and set aside.
5. In a cast iron heavy skillet, heat oil to 355 degrees over medium-high heat. (Use a candy or fry thermometer for accuracy or heat until a little flour flicked into the oil sizzles.)
6. Dip tomatoes in buttermilk, then dredge tomatoes in frying flour. Dip back into milk mixture and dredge again in frying flour, coating tomatoes thoroughly.
7. Fry tomatoes in small batches (about 4 slices at a time) until golden brown, approximately 2 minutes on each side, turning once during cooking.
8. Drain on a paper bag on a cookie sheet. Place fried tomatoes in oven while others are cooking. When all batches are completed, serve immediately with WOW Sauce.

LuLu Clue: Not only is "double-dipping" allowed, it's "a-mandatory" in turning this not-ripe vegetable into a mouth-watering Southern delicacy.

Jerk seasoning was very trendy when I started LuLu's and was perfect for our tropical theme. Over the years, it has become less in demand but is still a favorite of mine, transporting me to the beach in Mo-Bay (that's Montego Bay, not Mobile Bay). So I created a jerk seasoning with a Southern flair, added it to our shrimp and chicken, and stuck it right in the middle of our scrumptious quesadilla to satisfy my south-of-the-border/Caribbean cravings. Unless you have a large flattop commercial grill, you can only cook one of these at a time, so it's great to make and serve as you go for a large group. I serve mine with my Chunky Cherry Tomato Salsa and a large dollop of sour cream.

LuLu's Jerk Chicken Quesadillas

MAKES 4 SERVINGS

12 chicken breast tenders

6 tablespoons olive oil, divided

2 tablespoons LuLu's Jerk Seasoning (page 51)

2 medium sweet yellow onions, sliced

3 medium green bell peppers, sliced

Pinch of kosher salt

Pinch of black pepper

4 (12-inch) flour tortillas

4 cups shredded Monterey Jack/ Cheddar cheese blend

LuLu's Chunky Cherry Tomato Salsa (page 177)

Sour cream

1. Toss chicken strips with 1 tablespoon olive oil and jerk seasoning.
2. Brush a heavy skillet with 2 tablespoons olive oil and heat until just about to sizzle.
3. Add chicken tenders and sauté for 4 minutes on each side or until browned. Remove from heat and chop into bite-size pieces.
4. In same skillet, heat 2 tablespoons of olive oil.
5. Add onions, green peppers, salt, and black pepper. Sauté until soft and slightly browned on the edges. Remove and let cool.
6. Heat another large heavy skillet over medium heat for 2-3 minutes.
7. To make one quesadilla: brush one side of tortilla with a little of the remaining 1 tablespoon olive oil. Place tortilla, oil-side down, in hot skillet.
8. Layer one-fourth of the cheese, onions, and peppers over entire tortilla. Put one-fourth of the chicken on half of tortilla.
9. Fold tortilla over chicken and cook until bottom is lightly browned. Flip to other side and continue cooking until brown and edges are crisp.
10. Slice into wedges. Top with salsa and a large dollop of sour cream.

 LuLu Clue: For Southern Jerk Shrimp Quesadilla, substitute 1 pound medium shrimp, peeled and deveined.

When Chef Paul

Prudhomme introduced his Blackened Redfish recipe back in the 70's, the concept took the entire country by storm. Somehow, however, the recipe became distorted by the notion that the fish or shrimp or chicken had to be encrusted in seasoning. That is not at all how Chef Paul serves his dish. The seasoning is meant to flavor and flirt with the protein, not overpower it. I love blackened seasoning, as long as it's subtle. If you're a die-hard-no-remaining-taste-buds type, you can crank up the heat with LuLu's Mean Green Hot Sauce™.

Creola Blackened Shrimp Quesadillas

MAKES: 4 SERVINGS

1 pound medium shrimp, peeled and deveined

6 tablespoons olive oil, divided

2 tablespoons LuLu's Crazy Creola Seasoning™ (page 50)

2 medium yellow onions, sliced

3 medium green bell peppers, sliced

Pinch of salt

Pinch of black pepper

4 (12-inch) flour tortillas

4 cups shredded Monterey Jack/ Cheddar cheese blend

LuLu's Chunky Cherry Tomato Salsa (page 177)

Sour cream

1. Toss shrimp in 1 tablespoon olive oil and Creole seasoning. Set aside.
2. In a cast iron or heavy skillet, heat 2 tablespoons olive oil over medium-high heat.
3. Add shrimp and sauté for 3 to 4 minutes or until shrimp are pink and tender. Do not overcook; remove from heat immediately and set aside.
4. In the same skillet, heat 2 tablespoons olive oil.
5. Add onions, bell peppers, salt, and black pepper. Sauté until soft and slightly browned on the edges. Remove and set aside.
6. Heat another large heavy skillet over medium high heat.
7. To make one quesadilla: brush one side of tortilla with a little of the remaining 1 tablespoon olive oil. Place tortilla, oil-side down, in hot skillet.
8. Layer one-fourth of cheese, peppers, and onions over entire tortilla. Put one-fourth of the shrimp (approximately 8) on half of tortilla.
9. Fold tortilla in half and cook until bottom is lightly browned. Flip to other side and cook until brown and crisp.
10. Slice into wedges. Top with salsa and sour cream.

LuLu Clue: Also great as a Blackened Chicken Quesadilla.

Deep Fried Okra

2 cups LuLu's Crazy Frying Flour
(page 52)

2 cups whole milk

1 tablespoon LuLu's Perfect
Pepper Hot Sauce™

4 cups fresh okra, cut into ¼-inch
pieces

6 cups peanut or vegetable oil, or
enough to fill skillet about
2 inches deep

LuLu's WOW Sauce™ (page 173)

1. Place flour in a bowl.
2. Combine milk and hot sauce in another bowl.
3. In a cast iron or heavy skillet, heat oil to 355 degrees over medium-high heat. (Use a candy or fry thermometer for accuracy or heat until a little flour flicked into the oil sizzles.)
4. Dredge okra through flour, dip into milk mixture, and dredge again in flour, coating okra thoroughly.
5. Gently drop a handful of okra into hot oil. Fry in small batches until golden brown.
6. Drain on paper towels and serve immediately with WOW Sauce.

Jalapeño Hushpuppies

MAKES ABOUT 2½ DOZEN PUPPIES

1½ cups self-rising buttermilk
cornmeal mix

½ cup all-purpose flour

1 teaspoon baking powder

1 teaspoon salt

1½ teaspoons LuLu's Crazy Creola
Seasoning™ (page 50)

2 eggs, beaten

1½ teaspoons LuLu's Perfect
Pepper Hot Sauce™

1 cup whole milk

¼ cup finely chopped sweet onions

2 fresh jalapeño peppers, finely
chopped

6 cups peanut or vegetable oil, or
enough to fill skillet about
2 inches deep

1. In a large mixing bowl, combine corn meal, flour, baking powder, salt, and 1 teaspoon seasoning, set aside.
2. In a separate bowl, combine eggs, hot sauce, and milk and mix well.
3. Gradually add liquid mixture to dry ingredients and mix well.
4. Gently fold in onions and jalapeño peppers.
5. Heat oil in heavy Dutch oven. Add a drop of batter and wait until it sizzles to indicate oil is ready.
6. Drop a tablespoon of batter into hot oil, 4 to 6 at a time.
7. Roll each hushpuppy around in frying oil for 2 to 3 minutes or until evenly browned on all sides.
8. Drain on paper towels, sprinkle remaining ½ teaspoon seasoning mix over puppies, and serve hot!

Maybe these chicken fingers

taste homemade because they are! Whether grilled or fried, they are so versatile and delicious; we put them in sandwiches, wraps, and salads. They're perfect for the boat, the beach, the game, or the lunch box. I'm a sucker for the fried ones because they taste just like my Daddy's fried chicken. When you slather them in LuLu's Bad Girl Buffalo Sauce, they are out of this crazy world!

Crazy Chicken Fingers – Grilled

MAKES 4 SERVINGS

12 chicken breast tenders

1 cup LuLu's One Heart Marinade (page 48)

1 tablespoon olive oil

1. Place chicken, marinade, and olive oil in a shallow baking dish or a zip-top bag and refrigerate for 1 hour.
2. Place on a hot charcoal or gas grill and cook chicken for 4 minutes on each side or until cooked through.

LuLu Clue: If a grill is unavailable, heat olive oil in a heavy skillet and pan sauté.

Crazy Chicken Fingers – Fried

MAKES 4 SERVINGS

2 cups LuLu's Crazy Frying Flour (page 52)

2 cups whole milk

LuLu's Perfect Pepper Hot Sauce™

6 cups peanut or vegetable oil, or enough to fill a skillet about 2 inches deep

12 chicken breast tenders

1. Place frying flour in a bowl.
2. Combine milk and pepper sauce in another bowl.
3. In a cast iron or heavy skillet, heat oil to 355 degrees over medium-high heat. (Use a candy or fry thermometer for accuracy or heat until a little flour flicked into the oil sizzles.)
4. Dredge tenders through flour. Dip in milk, then dredge through flour again.
5. Fry chicken, turning once during cooking, for 3 to 4 minutes on each side or until golden brown. Drain on paper towels and serve immediately.

This recipe earns the Buffett "Clean Plate Award" because

every time I serve it, not so much as a morsel remains on the plate. And it is politically correct — it transcends age and gender as a crowd pleaser!

LuLu's Mexi-Loco Pie

MAKES 8-10 SERVINGS

2 cups sour cream

2 tablespoons LuLu's Chipotle Taco Seasoning (page 49) or any taco seasoning mix

¼ cup LuLu's Sassy Salsa™ (page 178)

1 ripe avocado

1 tablespoon freshly squeezed lime juice

2 (15-ounce) cans black beans, rinsed and drained

1 cup cherry tomatoes, quartered

½ cup thinly sliced green onions, including green tops

½ cup sliced black olives

¼ cup finely chopped fresh cilantro

3 cups shredded sharp Cheddar cheese

1. Combine sour cream, seasoning mix, and salsa. Refrigerate.
2. Peel and chop avocado. Toss with lime juice in a glass bowl. Set aside.
3. Spread black beans in the bottom of a 12-inch glass pie plate.
4. Spread sour cream mixture over beans.
5. Layer cherry tomatoes, green onions, and black olives on top of beans.
6. Drain avocado and spread on top of other layers.
7. Sprinkle cilantro over the top and cover completely with shredded cheese. Best served immediately with tortilla chips.

LuLu Clue: If you want to prepare this a couple of hours in advance, cover with plastic wrap and refrigerate. When ready to serve, let pie sit for fifteen minutes to allow the cheese to soften.

The first time I ever

had this dish was as a child at Pascal's Manale in New Orleans. I loved how messy and obscene it was. As a true Southern girl, any food that requires me to lick my fingers and use up a pine-tree load of napkins easily earns five big stars. "Sopping," as it's known down South, is absolutely essential with this dish (if you aren't in New Orleans with easy access to authentic French bread, try my improvisation: toasted hot dog buns). When I entertain lots of folks at my riverside home, I like to serve it outdoors on a paint-chipped picnic table covered in newspaper where we can stand around, eat, sop, and guzzle cold beer. It is messy and fun food. It doesn't get better than this.

Sloppy Shrimp

MAKES 4 SERVINGS

SLOPPY SEASONING MIX

2 teaspoons salt

1 teaspoon black pepper

½ teaspoon white pepper

½ teaspoon cayenne pepper

½ teaspoon crushed red pepper flakes

1 teaspoon onion powder

2 teaspoons paprika

1 stick, plus 2 tablespoons unsalted butter, divided

½ cup olive oil

2 tablespoons finely chopped fresh garlic

2 tablespoons finely chopped fresh rosemary

½ cup dark beer, room temperature

½ cup Shrimp Stock (page 57)

2 pounds large headless shrimp in the shells

1 tablespoon LuLu's Perfect Pepper Hot Sauce™

1 tablespoon Worcestershire sauce

Juice of 1 lemon

Zest of 1 lemon

2 tablespoons minced fresh parsley

1 loaf French bread or 4 hot dog buns

1. In a small bowl, combine all seasoning mix ingredients. Set aside.

2. Melt 1 stick of butter with olive oil over medium-high heat in a heavy skillet large enough to fit shrimp without overcrowding.

3. When butter and oil begin to sizzle, add garlic and rosemary. Stir once.

4. Add seasoning mix and stir once.

5. Add beer and shrimp stock, shaking skillet to marry the oil and liquid. Bring to a boil over medium-high heat, stirring or shaking the skillet constantly.

6. Add shrimp. Stir to coat and sauté or shake pan, turning shrimp, for 2 to 3 minutes or until they begin to turn pink.

7. Add remaining 2 tablespoons butter, hot sauce, Worcestershire sauce, lemon juice, lemon zest, and parsley. Stir well and cook for 1 minute. Do not overcook shrimp!

8. Quickly remove shrimp with a slotted spoon to 4 soup bowls. Ladle liquid over shrimp and serve immediately with crusty French bread and a roll of paper towels.

 LuLu Clue: It is especially important not to overcook the shrimp in this dish. If you see that the shells are turning opaque, they have cooked too long and will be difficult to peel.

 LuLu Clue: I use a little olive oil with the butter to allow it to get to a higher temperature without burning. Shaking the pan allows the juices to emulsify instead of separating. If I'm in a pinch without a back up of shrimp stock in my freezer, I use bottled clam juice or more beer.

Crispy Coconut Fried Shrimp

MAKES 2 SERVINGS

1 pound large headless shrimp in the shells

1 (12-ounce) can Coco Lopez® cream of coconut

1 egg, lightly beaten

2½ cups sweetened coconut flakes

½ cup self-rising flour

1 tablespoon sugar

1 teaspoon cayenne pepper

½ teaspoon salt

6 cups peanut or vegetable oil, or enough to fill a skillet about 2 inches deep

Orange Horseradish Dipping Sauce (page 174)

1. Peel shrimp, leaving tails on. Devein and place shrimp in a bowl of ice. Refrigerate until ready to bread.
2. Place Coco Lopez®, beaten egg, and coconut in three separate bowls.
3. Combine flour, sugar, cayenne pepper, and salt in a shallow baking pan.
4. Fix a big cocktail or take a deep breath and do a yoga stretch.
5. Holding shrimp by the tails, dredge in Coco Lopez®, then in flour mixture, and then in egg.
6. Roll shrimp in coconut, pressing firmly to coat completely. Place on a baking sheet and refrigerate for a minimum of 15 minutes.
7. In a cast iron or heavy skillet, heat oil to 355 degrees over medium-high heat. (Use a candy or fry thermometer for accuracy or heat until a little flour flicked into the oil sizzles.)
8. Fry shrimp in small batches, turning once during cooking, for 1½ to 2 minutes on each side or until golden.
9. Drain on paper towels and serve immediately with Orange Horseradish Dipping Sauce.

 LuLu Clue: These also work well when prepped and frozen. In fact they seem to stay together better when frozen, but you don't want to fry too many of them at one time because it takes more time for the oil to get back to the magic frying temp of 355 degrees between batches.

I had to include

this recipe in the cookbook, because Coconut Fried Shrimp was once on the menu, and I absolutely love to eat it...but it's a recipe that I absolutely "hate" to love.

If you were raised to go to confession or Temple on Saturday...

If your mother and grandmother tried to "out-martyr" each other...

If you believe that something has to be extremely hard and frustrating to be valid...

If you love to whine about how hard life is...

If you are NOT obsessive-compulsive about cleanliness while you cook...

If nothing you do is ever good enough...then this is the recipe for you!

   It is messy. It is hard to cook. It has to be cooked in batches so you can really only make enough for 2 servings at a time. It might fall apart, and coconut sometimes gets in the bottom of the fryer and burns before you are finished. But if you do it and do it right, IT IS DELICIOUS! One of the best recipes in the book. Good luck!

Our courageous friend, Kevin Holloran. It's tough, but someone's got to do it!

There are times in my life (sometimes as often as a couple of times a week)

when nothing satisfies my heart, soul, and belly more than chips, salsa, and a warm, spicy, cheesy, queso dip...and, of course, a margarita to wash it all down. Ah, the simple pleasures of life! It's one of my all-time favorite comfort foods, and my restaurant wouldn't be "me" without it on the menu!

Crazy Cheesy Queso Dip

MAKES 6-8 SERVINGS

4 tablespoons butter

½ sweet yellow onion, finely chopped

½ red bell pepper, finely chopped

½ green bell pepper, finely chopped

1 (4-ounce) can diced green chili peppers

1 pound white American cheese

1 cup whole milk

½ teaspoon ground cumin

½ teaspoon ground coriander

½ teaspoon white pepper

Salt to taste

1. Melt butter in a heavy skillet. Add onions and all bell peppers. Sauté 2 minutes or until vegetables are soft.
2. Add chili peppers and cook another 2 minutes. Remove from heat and set aside.
3. Cut cheese into 1-inch cubes. Place cheese and milk in the top of a double boiler and melt over medium-high heat.
4. Add onion and bell pepper mixture. Mix thoroughly.
5. Add cumin, coriander, and white pepper. Salt to taste.
6 Serve immediately with tortilla chips.

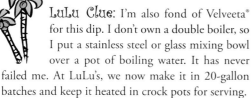 LuLu Clue: I'm also fond of Velveeta® for this dip. I don't own a double boiler, so I put a stainless steel or glass mixing bowl over a pot of boiling water. It has never failed me. At LuLu's, we now make it in 20-gallon batches and keep it heated in crock pots for serving.

This is absolutely scrumptious! Of course, it is… it's

full of fat but worth every calorie! It is versatile enough to be served either hot or cold and can be used as a dip or a sandwich spread. Caramelizing the onions gives it a sweet, almost smoky flavor. There is always a container of this dip in my fridge. It keeps well and makes a quick appetizer for friends who drop by. This recipe makes a big batch, so it can be halved.

Caramelized Onion and Spinach Dip

MAKES 7 CUPS

1 stick unsalted butter

2 sweet yellow onions, coarsely chopped

2 tablespoons sugar

2 teaspoons kosher salt, divided

2 (10-ounce) packages frozen chopped spinach, thawed and completely drained

1 (12-ounce) jar marinated quartered artichoke hearts, drained and coarsely chopped

1 (8-ounce) can water chestnuts, drained and coarsely chopped

4 ounces cream cheese, softened

1 cup sour cream

1 cup mayonnaise

¼ cup heavy cream

8 whole cloves garlic, peeled

1 teaspoon black pepper

1 tablespoon lemon pepper

1 teaspoon crushed red pepper flakes

2 teaspoons LuLu's Perfect Pepper Hot Sauce™

1 tablespoon freshly squeezed lemon juice

2 cups shredded Parmesan cheese

1. Melt butter in a heavy fry pan over medium heat. Add onions, sugar, and 1½ teaspoons salt. Sauté until onions begin to brown and caramelize. Place in large mixing bowl and let cool.

2. Meanwhile, place spinach in a colander and press to drain liquid. Squeeze drained spinach tightly in small handfuls until almost dry. Add to onions.

3. Add artichokes and water chestnuts to vegetable mixture. Set aside.

4. In the bowl of a food processor, combine cream cheese, sour cream, mayonnaise, cream, garlic, remaining ½ teaspoon of salt, black pepper, lemon pepper, crushed red pepper flakes, hot sauce, and lemon juice. Pulse several times until mixture is blended together.

5. Add Parmesan and pulse only a couple of times. Mixture should have a coarse texture.

6. Fold into vegetable mixture and mix thoroughly. Serve at room temperature, or heat in a 350 degree oven until it bubbles and is slightly browned on top.

LuLu Clue: If I serve my dips with salty crackers like bagel chips, I decrease the salt in the recipe. Using shredded instead of grated Parmesan gives the dip body.

LuLu Clue: One of my quick and favorite dinners is to take a flour tortilla or flat bread and bake it in a 350 degree oven until slightly crisp. Remove and spread with Caramelized Onion and Spinach Dip. Top with sliced tomatoes, sliced kalamata olives, and a little bit of shredded white Cheddar cheese. Return it to the oven until the mixture bubbles and the tortilla edges are crisp. Just delicious!

Blue crab is one of the Gulf Coast's most delicious treasures; catching them is as challenging and fun as learning to clean and eat them. A meal of crabs boiled at the end of the pier and eaten over a weathered picnic table is the definition of summer living on Mobile Bay.

There are as many variations on this coastal standard as there are crabmeat lovers. I like mine filled with lots of crabmeat, using just enough breadcrumbs to hold the cake together. You'll find this recipe full of LuLu's flavor yet the crabmeat is still the star of the show. I prefer to make my own breadcrumbs; they produce a heartier texture, but canned breadcrumbs are also acceptable. Use the best jumbo lump crabmeat you can find, but claw meat will work in a pinch. Make sure to serve these tasty morsels with LuLu's WOW Sauce™.

Lucy B. Goode's Crabcakes

MAKES 4 SERVINGS

1 pound jumbo lump crabmeat

2 tablespoons extra virgin olive oil

⅓ cup finely chopped red bell pepper

⅓ cup finely chopped yellow bell pepper

3 green onions, finely chopped

1½ cups coarse breadcrumbs, divided

¼ cup mayonnaise

1 egg, lightly beaten

1 tablespoon LuLu's Crazy Creola Seasoning™ (page 50)

1 teaspoon dry mustard

1 teaspoon salt

½ teaspoon black pepper

1 tablespoon fresh tarragon, finely chopped or 1½ teaspoons dried tarragon

1½ teaspoons Worcestershire sauce

2 tablespoons finely chopped parsley

2 tablespoons fresh lemon juice

⅔ cup vegetable oil

1. Pick through crabmeat for shells very gently and carefully, leaving large lumps as intact as possible.
2. In a heavy skillet, heat olive oil.
3. Over medium heat sauté all bell peppers and green onions for 2 minutes or until just soft. Remove from heat and set aside to cool completely.
4. In a large mixing bowl, combine 1 cup breadcrumbs, crabmeat, sautéed vegetables, mayonnaise, beaten egg, seasoning mix, dry mustard, salt, pepper, tarragon, Worcestershire, parsley, and lemon juice. With extreme caution, tenderly mix together using your hands, but don't lose your wedding ring!
5. Gently form into small cakes using about ½ cup mixture per cake. Dredge cakes in remaining ½ cup breadcrumbs to lightly coat. Place on a baking sheet and refrigerate for at least 1 hour.
6. In a heavy skillet heat vegetable oil over medium heat until a pinch of the crab mixture placed in skillet begins to sizzle. Pan-fry cakes for about 3 minutes per side or until golden brown. Adjust heat as necessary to insure that cakes are done in the middle.

I prefer sweet pickles

to dill, so this is LuLu's version of a compromise in pickle paradise. There is enough sugar in this recipe to keep your dentist driving a BMW for a lifetime. This is my version of the classic icebox sweet pickle; it is deliciously sweet, sour, and sure enough sassy!

Sweet and Sassy Icebox Pickles

MAKES 8 PINTS

1 (1-gallon) jar whole kosher dill pickles

4 medium-size yellow onions, thinly sliced

20 cloves garlic, peeled and sliced in half lengthwise

⅔ cup fresh gingerroot, peeled and sliced in thin half moons

¼ cup prepared horseradish

1 tablespoon red pepper flakes

1 tablespoon mustard seed

½ teaspoon turmeric

8 cinnamon sticks

4 cups sugar

4 cups light brown sugar, firmly packed

1 cup apple cider vinegar

1. Drain and cut dill pickles into ¼-inch slices. (You can save the pickle juice and use it to marinate oysters before frying them.)
2. Place pickles and remaining ingredients in a big ol' stainless steel bowl or large plastic container with an airtight lid.
3. Using your hands, toss well, cover, and refrigerate overnight. The pickles will reduce in volume, so the next day you can return them to the jar for easier storage.
4. Refrigerate for at least a week, turning topsy-turvy every day. Pickles are ready when sugar has dissolved and all dill flavor has vanished.

 LuLu Clue: These pickles will keep in the refrigerator indefinitely. I have canned them to make them shelf stable in order to give as Christmas gifts. When I do, I remove the cinnamon sticks before placing pickles in canning jars because the heat from the hot water bath releases too much cinnamon flavor.

I came up with this recipe

while I was executive chef on the Motor Yacht "Mariner III" in New York City. We held dinner parties, sometimes for up to a hundred folks a night, while cruising down the Hudson River, past the Statue of Liberty and around Manhattan up the East River. In homage to her home-port of Biloxi, Mississippi, I made sure my menus for MYMariner III were heavily influenced by Gulf Coast cuisine. Naturally, shrimp was a featured ingredient.

This tasty butter can be used to complement crusty French bread or as a dip with crispy crackers. Enjoy the inevitable "Oooohs" and "Aaaahs" from your guests as they taste the finely-mingled flavors. I can't take too much credit for how delicious it is; it's a no-brainer when the main ingredients are butter, shrimp, and garlic!

Shrimp Butter

MAKES 2 CUPS

1 pound boiled shrimp, peeled and deveined

2 sticks unsalted butter, softened

2 green onions, chopped

4 whole cloves garlic, peeled

3 tablespoons sherry or sweet wine such as sake or white Zinfandel

1 tablespoon freshly squeezed lemon juice

1 teaspoon salt

½ teaspoon white pepper

1 tablespoon plus 1 teaspoon chopped fresh parsley

1. Place shrimp in the bowl of a food processor. Pulse a few times until shrimp are finely ground.
2. Add butter, green onions, garlic, sherry, lemon juice, salt, white pepper, and 1 tablespoon of parsley. Process until all ingredients are thoroughly blended to the consistency of a smooth spread.
3. Spoon into glass ramekins and sprinkle remaining parsley over top for garnish.
4. Cover and refrigerate for at least 2 hours. Remove from refrigeration 30 minutes before serving so that it will be easy to spread.

LuLu Clue: There are so many ways you can use this spread. It is brilliant slathered over a piece of grilled fish or steak. Spread it on slices of baguette and broil for a great appetizer.

Pimento cheese

is as much a Southern staple as biscuits or fried chicken. When I was a child, pimentos were considered exotic, fancy, and only for the "grown-ups." "Pa-menna Cheese" (how we pronounce it) always reminds me of lunch with my mother on her sun porch overlooking Mobile Bay. She loved pimento cheese tea sandwiches and began a great tradition with the Buffett granddaughters, taking them to "high tea" in New York and New Orleans. As the girls sipped tea, she and I would sip pink champagne, turning a Southern family favorite into a genteel ladies' delicacy.

Pimento Party Cheese

MAKES 2 CUPS

¼ cup dark beer

1 (4-ounce) jar pimentos, drained and chopped

1 pound extra-sharp Cheddar cheese, shredded

1 tablespoon finely chopped garlic

2 tablespoons grated sweet onion

½ teaspoon salt

½ teaspoon coarsely ground black pepper

½ cup mayonnaise

3-4 dashes LuLu's Perfect Pepper Hot Sauce™

1. In a small saucepan, bring beer to a boil for about a minute. Remove from heat and cool completely. (Don't ask why I boil the beer — it makes it taste better. Also, I find drinking the remaining bottle of beer makes it taste better, too.)
2. Combine pimentos, cheese, garlic, onion, salt, and pepper.
3. Fold beer and mayonnaise into cheese mixture. Add hot sauce and stir well. Don't fret if mixture is a little runny.
4. Refrigerate for at least 2 hours or overnight so that the flavors can marry and the mixture will thicken.

 LuLu Clue: Make sure it sits out for at least half an hour before serving so that it can soften and is easy to spread. For a light and fluffy version, try whipping ingredients together in a food processor. The red pimentos disappear but the flavor is still there.

Gumbo Love &
Other Deep South Soups

LULU'S SUMMER SEAFOOD GUMBO

LULU'S WINTER GUMBO

LULU'S DAY AFTER THANKSGIVING TURKEY GUMBO

SHRIMP AND CRAB BISQUE

OYSTER STEW À LA LULU

LuLu's Roux — Taking It to the Edge!

My first experience with gumbo was in my grandmother's kitchen in Pascagoula, Mississippi. Hilda Buffett was a great cook of regional dishes, and her kitchen stove always had a big pot of something on it. On Fridays, what with "Mom" Buffett being a good Catholic woman, it was usually filled with a seafood gumbo so dark and rich that the tantalizing aroma traveled all the way down the driveway into the neighborhood. Gumbo is a very personal thing. Everybody's is different and everybody's is the best, particularly if your grandmamma made it. Hers was thick with crab, shrimp...and plenty of attitude.

Although gumbo-making isn't rocket science, neither is it for the faint of heart. But then, neither is living a fulfilled life. Both endeavors require courage and a willingness to risk for the good of the soul. The first time I attempted to cook gumbo I wasn't quite twenty. I was too naïve to be intimidated by a recipe with a million steps and ingredients. After all, I had been a teenage bride with two small daughters before I was eighteen years old. Cooking a pot of soup seemed an easy task compared to going to school, working, and taking care of a home and a family. I'm glad I learned at a young age before I knew better!

Over the years, I refined my technique and the pots grew larger as my gumbo became a social event for friends — always an excuse for a party. With just about a different variation for every season or special occasion, my gumbos have always been an opportunity to experiment (and how much do I love that?) There's the Easter Duck & Sausage Gumbo; the 4th of July Gumbo with Whole Crab; and a couple of traditional summer birthday gumbos loaded with shrimp, crab and oysters, fresh okra and tomatoes. In the fall, I always do our Day-After Thanksgiving Turkey Gumbo, and one Christmas I made the best gumbo I'd ever cooked in my life, which has now become my celebrated Winter Gumbo. It's filled with shrimp, oysters, andouille sausage, and chicken. There is no tomato or okra in the savory, rich broth; rather, it is thickened with filé powder (from the leaves of the sassafras tree).

Cooking gumbo can (and should) take all day, and it tends to call up a unique vibration of festivity. Typically I start early in the morning, listening to lots of James Taylor while I prep vegetables with my girlfriends. Toward noon, we might break into Bloody Marys, and by the end of the day, with clothes and hair reeking of roux and seasonings, we have solved most of the problems of the world. By suppertime, we don't have a care in the world. If more women knew how to cook gumbo, I swear they wouldn't need antidepressants.

There are two secrets to making a good gumbo. First, you gotta love to do it. If you try to rush the Divine timing of gumbo-making or get distracted by something other than the task at hand, the first whiff of burnt flour will immediately tell you the roux is doomed and you'll have to start all over again. And believe me, denial such as trying to "fix it" or thinking, "It'll be alright," won't work. I've learned after many failures that it's best just to surrender, take a deep breath, put on some more good music, and start all over again. Gumbo made in a hurry or under a cloud of resentment is sure enough going to burn somebody's tongue.

The other secret is the roux itself. Although the word sounds fancy, it's simply a French word for fat and flour. Folks used to use lard or bacon grease, but in today's health conscious world, any oil will do except olive oil. A good roux has to be taken to the edge of darkness, and olive oil can't tolerate the heat. I like a deep brown, almost black roux for my gumbos. It takes constant stirring for sometimes a half an hour or more. Steely persistence is required to bring roux just to the edge of disaster — that heinous, ever-looming scorch. When it feels like your arm is about to fall off, you're almost ready to throw in the "holy trinity," New Orleanian patois for the combination of chopped onions, bell peppers, and celery. It takes presence, judgment, and trust to listen to the simple inner-knowing that tells you when to add the trinity to keep the roux from ruin. Good gumbo cooks have roux scars on their hands or arms and wear them with honor, like badges of courage.

Gumbo is a family affair among the Buffetts, with the roots of roux stretching back to "Mom" Buffett and beyond. At my daughter Melanie's wedding party, I happened to overhear a young cousin remark to his daddy, my cousin, over the cup of gumbo he was eating, "Hey, Daddy, this tastes just like yours!" No surprise, but a cherished compliment. When my older daughter, Mara, was in her twenties, she decided that she would make a pot of gumbo to take to her boyfriend's family Christmas dinner. She called me from New Orleans about a hundred times that day as I walked her through the steps, even though she had helped me countless times in her youth. She was wary of making the roux because she had witnessed me scorch it many times, and she knew what that meant. She called at every stage: when it was light brown and thick...when it turned a pretty red-brown the color of a copper penny... when it started to get dark brown and gave off a roasted nutty aroma.

"Should I put in the trinity now?" she asked nervously.

"Baby, take it to the edge," I replied. And she laughed; she had seen me do that all of her life.

Making gumbo

is an all-day event in my home. First and foremost, it requires tons of prepping, so ingredients must be available and ready before cooking the roux. I organize bowls filled with colorful ingredients lined up in order of usage. This makes it easier to assemble, and since I tend to make a day of it, inviting friends and family for Bloody Marys, helps keep the cooking (or rather the cooks) on track.

LuLu's Summer Seafood Gumbo

MAKES 25 CUPS

3 pounds medium shrimp, heads on

2 pounds claw crabmeat, picked for shells

4 crab bodies, if available

4 large ripe tomatoes, peeled and chopped, or 1 (28-ounce) can whole tomatoes, coarsely chopped in their juice

2 large onions, coarsely chopped

2 green bell peppers, coarsely chopped

1 medium head celery, coarsely chopped including leaves

2½ pounds okra, fresh if available, cut in ¼-inch pieces, or frozen cut okra, thawed

¾ cup vegetable oil or bacon grease

1 cup all-purpose flour

8 cups shrimp or seafood stock, heated

2-3 teaspoons salt, or to taste

1 tablespoon black pepper

¼ teaspoon cayenne pepper

2 tablespoons dried thyme

4 bay leaves

1 teaspoon dried oregano

1 teaspoon dried basil

2 tablespoons LuLu's Crazy Creola Seasoning™ (page 50)

1. Dehead, peel, and devein shrimp. Reserve heads and shells for later use. Pick through crabmeat carefully for shells. Refrigerate shrimp and crab until ready to use.

2. Fill a medium-sized saucepan with water. Bring to a boil. Drop tomatoes carefully into boiling water and cook for 1 minute. Remove with a slotted spoon and let cool. Skins will slip off easily. Remove cores and coarsely chop tomatoes over a bowl to retain as much juice as possible. Set aside. (If using canned tomatoes, I cut them up in eighths.)

3. Place chopped onions, bell peppers, celery, and okra in separate bowls. Set aside.

4. To make the roux, heat vegetable oil or bacon grease in a 10-quart heavy stockpot over medium-high heat. When oil is hot, gradually add flour, whisking continuously. Continue to whisk roux, adjusting heat as necessary to keep from burning. This may take 25 to 35 minutes or until your arm feels like it is about to fall off and the roux is a dark mahogany color. Be careful; if the roux burns, you will have to start all over again!

5. Carefully add chopped onions to roux and continue stirring with a large wooden spoon for 2 to 3 minutes. Onions will sizzle and steam when they hit the hot roux so caution is advised. Seasoned gumbo cooks have roux battle scars on one or both arms.

6. Add bell peppers and continue stirring for another 2 to 3 minutes; add celery continuing to stir constantly for another 2 to 3 minutes. The mixture should now resemble a pot of black beans.

7. Add tomatoes and stir well.

8. Slowly add the heated stock.

CONTINUED

2-3 tablespoons LuLu's Perfect Pepper Hot Sauce™

2 tablespoons Worcestershire sauce

2 cups green onions, finely chopped

½ cup fresh parsley, finely chopped

½ cup freshly squeezed lemon juice

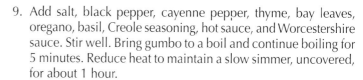

LuLu Clue: You can never put too much seafood in gumbo. I love to use crab bodies when I can get them. There is nothing better than getting to the bottom of the bowl and picking the crabmeat with your fingers.

9. Add salt, black pepper, cayenne pepper, thyme, bay leaves, oregano, basil, Creole seasoning, hot sauce, and Worcestershire sauce. Stir well. Bring gumbo to a boil and continue boiling for 5 minutes. Reduce heat to maintain a slow simmer, uncovered, for about 1 hour.

10. Add okra and bring back to a boil for 5 minutes. Reduce heat again to maintain a slow simmer, uncovered, for 30 minutes or a day (until okra has lost its bright green color and is cooked down like the other vegetables). If gumbo gets too thick, add a little water. If it is too thin, continue to simmer uncovered.

11. At this point, you can cool the gumbo. It's always better the day after it has been cooked, although I've never had a complaint when I served gumbo the day I made it. Remove from heat and let it sit for about 30 minutes. Then place pot, uncovered, in an empty sink. Fill the sink with water and ice around the stockpot. Stir gumbo every 15 minutes to move the liquid around to facilitate cooling. Gumbo will spoil if cooled improperly. (At the restaurant, we have cooling cylinders that look like baseball bats that are frozen and placed in the middle of five-gallon stockpots.) When completely cool, refrigerate it, uncovered, for a couple of hours before placing in an airtight container.

12. Reheat gumbo slowly to simmering. Thirty minutes before serving, add green onions, parsley, and lemon juice. Cover and cook for 15 minutes. Add shrimp and crabmeat. Mix well. Cover and turn off heat. Let sit for at least another 15 minutes while seafood cooks. It will stay hot for a long time. Adjust seasonings and serve over cooked white rice with French bread and butter.

OTHER DEEP SOUTH SOUPS

This recipe uses ingredients that are readily available in the wintertime — oysters and andouille sausage, a Gulf Coast staple for making gumbos and jambalayas. Pronounced "ahn-doo-ee," it's a heavily smoked pork sausage with French origins; I like the Cajun version that is also spicy and fragrant. The aroma and flavor are absolutely heavenly, especially on a cold winter day.

LuLu's Winter Gumbo

MAKES 25 CUPS

1 whole chicken (about 2 pounds cooked meat)

1 pound andouille sausage or any good quality smoked sausage, sliced into ⅛-inch thick rounds

2 large onions, coarsely chopped

2 green bell peppers, coarsely chopped

1 medium head celery, coarsely chopped including leaves

¾ cup vegetable oil or bacon grease

1 cup all-purpose flour

8 cups chicken stock, heated

1. Place whole chicken in a large stockpot. Cover with water, add 2 bay leaves, and boil chicken until tender. Remove from broth and cool.

2. Remove and discard chicken skin and bones. Chop chicken into large bite-size pieces. Set aside.

3. Heat a cast iron or heavy skillet and cook sausage over medium heat until browned. Drain on paper towels.

4. Place chopped onions, bell peppers and celery, including leaves, in separate bowls. Set aside.

5. To make the roux, heat vegetable oil or bacon grease in a 10-quart heavy stockpot over medium-high heat. When oil is hot, gradually add flour, whisking continuously. Continue to whisk roux, adjusting heat as necessary to keep from burning. This may take 25 to 35 minutes or until your arm feels like it is about to fall off and the roux is a dark mahogany color. Be careful; if the roux burns, you will have to start all over again!

6. Carefully add chopped onions to roux and continue stirring with a large wooden spoon for 2 to 3 minutes. Onions will sizzle and steam when they hit the hot roux so caution is advised. Seasoned gumbo cooks have roux battle scars on one or both arms.

7. Add bell peppers and continue stirring for another 2-3 minutes; add celery continuing to stir constantly for another 2 to 3 minutes. The mixture should now resemble a pot of black beans.

8. Add chicken and sausage and stir well.

9. Slowly add heated stock and stir well.

CONTINUED

- 1 tablespoon salt
- 2 teaspoons black pepper
- 1 tablespoon dried thyme
- 4 bay leaves
- 1 teaspoon dried oregano
- ½ teaspoon dried sage
- 1 tablespoon LuLu's Crazy Creola Seasoning™ (page 50)
- 2 tablespoons Worcestershire sauce
- 2 cups finely chopped green onions
- ½ cup finely chopped fresh parsley
- 1 quart fresh oysters, drained
- 2 pounds medium shrimp, peeled and deveined
- 2-3 tablespoons LuLu's Perfect Pepper Hot Sauce™
- Filé powder, optional

10. Add salt, black pepper, thyme, bay leaves, oregano, sage, Creole seasoning, and Worcestershire sauce. Stir well. Bring gumbo to a boil and continue boiling for 5 minutes. Reduce heat to maintain a slow simmer, uncovered, for about 1 hour or an entire day. If gumbo gets too thick, add a little water. If it is too thin, continue to simmer uncovered. Because there is pork sausage in this gumbo, skim off any excess oil that rises to the top.

11. At this point, you can cool the gumbo. It's always better the day after it has been cooked, although I've never had a complaint when I served gumbo the day I made it. Remove from heat and let it sit for about 30 minutes. Then place pot, uncovered, in an empty sink. Fill the sink with water and ice around the stockpot. Stir gumbo every 15 minutes to move the liquid around to facilitate cooling. Gumbo will spoil if cooled improperly. At the restaurant, we have cooling cylinders that look like baseball bats that are frozen and placed in the middle of 5-gallon stockpots. When completely cool, refrigerate it, uncovered, for a couple of hours before placing in an airtight container.

12. Reheat gumbo slowly to simmering. Thirty minutes before serving, add green onions and parsley. Cover and cook for 15 minutes. Add oysters and shrimp. Continue simmering for 2 minutes or until oysters begin to curl.

13. For a spicy flavor, add hot sauce. Remove from heat and cover. Let sit for 10 minutes. It will stay hot for a long time. Adjust seasonings and serve over cooked white rice with filé powder and French bread and butter.

LuLu Clue: Filé powder is a flavoring and thickening agent for gumbo made out of the ground leaves of sassafras trees, abundant along the Gulf Coast. Okra was not available in the winter in Louisiana, so the Cajuns, who learned from the Choctaw Indians, used filé powder in their gumbos. Filé is always added at the end of cooking since it can become stringy if boiled. Since I always make enough gumbo to feed an army, I put the filé powder on the table for individual seasoning.

Marketing & PR Director
Gumbo Schlepper
Debra Bigge-Holloran

 OTHER DEEP SOUTH SOUPS

Cousin Mark's Day After Thanksgiving Turkey Gumbo

MAKES 25 CUPS

1 turkey carcass and any leftover turkey meat

3 quarts water

1 pound andouille sausage or any good quality smoked sausage, cut into ⅛-inch rounds

2 large onions, coarsely chopped

2 green bell peppers, coarsely chopped

1 medium head celery, coarsely chopped including leaves

¾ cup vegetable oil or bacon grease

1 cup all-purpose flour

1 (28-ounce) can whole tomatoes, drained and coarsely chopped

1 tablespoon salt

1 tablespoon black pepper

2 tablespoons dried thyme

4 bay leaves

1 teaspoon dried oregano

1 teaspoon dried basil

1 tablespoon LuLu's Crazy Creola Seasoning™ (page 50)

2 tablespoons Worcestershire sauce

2 pounds frozen okra

2 cups finely chopped green onions

½ cup finely chopped fresh parsley

2-3 tablespoons LuLu's Perfect Pepper Hot Sauce™

1. Place turkey carcass and leftover turkey into a large stockpot. Cover with 3 quarts of water. Bring to a boil. Reduce heat to medium to maintain a vigorous simmer.

2. As you prep your vegetables for the gumbo, add trimmings to simmering stock. Skim foam as needed while stock reduces.

3. Heat a cast iron or heavy skillet and cook sausage over medium heat until browned. Drain on paper towels.

4. Place chopped onions, bell peppers and celery, including leaves, in separate bowls. Set aside.

5. To make the roux, heat vegetable oil or bacon grease in a 10-quart heavy stockpot over medium-high heat. When oil is hot, gradually add flour, whisking continuously. Continue to whisk roux, until it is reddish like a copper penny, adjusting heat as necessary to keep from burning.

6. Carefully add chopped onions to roux and continue stirring with a large wooden spoon for 2 to 3 minutes. Onions will sizzle and steam when they hit the hot roux so caution is advised. Seasoned gumbo cooks have roux battle scars on one or both arms.

7. Add bell peppers and continue stirring for another 2 to 3 minutes; add celery continuing to stir constantly for another 2 to 3 minutes.

9. Pour stock through a large strainer. Discard any skin, bones and trimmings.

10. Add turkey meat and sausage to roux mixture and stir well.

11. Slowly add 8 cups of strained stock and tomatoes, stirring well.

12. Add salt, black pepper, thyme, bay leaves, oregano, basil, Creole seasoning, and Worcestershire sauce. Stir well. Bring gumbo to a boil and continue boiling for 5 minutes. Reduce heat to maintain a slow simmer, uncovered, for about hour or an entire day.

13. Add okra and bring back to a boil for 5 minutes. Reduce heat again to maintain a slow simmer, uncovered, for a minimum of 30 minutes. The longer it simmers the better it gets. If gumbo gets too thick, add a little water. If it is too thin, continue to simmer uncovered. Because there is pork sausage in this gumbo, skim off any oil that rises to the top.

14. Thirty minutes before serving, add green onions and parsley to gumbo. Cover and cook for 15 minutes.

15. For a spicy flavor, add hot sauce. Turn off gumbo and cover. Let sit for 10 minutes. It will stay hot for a long time. Adjust seasonings and serve over cooked white rice with French bread and butter.

 GUMBO LOVE AND

LuLu's Day After Thanksgiving Turkey Gumbo

By my Mississippi cousin, Mark Lumpkin

In our family, cooking is as important as eating, just like music is as important as the dance. As a result of working in her mother's boarding house on the banks of the Pascagoula River, my grandmother, "Mom" Buffett, learned the music of cooking.

There must be some truth to that old adage that the road to a man's heart is through his stomach because she met her seafaring future husband around the dining table of that old boarding house. He had sailed into Pascagoula to pick up a load of lumber. Fifty years later, they still had a plaque in their home that read "Good lovin' don't last but good cookin' do."

And she sure could cook... seafood gumbo, eggplant casserole with crab and shrimp, stuffed crabs, boiled okra and tomatoes, garlic-stuffed roast beef and gravy, boiled crabs, boiled shrimp, soft-shell crabs... She made "Depression" burgers mixing bread crumbs, pork sausage, and bell peppers with the ground beef. Mom could stretch food money without cutting the taste.

I learned about the Trinity from her as she dragged Richard, our cousin, and me to 6 a.m. weekday mass at Our Lady of Victories. But she also taught the trinity of Creole cooking (bell peppers, celery, and onion), as well as the patience for creating roux.

Seafood gumbo was expensive so it was not made regularly. It was a special day and cause for celebration when she made hers. Her After-Thanksgiving Turkey and Oyster Gumbo was also fantastic. To this day, I make sure to save the carcass of our Thanksgiving smoked turkey to use for stock the next day to honor this special tradition.

Mom spoiled me, and I am still hesitant to eat "store-bought" gumbo; it almost never measures up to hers. But I know I'll get as good as Mom gave when I visit my cousin Lucy's LuLu's. We both learned from the same maestro, and in this cookbook I think Lucy has captured this dance we love to do.

The Buffett Family Table — every mouth open!

This silky bisque is to die for. Try to get your shrimp heads-on so you can use the heads for the stock; it's an important step and really adds to the flavor. We got our shrimp from a roadside vendor (a common sight in these parts), who goes to Bayou la Batre every morning to pick up a fresh haul from our local shrimpers. She advertises simply with her "Pretty Shrimp" sign, hand-lettered with the magic words we know to mean, real damn good fresh shrimp! I mean, really...don't you just love "Pretty Shrimp"?

Shrimp and Crab Bisque

Recipe by Carol Garrett, Former Kitchen Manager, Old LuLu's

SERVES 10

½ gallon water

2 pounds medium shrimp, shells on

6 tablespoons unsalted butter, divided

⅓ cup dry sherry

½ cup plus 3 tablespoons finely chopped shallots, divided

2 cloves garlic, minced

3 tablespoons tomato paste

2½ cups dry white wine

1 teaspoon dried tarragon

1 tablespoon finely chopped fresh thyme, or 1 teaspoon dried thyme leaves

¼ teaspoon red pepper flakes

2 bay leaves

3 tablespoons all-purpose flour

2½ cups whole milk

¾ cup heavy cream

2 teaspoons salt

White pepper to taste

2 egg yolks

4 cups hot Shrimp Stock (page 57)

1 pound lump crabmeat, well picked to remove shells

1. Bring water to a boil in large stockpot. Add shrimp, cook for 3 minutes and remove from water with a slotted spoon. Set aside to cool.
2. Peel shrimp and finely chop. Save shells and set aside.
3. Melt 3 tablespoons of butter in a large skillet over medium heat.
4. Add shrimp shells and sherry.
5. Stir in ½ cup shallots, garlic, tomato paste, wine, and 4 cups shrimp stock.
6. Add tarragon, thyme, red pepper flakes, and bay leaves.
7. Simmer, uncovered, for 30 minutes. Strain through a sieve into a large bowl and set aside.
8. Melt remaining 3 tablespoons butter in a heavy stockpot over medium heat.
9. Add remaining 3 tablespoons shallots and sauté for 2 minutes.
10. Add flour and whisk constantly for 1 minute.
11. Gradually whisk in strained shrimp stock until well blended.
12. Add milk and heavy cream. Reduce heat if necessary; do not bring to a boil.
13. Add salt and white pepper
14. In a separate bowl, whisk egg yolks together. Add ½ cup of hot soup stock to temper the yolks, then add back to soup pot. (This will warm the eggs slightly, but not enough to cook them before adding to hot soup...you don't want to end up with egg-drop soup!)
15. Stir in chopped shrimp and lump crabmeat. Heat for several minutes. Serve piping hot!

This recipe is rich

and exotic, using a triple-cream fancy cheese and was inspired by a dish I once had at K-Paul's in New Orleans. But the star of this dish remains the delectable fresh oysters that are plentiful along the Gulf Coast in the "R" months. I love that the liquid which runs off when the oysters are shucked is called "liquor." Perhaps it is because, like that other kind of liquor, oysters have a mystical reputation for enhancing sensuality...maybe not, but I've known pals who have ended up in the backseat of a car after too much of either! I just know that almost nothing is better on any Deep South day when the thermometer dips below a chilly 70° than a bowl of oyster stew and a slice of toasted Bunny bread for dipping.

Oyster Stew à la LuLu

SERVES 10

1 quart oysters in oyster liquor

Ice water

1 stick unsalted butter

4 cloves garlic, finely chopped

1 cup finely chopped celery

1 cup finely chopped white onion

½ cup thinly sliced small button mushrooms

2 cups heavy cream

½ teaspoon salt

½ teaspoon white pepper

¼ teaspoon cayenne pepper

½ pound Brie cheese or any soft triple-cream cheese, like St. Andre, rind removed

½ cup dry white wine

¾ cup finely chopped green onions

2 tablespoons finely chopped fresh parsley

Generous dash of LuLu's Perfect Pepper Hot Sauce™

1. Drain oysters and refrigerate until ready to use. Reserve liquor and add enough ice water to yield 3 cups of liquid. Set aside.
2. In large saucepan, melt butter over medium heat until it is just sizzling. (It is important not to let the butter brown at all.)
3. Add garlic and cook until soft, but not brown.
4. Add celery, onions, and mushrooms and continue to sauté until soft.
5. Add oyster liquor-water mixture then heavy cream. (Do not add heavy cream first or it might scorch.)
6. Add salt, white pepper, and cayenne. Cook for about 5 minutes, or until stew is just about to boil. Reduce heat to low and cover. Continue simmering for another 5 minutes.
7. Add cheese and wine, stirring constantly until cheese melts.
8. Add oysters and green onions. Cover and continue to cook for 2 to 3 minutes or until edges of oysters curl.
9. Add parsley and hot sauce. Adjust seasonings and serve immediately.

 LuLu Clue: When we counted out a quart of oysters at the restaurant, it yielded 39 oysters and 2 cups of liquor. Of course, this is all dependent upon the size of the oysters. I favor the smaller ones, and if they are really salty, you might not want to add the salt until the end when you adjust the seasonings. I don't use milk as my liquid as many oyster stew recipes do, because it can curdle.

SASSY CAESAR

CREOLA BLACKENED GROUPER SALAD

CHICKEN TOSTADA SALAD

GULF COAST GREEK SALAD WITH GRILLED SHRIMP

LULU'S WACKY WEDGE

LULU'S JERK-CHICK DELI SALAD

FRIDAY SHRIMP SALAD À LA LULU

LULU'S TRIED AND TRUE COLESLAW

SPICY ASIAN SLAW

CRAZY EASY ASIAN SLAW

SWEET AND SAVORY SPINACH SALAD

The Salad Days of Summer

In the Deep South, summertime demands lighter and colder foods. It's just about 100 degrees in Key West as I write this, therefore appropriate for a discussion of salads — the essential summertime food.

In the summer of 1998, I had just returned to Alabama from California, a state that grows nearly 80% of all produce for the country. On Wednesdays in Santa Monica, farmers bring in their weekly yield, and the city closes down two prominent streets for the Santa Monica Farmers' Market. The variety of produce and flowers is breathtaking, cart after cart lining the street. It is a beautiful experience, and I dream of having a monthly farmers' market at LuLu's.

More than anything, I would like to have my own tomato patch that can service my restaurant during the summer. If lettuce is the mainstay of a salad, then a juicy red ripe homegrown tomato is the crown jewel. At my home, tomatoes are always ripening on the windowsill. Sometimes we bite into them like apples. Other times I pan sear slices for breakfast to accompany scrambled eggs. Fresh slices invariably end up at most of my meals. My mother had a tomato sandwich every day of her life; my sister has homegrown Baldwin County tomatoes Fed-Exed to her ranch in Montana.

The endless supply of fresh ingredients readily available in the summertime allows for many variations on my favorite meal — the salad. My body craves a salad at least every other day like a dog craves a bone. Mac teases me when he sees the salad I concoct for a "light lunch." Generally prepared in the large salad bowl (you know, the one meant to serve a party of 8!), my "light salad" takes up the whole bowl and can be filled with baby romaine or field greens and topped with whatever is left in the refrigerator: roasted or grilled vegetables, left-over boiled or sautéed shrimp, a fresh homegrown tomato (of course), black olives, and all kinds of cheese, especially my favorites, Parmesan and goat cheese.

After ten years in Los Angeles, I hate to admit it, but I became a lettuce snob. Long gone was the concept that iceberg lettuce slathered in thick dressing is the only choice on the menu. Don't get me wrong; I love a wedge as much as the next gal, but salads have evolved into full meals with a wide variety of greens and ingredients. I will never fully abandon the iceberg lettuce of my childhood. My cravings do occasionally call for a great chopped or Cobb salad, and, of course, it is a must that they are made with good old iceberg.

Yet, I had become seduced by the wonderful varieties of lettuces that I had never heard of, especially the "mesclun mix," a combination of fresh spring field-greens and baby lettuces such as butter lettuce, baby romaine, frisée, oakleaf, endive, arugula, and dandelion leaves (oh my!), all of them leafy and delicate. When I opened LuLu's in 1999, "fancy" leaf lettuces were not commonplace in our little corner of the world. While creating the menu, I decided that I would serve a traditional iceberg salad with homemade Thousand Island dressing just like I ate every night as a child. But I also decided to do a wild and crazy thing — introduce a salad with some of the lettuces I learned to love in California. LuLu's house salad became a mix of baby greens garnished with cherry tomatoes, slices of purple onions, and sections of Mandarin oranges.

The two salads took off like gangbusters. A few old-timers balked at the funny looking lettuce on their plates but these main-course salads quickly became top sellers, especially during our extremely hot summer months. Soon after, when we did our food inventories, we had to throw away iceberg lettuce that had spoiled. Eventually, we took it off of the menu; it had become such a slow seller. It gave me a sense of accomplishment that my little "high-class dive" could help open minds to a new idea. We have re-introduced the iceberg salad of old on LuLu's new menu as a classic wedge sprinkled with bleu cheese and bacon crumbles.

There are many variations of "salad," but what they all have in common really is one thing — refreshment. When the mercury hits triple digits, the humidity is 88% and you can't bear to move your bones off the sofa, the only thing you can eat is something cool and light. And so I'm off to Louie's for a nice, refreshing salad.

Sassy Caesar

MAKES 6 SERVINGS

½ cup unsalted butter

3 tablespoons finely chopped garlic, divided

½ teaspoon LuLu's Crazy Creola Seasoning™ (page 50)

½ loaf French baguette, sliced into 1-inch rounds

2 large heads romaine lettuce

⅓ cup freshly squeezed lemon juice

Juice of ½ small orange

½ teaspoon orange zest

1 tablespoon Dijon mustard

1 teaspoon Worcestershire sauce

2-3 tablespoons anchovy paste

1 teaspoon kosher salt

1 teaspoon coarsely ground black pepper

½ teaspoon sugar

½ cup olive oil

3-4 dashes LuLu's Perfect Pepper Hot Sauce™

½ cup shredded Parmigiano-Reggiano cheese, divided

1. Melt butter over low heat. Add 1 tablespoon garlic and Creole seasoning. As soon as butter begins to sizzle, remove from heat.

2. Spread melted butter mixture over both sides of bread rounds. Place on a nonstick baking sheet under broiler. Toast both sides and remove from broiler once browned. Set aside.

3. Wash and dry lettuce and tear into medium-sized pieces. Cover with a damp paper towel and refrigerate until ready to serve.

4. In a mixing bowl, combine lemon juice, orange juice, orange zest, mustard, Worcestershire sauce, anchovy paste, salt, pepper, sugar, olive oil, hot sauce, and ¼ cup Parmesan cheese, whisking well to make a dressing.

5. Immediately before serving, drizzle dressing over lettuce and toss well.

6. Sprinkle remaining cheese over dressed lettuce and top with the freshly baked crouton rounds.

 LuLu Clue: Some recipes will call for you to remove the ribs of romaine lettuce. I don't. The spine of the lettuce leaf adds crunch and body to the salad. In "the world of me," I don't put too much stock in the notion that you shouldn't chop lettuce — it's easier, faster, and doesn't seem to mind being "bruised" anyway. If you're a stickler for such things, tear the lettuce into small pieces instead.

Creola Blackened Grouper Salad

MAKES 4 SERVINGS

4 grouper fillets

6 tablespoons olive oil, divided

2 tablespoons LuLu's Crazy Creola Seasoning™ (page 50)

2 bags mixed spring greens or fresh arugula, thoroughly washed and dried

½ cup Ginger Lime Salad Dressing (page 180)

½ red onion, very thinly sliced

4-6 radishes, very thinly sliced

1 cup cherry tomatoes, halved

1 yellow bell pepper, sliced in strips

½ cup Mandarin orange slices, optional

1. Preheat oven to 250 degrees.

2. Toss grouper with 2 tablespoons olive oil and Creole seasoning. Set aside.

3. In a large cast iron or heavy skillet, heat remaining 4 tablespoons olive oil over medium-high heat until it sizzles. Gently place grouper fillets in skillet. Cook on one side for 3 to 4 minutes. Carefully turn fish fillets and continue cooking for another 3 to 4 minutes or until fish is cooked through. If you can easily insert a toothpick into the fish, it is done. Remove to an ovenproof platter or baking dish. Place in oven to keep warm while cooking remaining fillets.

4. While fish is cooking combine salad greens with dressing. Toss thoroughly. Divide greens among four dinner plates.

5. On top of salads, sprinkle red onions, radishes, cherry tomatoes, and bell pepper strips.

6. Top each salad with a grouper fillet, garnish with Mandarin orange slices and serve immediately.

 LuLu Clue: When I'm making any salad, I always wash, prep, and dry my greens first. (I suggest investing in a "salad spinner" — it's the easiest method to remove all excess water from the greens.) Then, covered with a damp paper towel in a salad bowl, into the fridge they'll go to chill until I'm ready to serve. I never dress salad greens until right before I'm ready to serve so that they won't get soggy. I also caution against overdressing any salad. You want your salad skinny-dippin', not swimming in dressing.

Melanie enjoying her daily obsession.

MELANIE'S GROUPER SALAD OBSESSION

Melanie Buffett, Lucy's younger daughter, is a disciplined, driven young woman. She is a dedicated yoga practitioner and instructor, a devoted Catholic, an adoring wife, a seafood-only vegetarian and a 99.9% teetotaler. She's also very funny and a little bit more than slightly kooky. Sometimes her quirks play out in interesting ways. In the early days of LuLu's, Melanie had come home to roll up her sleeves and pitch in. But her dietary inclinations didn't run to fried food and cheeseburgers. There were, to be fair, only a few items on the menu that suited her diet. What began as simply a lunchtime selection, by process of elimination, became Melanie's obsession. For its fresh, blackened fish and flavorful ginger lime dressing over baby spring greens, Melanie ordered LuLu's wildly popular and beloved Creola Blackened Grouper Salad for lunch. Every day. For a year. Try this yourself and see if you don't get hooked.

-Diva

Chicken Tostada Salad

MAKES 4 SERVINGS

12 chicken tenders

3 tablespoons olive oil, divided

2 tablespoons LuLu's Chipotle Taco Seasoning (page 49) or any taco seasoning

½ bag tortilla chips

2 cups Cuban Black Beans (page 273)

½ head iceberg lettuce, torn in pieces

½ head romaine lettuce, torn in pieces

1 large tomato, cut into wedges

1 avocado, sliced

½ red onion, thinly sliced

2 cups shredded Cheddar cheese

¼ cup sliced black olives

Chipotle Cream Sauce (page 183)

1. Toss chicken strips with 2 tablespoons olive oil and seasoning.
2. Brush a heavy skillet with remaining 1 tablespoon olive oil and heat until just about to sizzle.
3. Add chicken tenders and pan-sauté or grill 4 minutes on each side or until browned. Remove from heat and chop into bite-sized pieces.
4. In a large salad bowl, layer tortilla chips, black beans, lettuces, tomatoes, avocados, red onion, cheese, chicken, and black olives.
5. Top with Chipotle Cream Sauce.

LuLu Clue: At the restaurant, we fry up fresh tortilla bowls to use for this salad instead of the chips; you can find them ready-made at your local grocery store. For a speedy prep, you can substitute a can of black beans, drained and rinsed, for the Cuban Black Beans.

Gulf Coast Greek Salad with Grilled Shrimp

1 pound large headless shrimp, shells on

7 tablespoons olive oil, divided

1 tablespoon LuLu's Crazy Creola Seasoning™ (page 50)

1 head romaine lettuce, rinsed, dried, and chopped

1 small red onion, thinly sliced

¾ cup kalamata olives

1 green bell pepper, chopped

1 red bell pepper, chopped

2 large tomatoes, chopped

1 cucumber, sliced

1 cup crumbled feta cheese

1 teaspoon dried oregano

Juice of 1 lemon

Coarsely ground black pepper

1. Peel shrimp, leaving tails intact. Toss shrimp with 1 tablespoon olive oil and Creole seasoning. Skewer shish-kabob style onto metal or wooden skewers.

2. To grill shrimp, fire up the grill to high heat and cook shrimp for 1½-2 minutes on each side.

3. In a large salad bowl, combine romaine lettuce, onion, olives, all bell peppers, tomatoes, cucumber, and cheese.

3. In a separate bowl, whisk together remaining 6 tablespoons olive oil, oregano, and lemon juice.

4. Toss salad with dressing and mix well.

5. Top with shrimp and black pepper to taste.

LuLu Clue: If using wooden skewers, make sure to soak them well in water before you grill.

The wedge salad…

how I love thee. So simple, so humble, so easy, and always so good! Cool iceberg lettuce paired harmoniously with the freshest summer tomatoes, the crispiest bacon, and the creamiest blue cheese dressing. Nothing fussy, simply delectable. I have spent most of my life experimenting with food, with tastes, and different culinary techniques. But in life, as in cooking, I gravitate back to the basics, the tried-and-true. This salad is a wonderful case in point. You simply cannot mess up the wedge.

LuLu's Wacky Wedge

MAKES 4 SERVINGS

4 slices thick-cut bacon

**1 large head or 2 small heads
    iceberg lettuce**

**1 cup cherry tomatoes, halved, or
    1 whole home-grown tomato,
    sliced into wedges**

**Stilton Blue Cheese Salad Dressing
    (page 179)**

1 cup crumbled Stilton cheese

**Coarsely ground black
    pepper**

1. Fry bacon in a cast iron or heavy skillet over medium heat. As bacon begins to sizzle, lower heat to keep it from smoking or burning. As bacon begins to brown, turn once. When crispy, remove from skillet and drain on paper towels.

2. Core lettuce head by smashing it (yes, smashing) straight down on its root/stem end (you know, the round "nubby" thing) onto a hard surface. This loosens the hard center, making it easy to remove.

3. Quarter (or halve) lettuce head.

4. Crumble bacon into pieces.

5. Top lettuce wedge with tomatoes, dressing, bacon, cheese, and pepper to taste.

LuLu's Jerk-Chick Deli Salad

3-4 boneless, skinless chicken breasts

1 cup white wine

1 cup water

Salt and pepper to taste

½ cup unsalted pecan pieces

½ cup chopped red onions

1 cup chopped celery

¼ cup chopped green bell peppers

1 cup sour cream

1 tablespoon honey mustard

1 teaspoon salt

1 teaspoon white pepper

1 tablespoon freshly squeezed lemon juice

½ teaspoon LuLu's Jerk Seasoning (page 51)

2 tablespoons finely chopped fresh parsley

1. Preheat oven to 350 degrees.
2. Place chicken breasts in a baking dish and cover with white wine and water. Sprinkle with salt and pepper and bake 50 to 60 minutes or until chicken is thoroughly cooked.
3. Spread pecan pieces on a baking sheet and bake for 5 to 7 minutes or until browned.
4. Remove chicken from baking dish and cool thoroughly. Cut into bite-sized chunks.
5. In a large mixing bowl, combine chicken chunks, red onions, celery, bell peppers, and pecans.
6. Mix in sour cream, honey mustard, salt, white pepper, lemon juice, and Jerk seasoning.
7. Add fresh parsley and chill in refrigerator for 2 hours before serving.
8. Serve with crackers, on a sandwich, or on top of spring greens.

We start our weekends early during the summer, so every Friday we plan a boating trip that ends floating by the channel buoy at the mouth of Weeks Bay to watch the sunset. That's when we pop a little champagne or cold white wine and nibble on shrimp salad and saltine crackers. Lots of times we just use our fingers and jump in the bay to wash off before heading back home up Fish River.

Friday Shrimp Salad à la LuLu

MAKES 6 TO 8 SERVINGS

3 pounds LuLu's Perfect Peel and Eat Shrimp (page 95), peeled and chopped into medium to large pieces

1 cup chopped celery

¾ cup chopped red onion

½ cup chopped green onions

3 hard boiled eggs, chopped

2 tablespoons finely chopped parsley

1 teaspoon salt

1 teaspoon white pepper

1 teaspoon LuLu's Crazy Creola Seasoning™ (page 50)

2 tablespoons Dijon mustard

½ cup mayonnaise

1 tablespoon freshly squeezed lemon juice

1. In a large mixing bowl, combine all ingredients, stirring gently.
2. Cover and refrigerate for 2 hours before serving.

LuLu Clue: At LuLu's we serve our shrimp salad with a duo of Fried Green Tomatoes (page 101) drizzled with our famous LuLu's WOW Sauce™ (page 173).

SASSY SALADS

Coleslaw is a mainstay

at any seafood restaurant and is one of our main side dishes at LuLu's. It is served with just about everything. There are many versions of this classic Southern side dish. Some folks like it finely chopped and seasoned with a vinegar-based dressing, but I like my slaw coarsely chopped and mixed with a delicate, sweet mayonnaise dressing. I must not be the only one who likes it that way — LuLu's customers rave about it.

LuLu's Tried and True Coleslaw

MAKES ABOUT 8 CUPS

1 head green cabbage, coarsely chopped

1½ cups coarsely grated carrots

2 tablespoons finely grated onion

1 cup mayonnaise

1 tablespoon cider vinegar

3 tablespoons sugar

Pinch of salt

1 teaspoon black pepper

2 teaspoons fresh horseradish

1. Combine cabbage, carrots, and onion in a large mixing bowl. Set aside.
2. In a small mixing bowl combine mayonnaise, cider vinegar, sugar, salt, black pepper, and horseradish. Whisk ingredients well, making sure sugar is dissolved.
3. Add enough dressing to cabbage mixture to moisten well.
4. Refrigerate for 30 minutes and serve immediately.

Spicy Asian Slaw

MAKES 12 CUPS

½ cup creamy peanut butter

¼ cup water or chicken broth

2 tablespoons rice wine vinegar

2 tablespoons honey

1 tablespoon soy sauce

½ teaspoon roasted sesame oil

2 tablespoons finely chopped garlic

2 tablespoons finely chopped fresh ginger

1 green onion, cut into 2-inch pieces

⅛-¼ teaspoon cayenne pepper

1 head green cabbage, coarsely chopped or shredded

½ head red cabbage, coarsely chopped or shredded

3 large carrots, shredded

½ cup coarsely chopped dry-roasted peanuts for garnish

1. In the bowl of a food processor, combine peanut butter, water or broth, rice wine vinegar, honey, soy sauce, sesame oil, garlic, ginger, green onion, and cayenne pepper. Pulse several times or until dressing is smooth and creamy. Set aside.

2. In a large mixing bowl, combine green cabbage, red cabbage, and carrots. Add dressing to cabbage and toss well to coat.

3. Top with dry-roasted peanuts and serve immediately.

SASSY SALADS

Crazy Easy Asian Slaw

MAKES 6 TO 8 SERVINGS

2 (3-ounce) packages chicken-flavored ramen noodles

½ cup slivered almonds

4 cups coarsely chopped or shredded green cabbage (about 1 medium head)

2 cups coarsely chopped or shredded purple cabbage (about ½ medium head)

¼ cup canola oil

⅓ cup rice wine vinegar

¼ cup sugar

1 tablespoon soy sauce

1 teaspoon toasted sesame oil

½ teaspoon salt

1 teaspoon black pepper

1 cup finely chopped green onions

1. Preheat oven to 350 degrees.
2. Break ramen noodles into pieces and place with almonds on a greased baking sheet. Reserve flavor packets to be used in dressing.
3. Bake for 12 minutes or until almonds turn a light brown. Cool thoroughly.
4. To clean and cut the cabbage, remove the thicker outer leaves and cut off the stem. Rinse the whole head under cool water. Cut into wedges and then chop coarsely.
5. In a small saucepan, heat oil, vinegar, sugar, soy sauce, sesame oil, salt, black pepper, and both flavor packets from ramen noodles until all dissolve. Remove dressing from heat and cool to room temperature.
6. In a large salad bowl, combine cabbage, green onions, noodles, and almonds.
7. Add dressing and toss well.

LuLu Clue: Best when chilled an hour before serving so cabbage can soak up the flavors of the dressing.

Getting ready for Hurricane Ivan

Sweet and Savory Spinach Salad

MAKES 4 TO 6 SERVINGS

2 bags fresh spinach

1 tablespoon butter

½ cup pecan halves

½ tablespoon sugar

⅓ cup Balsamic Bleu Dressing
(page 180)

½ red onion, very thinly sliced

2 oranges or 1 grapefruit, peeled
and sectioned

1 cup strawberries, sliced

⅓ cup oil-cured olives, pitted
and sliced

¼ cup crumbled Stilton cheese

1. Thoroughly wash and pat dry spinach, trim off stems. Place in a large salad bowl. Cover with damp paper towel and refrigerate.

2. In a heavy skillet, melt butter over medium-low heat. Add pecans and toss to coat. Add sugar and stir continuously until pecans are browned and glazed. Remove pecans from the skillet and transfer onto paper towels. As the pecans cool, the sugar will harden like candy.

3. Immediately before serving, toss spinach greens with dressing.

4. Top with onion slices, citrus fruit, strawberries, olives, and Stilton cheese. Sprinkle with candied pecans.

SASSY SALADS

BURGER BLISS

CLASSIC SHRIMP LOAF

MAMA'S FAVORITE OYSTER LOAF

CREOLA BLACKENED GROUPER SANDWICH
WITH FRIED GREEN TOMATOES AND WOW SAUCE

CRAB MELT

FRIED GREEN TOMATO B.L.T.

MEATLOAF SANDWICH

CRAZY SISTA'S JUICY POT ROAST SANDWICH

GRILLED CONECUH COUNTY SAUSAGE SANDWICH
WITH JEZEBEL SAUCE

ONE LOVE TUNA SANDWICH WITH SPICY ASIAN SLAW

GROWN-UP GRILLED CHEESE SANDWICH

SUMMERTIME HOMEGROWN TOMATO SANDWICH

MAHI SOFT TACOS
WITH CHIPOTLE CREAM SAUCE

Sandwich: Penance or Pleasure?

Iwas never a big fan of the sandwich. To be perfectly honest, my prickly relationship with sandwiches brought me close to eternal damnation.

Like most children, a sandwich was the staple of my daily lunch. Packed early in the morning, my lunches were a soggy, unappetizing mess, no doubt a result of the choices that my Mississippi-born mother made. Usually, she was running late (a gene that I unfortunately inherited) and would rush through the process relying on Dixie autopilot. I don't know about other parts of the country, but here in the South, folks eat a lot of funky sandwiches: white bread slices covered in mayo with a banana or pineapple squashed in between. When the cupboards were bare, only the mayo made it onto the bread.

Sometimes on Fridays my mother wanted to amuse me with the occasional tuna fish (a rare delicacy usually reserved for supper, tossed together with some Kraft® mac & cheese and that great American staple, cream of mushroom soup). She tried bologna once, and I threw up in the middle of Religion Class. I don't know if it was the mushy pink sandwich or the soul food seasoned with guilt that disagreed with me. She had to leave work (a mortal sin in our family) and pick me up from school, a harrowing inconvenience for her since she worked an hour away. End of bologna.

Finally, she just gave up, and it was peanut butter and jelly every day in my Barbie lunchbox for the remainder of her lunch-making career. Needless to say, most of the sandwiches found their way into the trash when the nuns weren't looking (another mortal sin), and by the time I was eight I was making my own lunch, a suitable penance for a rebellious youngster. A bag of Fritos and cookies seemed like the ideal lunch to me, and if I was going to hell, even as a child I knew to enjoy the ride.

Thankfully, as my legs grew longer (another gene I gladly inherited from her), so did my curiosity, and I ventured into the world of fast food and embraced the iconic American treasure, the hamburger. My favorite was from the Burger Chef, the short-lived McDonald's knock-off on the corner of Airport Boulevard and McGregor Street in Mobile, Alabama. My parents were relieved that I would eat anything with even a smidge of nutrition; this might have been the origin of my love affair with food and the end of my disdain for sandwiches.

In many areas of my life I have mellowed. For one thing, I have (hopefully!) gained a little knowledge over the years. I did learn that a turkey sandwich with cheese, tomatoes, and sweet pickles on wheat bread with a little wasabi mustard is a much better choice than a salad smothered in bleu cheese dressing. Sometimes when I am at LuLu's, I will opt for one of our specialty sandwiches, such as our amazing fish tacos, simply because life is short and I do my penance in other ways these days instead of depriving myself of living well.

Most Sundays, you can find me having…yes, a cheeseburger at the bar at LuLu's. There is something healing about a thick, juicy burger, crisp hot French fries, and a cold mug of beer, especially after a late night of frivolity. Add a slice of Cheddar, and by God, it becomes a famous song! (And besides, is there better hangover food?) We Americans love our cheeseburgers; at LuLu's we sell 100,000 of them annually. Suffice to say, we think our cheeseburger at LuLu's stands up to any of the others out there in paradise.

Burger Bliss & Other Blessings

I "Googled" the word "cheeseburger." There were more than 3.3 million possible results, and when I "Googled" "cheeseburger recipe," there were more than 600,000. Clearly, there are many, many ways to prepare and enjoy a good burger; it basically defies any hard and fast rules. Honestly though, if you don't know how to make one, it's probably easier just to head down the road to your favorite burger joint. I hope that would be LuLu's if you're in the neighborhood! But if you're going to give it a shot, here are some suggestions.

You should try for whatever reason, men simply have better grill skills. Or at least that's been my experience. Maybe it's that the women are smarter, staying indoors in the cool AC, slicing tomatoes and washing lettuce while the menfolk sweat it out over a hot grill. I'm just sayin' it's something to think about.

Don't skimp on the quality of the meat or the amount of fat in it. Now is no time to start second-guessing your decision to make a cheeseburger, and there's no such thing as a "diet" cheeseburger. Horrors such as turkey or veggie burgers have no bearing in this discussion and thus will be ignored completely. So you may as well buck up and make a nice, juicy one. The higher the fat content, the tastier the burger; sorry, but it's true.

I always like to butter my toasted buns. (Somehow that sounds naughty, but I'm okay with that.) I like my onions grilled, I choose Swiss for my cheese, and yes, I like a little Heinz 57®. The perfect burger is as personal as the perfect gumbo. Some people, like Anastasia, are super-picky and want theirs "just-so," others pile on every topping they can find, messy stains be damned. Whatever blows your skirt up, sister!

There are as many marinades and sauces on the market as there are opinions as to which is best. For the purposes of this recipe, I'm doing it my way. And my way, you may have figured out by now, tends to be the simple way. I don't dredge my burger in anything, no steak sauce, no Italian dressing, no soy sauce, or anything else. I simply salt and pepper the meat; once patties are made, the grill takes care of the rest, bringing out the meat's natural flavor.

Burger Bliss

2 pounds ground chuck (or) 2½ pounds ground beef, pattied into 8 burgers

8 large hamburger buns (believe it or not, I'm not crazy about the sesame seeds)

Toppings & Condiments (see list of suggestions)

1. Find a Helpful Man (if that's helpful).
2. Have him heat a charcoal or gas grill, whatever he prefers.
3. Mix him his favorite cocktail while he monitors the grill temp.
4. When he says the grill is ready, bring him the beautifully pattied burgers, arranged lovingly over waxed paper on a festive platter. Use waxed paper so that you can remove it after your Helpful Man has loaded the burgers onto the grill and, voilà, you have a clean serving platter ready once they're cooked.
5. Arrange toppings and condiments on platters and in bowls. Heat your buns.
6. Refresh your Helpful Man's drink as needed.
7. Provide him with toppings to be grilled and cheeses to be melted when requested.
8. When the burgers are ready to be served, be sure to praise your Helpful Man, thank him for his efforts and remind him to clean the grill.

LuLu Clue: Here are some suggested toppings and condiments. Play, get crazy!

TOPPINGS

- Cheese (almost any): Swiss, Cheddar, Havarti, Provolone, Monterey Jack, Bleu, Mozzarella, Feta
- Lettuce: Iceberg, Green Leaf, Romaine
- Onion: grilled or raw, sliced or chopped; red onion is pretty, Vidalias® are nice and sweet
- Tomato
- Bacon
- Avocado
- Mushrooms, sautéed in butter

- Sliced pickles
- Sweet relish
- Colored bell peppers
- Jalapeños
- Banana peppers
- Cole slaw
- Sauerkraut
- Potato chips
- Pepperoni
- Ketchup: Heinz® only
- Mustard: yellow – French's® only; Dijon, Creole, spicy or sweet

- Mayonnaise: Hellmann's® only
- Heinz 57®
- A.1.® Steak sauce
- Hot sauce
- Barbecue sauce
- Pizza sauce
- Ranch dressing
- Teriyaki sauce
- Gyro (yogurt cucumber) sauce
- Soy-ginger, pesto, wasabi, or chipotle mayonnaise

In other parts of the country, this kind of sandwich might be called a hoagie or sub (although I would imagine you don't run into a fresh fried shrimp hoagie too often in Chicago); in New Orleans it's known as a po'boy, but here on the brackish tidewaters of Lower Alabama it's a "loaf"...as in what we like to do on any given Sunday afternoon.

Classic Shrimp Loaf

MAKES 4 SANDWICHES

4 dozen medium shrimp, peeled and deveined

4 (8-inch) loaves New Orleans-style French bread or 1 baguette, cut into 4 pieces

2-3 tablespoons butter, softened

Mayonnaise to taste

Creole mustard to taste

Lettuce leaves

2 medium tomatoes, sliced

Sweet and Sassy Icebox Pickle slices (page 116)

LuLu's Perfect Pepper Hot Sauce™

1. Preheat oven to 200 degrees.
2. Fry shrimp (page 52) in batches and place cooked shrimp in oven to keep warm.
3. Slice French bread horizontally, about three-fourths of the way through, leaving one edge intact.
4. Spread a little butter on inside surface of French bread and toast. I like to place mine face-down, on a warm skillet or grill.
5. Spread mayonnaise on one side of toasted bread and Creole mustard on the other side.
6. Layer lettuce, tomato slices, and pickles on bottom side of bread.
7. Top with fried shrimp, using 10 to 12 shrimp per sandwich.
8. Add a few dashes of hot sauce to taste. Cut in half and serve.

My mother was oyster-crazed. She looked forward to

the months ending in "r" (oyster season) with as much eagerness and anticipation as a hunter awaiting the first day of duck or deer season. She loved them any-which-way they could be prepared, and her tastes enjoyed extensive scope. She loved them roasted with a Champagne-vinegar mignonette sauce; deep fried after marinating in pickle juice (a Southern secret); baked with herbs, cheese, and spinach; in soups, stews, casseroles; and especially cold, fresh, and raw on the half shell. This was my mother's favorite sandwich at LuLu's — a fact the staff knew well. They could often be counted on to have an oyster loaf ready for her by the time she was seated at "her" special table where she held court. Peets smiled a lot, generally, but this traditional Southern sandwich was always a sweet guarantee.

Mama's Favorite Oyster Loaf

MAKES 4 SANDWICHES

1 quart oysters

4 (8-inch) loaves New Orleans-style French bread or 1 baguette, cut into 4 pieces

2-3 tablespoons butter, softened

Mayonnaise to taste

Lettuce leaves

2 medium tomatoes, sliced

Sweet and Sassy Icebox Pickle slices (page 116)

LuLu's Perfect Pepper Hot Sauce™

1. Preheat oven to 200 degrees.
2. Fry oysters (page 54) in batches and place cooked oysters in oven to keep warm.
3. Slice French bread horizontally, about three-fourths of the way through, leaving one edge intact.
4. Spread a little butter on inside surface of French bread and toast. I like to place mine face-down, on a warm skillet or grill.
5. Spread mayonnaise on toasted bread.
6. Layer lettuce, tomato slices, and pickles on bottom side of bread.
7. Top with fried oysters, using about 8 oysters per sandwich.
8. Add a few dashes of hot sauce to taste. Cut in half and serve.

Creola Blackened Grouper Sandwich with Fried Green Tomatoes and WOW Sauce™

MAKES 4 SANDWICHES

4 grouper fillets

6 tablespoons olive oil, divided

2 tablespoons LuLu's Crazy Creola Seasoning™ (page 50)

8 green tomato slices

4 (8-inch) loaves New Orleans-style French bread or 1 baguette, cut into 4 pieces

2-3 tablespoons butter, softened

LuLu's WOW Sauce™ (page 173)

1. Preheat oven to 200 degrees.
2. Coat fish with 2 tablespoons olive oil and Creola seasoning. Set aside.
3. Fry tomatoes (page 101). Place cooked tomatoes in oven to keep warm.
4. In a large cast iron or heavy skillet, heat remaining 4 tablespoons olive oil over medium-high heat until it sizzles. Gently place fillets in skillet. Cook on one side for 3 to 4 minutes. Carefully turn fillets and continue cooking for another 3 to 4 minutes or until fish is cooked through. (If you can easily insert a toothpick into the fish, it is done.) Remove to an ovenproof platter or baking dish. Place in oven to keep warm.
5. Slice French bread horizontally, about three-fourths of the way through, leaving one edge intact.
6. Spread a little butter on inside surface of French bread and toast. I like to place mine face-down, on a warm skillet or grill.
7. Place a fillet on each sandwich bottom.
8. Top each with 2 fried green tomato slices and slather with WOW Sauce™. Fold tops over and cut in half. Enjoy!

Crab Melt

1 pound fresh crab claw meat

2 cups shredded Swiss cheese

½ cup finely chopped green onions

½ teaspoon salt

½ teaspoon black pepper

1½ cups mayonnaise

4 (8-inch) loaves New Orleans-style French bread or 1 baguette, cut into 4 pieces

1. Preheat oven to 350 degrees.
2. Carefully pick through crabmeat to remove any shells.
3. Combine crabmeat, cheese, green onions, salt, and pepper in a bowl. Add mayonnaise and gently mix.
4. Slice each French loaf in half, horizontally.
5. Spread crabmeat mixture generously over each piece of bread.
6. Transfer all 8 pieces to a baking sheet. Bake for 15 minutes or until hot and cheese starts to bubble.
7. Place under broiler for a few minutes until golden brown.

LuLu Clue: We serve this "open-faced" on French bread at the restaurant, but I have also made it as an hors d'oeuvre for parties on toast points or as an individual appetizer wrapped in phyllo dough... there are many ways to serve this rich, addictive dish. I also love it hot and bubbly in a small baking crock served with flatbread or pita crisps.

I thought it would be impossible to make a good, old-fashioned BLT any more

delicious, but I was wrong and found out just how wrong with my very first bite of this sandwich. We were working on changes for the LuLu's menu, and I asked the kitchen to make me a BLT with a fried green tomato to sample. I really did intend to have one bite, a taste...I ate the whole thing. It's a terrific twist on a classic.

Fried Green Tomato B.L.T.

MAKES 4 SANDWICHES

12 green tomato slices

12 strips thick-cut bacon

Lettuce leaves

2-3 tablespoons butter, softened

8 thick slices sourdough bread

LuLu's WOW Sauce™ (page 173)

1. Preheat oven to 250 degrees.
2. Fry tomatoes (page 101). Place cooked tomatoes in oven to keep warm.
3. Fry bacon in 2 batches in a cast iron or heavy skillet over medium heat. As bacon begins to sizzle, lower heat to keep it from smoking or burning. As bacon begins to brown, turn once. Drain on paper towels.
4. Butter bread slices on one side and broil until browned. Flip bread and toast unbuttered side.
5. Layer 3 slices fried tomatoes, 3 pieces fried bacon, and lettuce on buttered side of each piece of bread.
6. Slather with WOW Sauce™.
7. Top with remaining toasted slices, butter side down.
8. Cut in half and serve.

 LuLu Clue: If you're frying bacon, you might as well save the bacon grease and reserve it for making gumbo. I think it makes for a much more flavorful roux.

Poor meatloaf gets a bad rap. Nobody wants to admit that they love it. But they do. You show me someone who doesn't like meatloaf, and I'll show you someone who's maybe had it a bit too easy in this world. (Either that, or it's what they ate one too many times as a child.) It's simple, country food, about as American as you can get. When you have to stretch the grocery dollars as far as many people do these days, you have to have bang for your buck. And, as with so many comforting dishes, meatloaf is even better on day two. Prepare this dish specifically for sandwiches or pair it with Josie's Mac and Cheese (see recipe page 287) for a full-belly supper and save the leftovers.

Meatloaf Sandwich

MAKES 4 SANDWICHES

1 pound ground beef

1 small yellow onion, finely chopped

1 small apple, peeled, cored, and grated

Black pepper to taste

Chicken-n-a-Biscuit® crackers

1 egg, beaten

½ cup ketchup

4 tablespoons olive oil, divided

1 small onion, sliced

1 small green bell pepper, sliced

4 slices Swiss cheese

4 (8-inch) loaves New Orleans-style French bread or 1 baguette, cut into 4 pieces

2-3 tablespoons butter, softened

Jezebel Sauce (page 182), optional

White Horseradish Sauce (page 174), optional

1. Preheat oven to 350 degrees.
2. Combine beef, chopped onion, apple, and black pepper in a bowl.
3. Crush crackers with your hands to yield 1 cup of crumbs.
4. Add beaten egg and cracker crumbs by hand to meat mixture, kneading well.
5. Form into a loaf shape and place in a greased baking dish.
6. Spread ketchup over top of loaf.
7. Bake for 50 to 60 minutes.
8. Remove meatloaf from the oven and cool completely.
9. Refrigerate overnight.
10. Cut meatloaf into ½-inch-thick slices.
11. In a large sauté pan, heat 2 tablespoons olive oil until it begins to sizzle.
12. Add sliced onion and bell pepper and sauté until soft and slightly browned on the edges. Remove from pan and set aside.
13. In same sauté pan, add remaining 2 tablespoons olive oil and heat until it begins to sizzle.
14. Place meatloaf slices in pan and cook on one side for 2 minutes. Turn slices over and cook 2 minutes longer or until heated through.
15. Top meatloaf with Swiss cheese and cover. Cook until cheese is melted. Remove from heat.
16. Slice French bread horizontally, about three-fourths of the way through, leaving one edge intact.
17. Spread a little butter on inside surface of French bread and toast. I like to place mine face-down, on a warm skillet or grill.
18. Place meatloaf on toasted French loaves and top with grilled onions and peppers.
19. Serve with Jezebel or White Horseradish Sauce.

LuLu Clue: The crackers I use in this recipe are plenty salty; I don't suggest adding any more than you need to bind the mixture together.

Crazy Sista's Juicy Pot Roast Sandwich

1 (2-pound) beef chuck roast

8 whole cloves garlic, peeled

Cracked black pepper

1 (14-ounce) can beef broth

½ cup Allegro® Original Marinade

4 (8-inch) loaves New Orleans-style French bread or 1 baguette, cut into 4 pieces

4 tablespoons butter, softened, divided

1 yellow onion, sliced

1 green bell pepper, sliced

4-8 slices Swiss cheese

White Horseradish Sauce (page 174)

1. Preheat oven to 250 degrees.
2. Place pot roast in a baking dish just big enough to hold the meat.
3. Make 8 deep, little cuts throughout the roast and insert a whole clove of garlic into each one.
4. Season roast generously with cracked black pepper.
5. Pour beef broth and marinade over roast and cover tightly with a sheet of aluminum foil.
6. Bake for 5 to 6 hours. When roast is done, it will be so tender, the meat should literally fall apart.
7. Drain juices into a bowl or container to reserve for au jus dipping sauce.
8. Melt 2 tablespoons of butter in a cast iron skillet. Add onion and bell pepper and sauté until soft and slightly browned on the edges. Remove from skillet and set aside.
9. Slice French bread horizontally, about three-fourths of the way through, leaving one edge intact.
10. Spread remaining butter on inside surface of French bread and toast. I like to place mine face-down, on a warm skillet or grill.
11. Layer each toasted French loaf with shredded pot roast, Swiss cheese, and sautéed onion and bell pepper.
12. Drizzle generously with horseradish sauce.
13. Serve with a side of au jus for dipping (and plenty of napkins)!

NEVER FAIL POT ROAST REMEDY

If Lucy is known as "Crazy Sista," then our good friend-brother is "Ten-Times-As-Crazy Brotha."

He has many nicknames, but those who love him call him Danny Faulk. He's hardheaded as a mule — legend holds that he went through 7 Riddell ("unbreakable") helmets in his senior year on the high school football field. He is tougher than nails and is always up to the challenge, taking the hard road at every opportunity. Pain in the ass. And, he's a total softie. He knows everyone, loves everyone, and loves nothing more than taking care of folks. If you're ever broke and broken-down on a back road somewhere far-the-hell away, Danny's your man. He'll be there to pick you up in "two minutes." Should you happen to be a total stranger with no place to stay and odd piercings, you're probably sleeping on Danny's couch. God forbid you've just broken up with your boyfriend and need a shoulder to cry on...he'd feel up your ancient Aunt Edna given the chance! But in true times of need or sorrow, Danny can fix you up fast...well, at least in a couple of hours. This sandwich is on the menu at LuLu's in tribute to its former manager because this pot roast is Danny's super-powerful medicine for that which ails you. It never fails. It seems way easier than it should be, given its origin, but follow Charles Daniel-my-Brother's instructions and you'll be happier than "a mule eatin' briars."

-Diva

Danny Faulk flying high

There may not be a better smoked sausage than the rope sausage handmade in Conecuh (pronounced con-É-ka) County, Alabama. Of course, if you are unable to find the "real thing," go ahead and use the best quality sausage you can find. With online shopping and global availability, do yourself a favor and have it shipped to your front door. It really does make a difference. www.conecuhsausage.com

Grilled Conecuh County Sausage Sandwich with Jezebel Sauce

MAKES 4 SANDWICHES

2 pounds Conecuh® Smoked Sausage
4 tablespoons butter, divided
1 large onion, sliced
1 green bell pepper, sliced
4 hot dog buns
Jezebel Sauce (page 182)

1. Cut sausage into bun-length pieces and butterfly each piece, leaving halves connected.
2. Grill or fry sausage over medium heat in a skillet until brown and cooked through. Remove sausage from skillet and drain on paper towels. Wipe out skillet with paper towels.
3. Add 2 tablespoons butter to skillet over low heat; do not allow butter to burn.
4. When butter begins to foam, add onions and bell peppers and sauté until soft and slightly browned on the edges. Remove from heat and set aside.
5. Spread remaining butter on inside of hot dog buns. Toast open buns.
6. Place cooked sausage on buns.
7. Divide the sautéed onions and peppers evenly among the buns.
8. Spoon desired amount of Jezebel sauce over each.

One Heart Tuna Sandwich with Spicy Asian Slaw

MAKES 4 SANDWICHES

1 cup One Heart Marinade
  (page 48)

4 (6-ounce) fresh tuna fillets

2 tablespoons butter, softened

4 hamburger buns

Wasabi Mayonnaise (page 183)

Spicy Asian Slaw (page 147)

1. Marinate tuna for 20 minutes, turning fillets once halfway through.
2. To grill tuna, fire up the grill to high heat and sear tuna on each side for 2 minutes. Or, to pan-sear tuna, spray skillet with olive oil and heat to hot. Pan-sear tuna on each side for 2 minutes.
4. Spread a little butter on hamburger buns and broil to toast.
5. Spread toasted buns with wasabi mayonnaise.
6. Place about ¼ cup of slaw on the bottom of bun and top with tuna.

 LuLu Clue: These instructions will make a rare piece of tuna; if you prefer yours more well done, simply grill or pan-sear the fillets a little longer.

Nothing screams "comfort food" quite like a crispy-on-the-outside, gooey-warm-on-the-inside grilled cheese sandwich. I think it's fun to use different kinds of cheeses. So here's how it's done LuLu-style — all yummy goodness.

Grown-Up Grilled Cheese Sandwich

MAKES 1 SANDWICH

1 tablespoon butter, softened

2 thickly sliced pieces fresh rustic bread

¾ cup shredded sharp Cheddar cheese

1 thick slice Havarti cheese

1 slice Provolone cheese

1. Spread ½ tablespoon butter on each bread slice.
2. Place bread, buttered-side down, in nonstick skillet over medium-low heat.
3. Top with cheeses and remaining bread, buttered-side up.
4. Cook slowly until bottom is browned and cheeses are melted.
5. Press gently with a flat spatula, otherwise known as squishing, to bind together.
6. Flip and cook on other side until browned to perfection.

 LuLu Clue: You can put a lid on the skillet for the first minute or so to help melt the cheese.

Nothing reminds me of summer like the taste of a luscious, red, warm

homegrown tomato picked off the vine. We can't wait to plant our varieties each spring, but don't worry if you don't have the time or inclination to plant your own garden. I'm sure you can find a farmers' market in your hometown. In Baldwin County, Alabama, where I live, you can't drive a mile without encountering a road-side stand selling seasonal fruits and vegetables like tomatoes, Silver Queen corn, and strawberries. This sandwich is so perfect in its simplicity, it deserves the freshest tomatoes you can find.

Summertime Homegrown Tomato Sandwich

MAKES 1 SANDWICH

1 large "homegrown" ripe tomato
2 slices white bread
    (very important)
Real mayonnaise
Salt and pepper to taste

1. Cut tomato into thick slices.
2. Slather both slices of bread with mayonnaise.
3. Top bread with several slices of juicy tomato.
4. Sprinkle generously with salt and pepper.
5. Smile as the perfect juices dribble down your chin!

LuLu Clue: When I feel the urge to be exotic, I grab a few basil leaves from the garden and place them between the tomatoes.

Mahi Soft Tacos with Chipotle Cream Sauce

MAKES 6 SERVINGS

4 (8-ounce) fresh mahi-mahi fish
    fillets

4 tablespoons olive oil, divided

2 tablespoons LuLu's Chipotle
    Taco Seasoning (page 49)

1½ cups Cuban Black Beans
    (page 273)

1 cup shredded sharp Cheddar
    cheese

1 cup shredded Monterey Jack
    cheese

1 cup shredded white cabbage

1 cup shredded purple cabbage

12 (6-inch) corn tortillas

Chipotle Cream Sauce
    (page 183)

LuLu's Sassy Salsa™ (page 178)

1 fresh lime, cut into wedges

1. Preheat oven to 300 degrees.
2. Coat fish with 2 tablespoons olive oil and seasoning. Set aside.
3. Warm black beans.
4. Combine cheeses in a bowl.
5. In a separate bowl, mix cabbages.
6. Wrap tortillas in foil and warm in oven for 10 minutes.
7. In a large cast iron or heavy skillet, heat remaining 2 tablespoons olive oil over medium-high heat until it sizzles. Gently place fillets in skillet. Cook on one side for 3 to 4 minutes. Carefully turn fillets and continue cooking for another 3 to 4 minutes or until fish is cooked through. (If you can easily insert a toothpick into the fish, it is done.) Remove from heat and chop into bite-sized pieces.
8. To assemble taco, top warm tortilla with fish, black beans, cheese, and cabbage. Drizzle with Chipotle Cream Sauce and fold in half.
9. Serve with LuLu's Sassy Salsa™ and fresh lime wedges.

LuLu Clue: A can of black beans, rinsed and drained, can be substituted for Cuban Black Beans. At LuLu's, we also serve these great tacos with chicken or shrimp.

LULU'S WOW SAUCE

RED HORSERADISH SAUCE (COCKTAIL SAUCE)

WHITE HORSERADISH SAUCE

ORANGE HORSERADISH DIPPING SAUCE

TARTAR "NOT FROM A JAR" SAUCE

HONEY-HONEY MUSTARD

CHUNKY CHERRY TOMATO SALSA

SASSY SALSA

BAD GIRL BUFFALO SAUCE (SPICY!)

STILTON BLUE CHEESE SALAD DRESSING

GINGER LIME SALAD DRESSING

BALSAMIC BLEU DRESSING

JEZEBEL SAUCE

FRESH BASIL MAYONNAISE

WASABI MAYONNAISE

CHIPOTLE CREAM SAUCE

SAUCY & PROUD OF IT!

I've never cared for bland. Middle-of-the-road, ordinary, "normal" — what does any of that mean anyway? I've never been interested in whether someone thought I was "over the top." I am, and I'm happy to own that! I like my life in Technicolor® with a bright, sassy soundtrack. My life is dramatic and colorful, my loves all-encompassing, my energy vivid. I was taught at an early age to "live out loud," and I do.

My joie de vivre extends, as you've probably already surmised, to food. I believe food is for enjoyment, not just for sustenance. It is to be experienced, like life, not merely consumed for nutritional value. And there are so many ways to create delicious, flavorful foods that it seems like a sin to eat boring food. One of the easiest ways to put some zing in your meal is to use some sauce. Everything tastes better with a little something to slather on it or dip it in, especially if that "something" is more naughty than nice...more tart & tramp than sugar & spice. That's why I love Jezebel sauce so much. It lives up to its infamous name, with plenty of heat. Maybe there isn't much that's sexy about sauces and dressings, unless you count the finger-lickin' that goes along with them, but you'll definitely be taking a walk on the wild-child side with Bad Girl Buffalo Sauce.

I'm proud that LuLu's signature dressings and sauces are still homemade in the kitchen. Don't take the store-bought road if you don't have to — make sauces and dressings yourself! When I'm at home, I make all of my dressings and marinades from scratch; it's too easy not to. And besides that, putting bottled dressing over fresh seafood is like cheating at cards or not wearing underwear to church — in other words, a sin. If you don't have the time or the inclination, LuLu's is happy to supply you with our distinctive Fun Food line of vibrant, delicious sauces, salsas, and dressings. No worries. Be saucy & proud!

"Saucy" Lucy and her mama "Peets" Buffett, circa 1961

Honest to God,

people actually say "WOW!" when they take a bite of our famous Grouper Loaf with Fried Green Tomatoes topped with this wonderful sauce. It happens so often in fact, "WOW" finally became part of the dish's name, and "WOW Sauce" is much easier to say than "distinctive Creole mustard and horseradish sauce." Similar in flavor to a rémoulade sauce, the Creole mustard gives it a regional tang, and the horseradish accentuates beef dishes beautifully. We also serve it with both our BL&FGT (bacon, lettuce, and fried green tomato) Sandwich and our Pot Roast Sandwich.

LuLu's WOW Sauce

MAKES 1½ CUPS

2 whole fresh jalapeño peppers
1 tablespoon olive oil
1 cup mayonnaise
¼ cup Creole mustard
¼ cup horseradish

1. Coat peppers with olive oil. Char in a hot skillet or under a broiler. The trick is to blacken the skins evenly by turning them frequently.

2. Once peppers are charred, place them in plastic bag or covered bowl for about 15 minutes. As the peppers cool, the heat and moisture sweat the skins from the peppers. Once skins are removed, cut peppers in half, carefully remove seeds, and finely chop.

3. Combine chopped peppers, mayonnaise, mustard, and horseradish in a bowl. Mix thoroughly and refrigerate.

LuLu Clue: Caution: use plastic gloves or utensils when dealing with any hot, fresh peppers, unless your fingertips are well calloused from lots of cooking or ironing. Also, after fooling with hot peppers, don't go to the bathroom or stick your fingers near your eyes unless you are Catholic and it is part of your confessional penance.

Red Horseradish Sauce (Cocktail Sauce)

MAKES 2½ CUPS

2 cups ketchup

¾ cup prepared horseradish

2 tablespoons LuLu's Perfect
Pepper Hot Sauce™

¼ cup Worcestershire sauce

2 tablespoons Pickapeppa® sauce

1 tablespoon freshly squeezed
lemon juice

1. Combine all ingredients in a bowl.
2. Mix thoroughly and refrigerate.

White Horseradish Sauce

MAKES 2 CUPS

2 cups sour cream

½ cup prepared horseradish

1 teaspoon salt

½ teaspoon white pepper

1 tablespoon Worcestershire sauce

2 tablespooons freshly squeezed
lemon juice

2-3 dashes LuLu's Perfect Pepper
Hot Sauce™

1 teaspoon freshly chopped
rosemary, optional

1. Combine all ingredients in a bowl.
2. Mix thoroughly and refrigerate.

Orange Horseradish Dipping Sauce

MAKES ABOUT 1 CUP

1 cup orange marmalade

2 tablespoons prepared horseradish

1 tablespoon Dijon mustard

1 tablespoon freshly squeezed
lemon juice

½ teaspoon LuLu's Perfect Pepper
Hot Sauce™

½ teaspoon salt

1. Combine all ingredients in a bowl.
2. Mix thoroughly and refrigerate.

Tartar "Not From A Jar" Sauce

MAKES 2 CUPS

2 cups mayonnaise
¼ cup dill pickle relish
2 tablespoons sweet pickle relish
½ cup finely chopped yellow onion
½ teaspoon salt
1 teaspoon black pepper

1. Combine all ingredients in a bowl.
2. Mix thoroughly and refrigerate.

Honey-Honey Mustard

MAKES 2½ CUPS

¾ cup honey
¾ cup Creole mustard
¾ cup prepared yellow mustard

1. Combine all ingredients in a bowl.
2. Mix thoroughly and refrigerate.
3. Act as if it took all day long to make. Play hooky and catch the last half hour of Dr. Phil.

LuLu Clue: Serve Honey-Honey Mustard with chicken fingers and chicken wings. It's also great as a sweet salad dressing with the LuLu's Jerk-Chick Deli Salad (page 144). Perfect on a turkey sandwich.

I learned to make this salsa while I was executive chef on MYMariner III in Belize City. The boat had been chartered by Harrison Ford while shooting "The Mosquito Coast." Friday nights were always our "blow-out" nights after a grueling week on the set. One such night I had planned a dinner of fajitas and Cuban-style black beans. After drinking numerous cocktails, Ford, who is a master of many crafts, proceeded to instruct me on how to make real salsa. Fresh tomatoes, onions, salt, a little lime juice, and fresh cilantro. Inspired, we made margaritas which we drank until way... way after midnight. It was traditional for us to weigh anchor at 6 a.m. and take Harrison and his wife cruising for the weekend. The following morning I had to get back to my job! The seas were a violent two inches, not a puff o' wind. Never seasick before and never since, I was green that day. It did not, however, inspire me to avoid salsa!

Chunky Cherry Tomato Salsa

MAKES 4 CUPS

2 pints cherry tomatoes, quartered

¼ cup finely chopped fresh cilantro

½ cup finely chopped yellow onion

1 jalapeño, with seeds, finely chopped

3 tablespoons freshly squeezed lime juice

½ teaspoon salt

Freshly ground black pepper to taste

1. Combine all ingredients in a bowl.
2. Mix thoroughly and refrigerate.

LuLu Clue: This fresh salsa is almost too simple to prepare, but so lovely over fresh grilled fish, a light Sunday morning omelet, or with tortilla chips and a beer. Jalapeño seeds add heat; if you want a more mild salsa, remove the seeds.

177

I realize I have mentioned my chips and salsa "addiction" a few times in this cookbook, and it warrants mention again here. I am not biased when I say this is one of the better salsa recipes out there...believe me, I have sampled thousands. The ingredients are pretty standard, but something about the Rose's® lime juice adds a hint of something deliciously unique. I have toyed with the idea of starting a "chips and salsa support group." Instead, I bottled this particular recipe so other people can share my whole-hearted passion.

Sassy Salsa

MAKES ABOUT 3½ CUPS

1 (28-ounce) can diced tomatoes, undrained

2 jalapeño peppers, seeds removed

2 teaspoons Rose's® lime juice

2 teaspoons finely chopped cilantro leaves

2 cloves garlic, crushed

½ cup finely chopped yellow onions

1 teaspoon ground cumin

1 teaspoon salt

1 teaspoon sugar

1. Place tomatoes with their juice in the bowl of a food processor. Pulse a couple of times until slightly chunky. Transfer tomatoes to a large glass bowl.

2. Place jalapeños and lime juice in the bowl of a food processor. Process until puréed and add to the tomatoes.

3. Add cilantro, garlic, onions, cumin, salt, and sugar to tomatoes. Mix well. Cover and refrigerate for at least 2 hours before serving.

Bad Girl Buffalo Sauce (Spicy!)

MAKES 2 CUPS

SAUCE BASE

1 cup LuLu's Perfect Pepper Hot Sauce™ or any medium hot sauce (Crystal® also works great!)

2 tablespoons unsalted butter

1 cup honey

½ teaspoon liquid smoke hickory seasoning

¼ teaspoon salt

¼ teaspoon black pepper

1 teaspoon LuLu's Crazy Creola Seasoning™ (page 50)

ROUX

2 tablespoons unsalted butter

2 tablespoons all-purpose flour

1. In a large saucepan, heat hot sauce and butter over medium heat.
2. Add honey, liquid smoke, salt, pepper, and Creole seasoning. Stir until well blended. Simmer for 15 minutes.
3. To make roux, heat butter over medium-low heat in a small cast iron skillet.
4. Slowly add flour to melted butter, stirring constantly, for about 5 minutes until a blond color is achieved and flour comes away from the pan. It will have a paste-like consistency, but as you stir it will thin slightly. Make sure it does not burn...if it smokes and smells even a tiny bit burned, just start over.
5. Carefully add simmering hot sauce mixture to roux, stirring constantly. It will sizzle. Stir until well blended.
6. Remove from heat. Cool to room temperature and store, or serve piping hot with LuLu's Crazy Chicken Fingers (page 106).

Stilton Blue Cheese Salad Dressing

MAKES APPROXIMATELY 2½ CUPS

1 cup Stilton blue cheese

¾ cup mayonnaise

¾ cup buttermilk

1½ teaspoons water

1 teaspoon sugar

½ teaspoon minced garlic

Salt and pepper to taste

1. Crumble Stilton cheese into a small bowl.
2. Stir in mayonnaise until cheese and mayonnaise are creamy.
3. Add buttermilk and water until well blended.
4. Add sugar, garlic, and salt and pepper to taste.
5. Refrigerate or serve immediately.

 PERFECT SAUCES & SALAD DRESSINGS

I was skeptical

as to whether this "fancy" dressing was going to go over at my little "high-class dive" and happily surprised at how well it did! I was first introduced to it at a lunch with our friends Gail and Jim Laughner. They are part of the Fish River crew and two of the most interesting folks I've ever met. She made her version of a jerk chicken salad with ginger lime dressing, and I thought it was awesome. I put it on the menu at the restaurant, and it has endured for years, becoming a house favorite at LuLu's. There have been so many requests for the recipe that we started bottling it ourselves; it is the flagship of our LuLu's Fun Foods line.

Ginger Lime Salad Dressing

MAKES 1 CUP

2 tablespoons finely minced fresh gingerroot

¼ cup extra virgin olive oil

¼ cup canola oil

¼ cup freshly squeezed lemon juice

¼ cup freshly squeezed lime juice

1½ tablespoons fine sugar

1 teaspoon coarse black pepper

½ teaspoon salt

1. Place all ingredients in a glass jar or plastic container and shake well until dressing is combined. Refrigerate.
2. Stir or shake well before serving.

 LuLu Clue: This salad dressing keeps well and is delicious over blackened grouper or grilled shrimp salad. It can also be used as a marinade for grilling chicken or fish.

Balsamic Bleu Dressing

MAKES ABOUT 2 CUPS

½ cup olive oil

½ cup balsamic vinegar

2 tablespoons Dijon mustard

2 tablespoons lemon juice

1 cup crumbled bleu cheese

½ teaspoon sugar

½ teaspoon salt

¼ teaspoon black pepper

1. Combine all ingredients in a bowl.
2. Mix thoroughly and refrigerate.

Jezebel Sauce

is as provocative as it sounds. It's sweet, and it's hot! It's a classic Southern sauce traditionally served with ham. There are many versions, but all basically use the apple jelly and pineapple preserves with various mustards. I like it with my Grilled Conecuh County Sausage Sandwich.

Jezebel Sauce

MAKES 2 CUPS

1 (12-ounce) jar apple jelly

1 (12-ounce) jar pineapple preserves

½ cup dry mustard

½ cup prepared horseradish

1 teaspoon finely ground black pepper

1. Combine all ingredients in a bowl.
2. Mix thoroughly and refrigerate.

Fresh Basil Mayonnaise

MAKES 1 CUP

1 cup loosely packed fresh basil leaves

1 cup mayonnaise

1 teaspoon freshly squeezed lemon juice

½ teaspoon salt

½ teaspoon white pepper

1 whole clove garlic

1. Remove stems from basil, wash, and pat dry.
2. In a food processor, combine basil leaves, mayonnaise, lemon juice, salt, white pepper, and garlic. Pulse until well blended.
3. Mix thoroughly and refrigerate.

LuLu Clue: Absolutely perfect on our Summertime Homegrown Tomato Sandwich (page 168).

LuLu Clue: You can substitute butter for the mayonnaise to make Fresh Basil Butter, which is wonderful over steamed veggies or as a spread for tea sandwiches.

My husband loves wasabi. He would eat it on anything if he could.

One Christmas, my daughter gave him a fancy stocking-stuffer jar of wasabi mustard that may have been his favorite gift of all. I think he would try wasabi ice cream if the opportunity presented itself. I whipped up this simple but tasty mayo to spice up a tuna sandwich I made him for lunch one day. We discovered it goes great with quite a few dishes, drizzled on everything from hors d'oeuvres, meats, seafood, and sandwiches, or served as a simple dip with veggies and chips. We haven't put it on ice cream…yet.

Wasabi Mayonnaise

MAKES ABOUT 1 CUP

3 tablespoons dry wasabi powder

1½ tablespoons cold water, or as needed

1 cup mayonnaise

1 teaspoon freshly squeezed lime juice

1 teaspoon soy sauce

¼ teaspoon salt

1 tablespoon chopped fresh cilantro

1. Mix wasabi powder with just enough cold water to form a paste.
2. In a food processor, combine wasabi paste, mayonnaise, lime juice, soy sauce, and salt. Pulse until well blended.
3. Add cilantro and continue to pulse until well blended and light green in color.
4. Refrigerate and serve chilled.

LuLu Clue: Great with our One Heart Tuna Sandwich (page 167).

Chipotle Cream Sauce

MAKES 2 CUPS

4-5 whole chipotle peppers in adobo sauce (found in 7-ounce cans)

1 tablespoon freshly squeezed lime juice

1 teaspoon freshly squeezed lemon juice

½ teaspoon salt

¼ teaspoon ground cumin

¼ teaspoon LuLu's Chipotle Taco Seasoning (page 49)

2 cups sour cream

1. In a food processor, combine whole chipotle peppers, lime juice, lemon juice, salt, cumin, and seasoning. Blend until peppers are puréed.
2. Add the sour cream and blend thoroughly until smooth.
3. Refrigerate and serve chilled.

LULU'S BIG CHOCOLATE CHUNKY COOKIE

KEY LIME PIE WITH
GRAND MARNIER® WHIPPED CREAM

WEEDY'S MARGARITA CHEESECAKE

CHOCOLATE POUND CAKE WITH
MOCHA GLAZE

HOMEMADE BANANA PUDDIN' WITH
NILLA® WAFERS

KEY LIME SQUARES

GERMAN CHOCOLATE CAKE WITH
COCONUT-PECAN FROSTING

JOSIE'S RED VELVET CAKE WITH
CREAM CHEESE FROSTING

DESSERT FIRST

I like a little something sweet to finish supper. I don't need a lot (sweets aren't necessarily part of my food addiction), but I like a little taste. My husband Mac would eat ice cream every night if given the chance; my parents had to have dessert because supper just wasn't complete without some sort of confection. Both my mother and grandmother regularly kept a fresh cake, usually chocolate pound cake, on the sideboard cake pedestal. My daughters, my siblings, and I all grew up knowing it was alright to have a slice whenever we pleased. For her part, my maternal grandmother always liked to have a tray of petit-fours on hand. I was blessed to have in Peets a mother with an abiding appreciation for quality of life.

Usually by the time I reach the end of the meal, unfortunately, I've already feasted on so much food I rarely have room to spare, which leads me to believe that maybe I should just have it first! There's a beautiful sailboat plying the waters around the Pensacola area, a glorious black Freedom yacht; her name is *Dessert First*. What a fabulous name for a boat! What a delicious attitude! I can only assume the captain and crew are familiar with the ideals of the LuLu's Lifestyle — carefree fun and celebrating joy.

Wouldn't life be just a little sweeter if we cherished its delights more than we fixated on its trials and tribulations? Having fun is a birthright; it isn't something you have to earn or save up for. In fact it's probably the healthiest thing you can do for yourself. Haven't you ever laughed so hard you couldn't quit? Or run headlong into the surf, screaming with glee? What about trying to tell a great joke and not being able to get through it because you've cracked yourself up? To quote Arthur Bach from the hilarious movie *Arthur*, "Isn't fun the best thing to have?" I would so much rather be an old lady with laugh lines than one with wrinkles from frowning my way through life. Another great quote I love is, "Life is not a journey to the grave with the intention of arriving safely in a pretty and well preserved body, but rather to skid in broadside, martini in one hand, Godiva chocolates in the other, thoroughly used up, totally worn out, and loudly proclaiming 'WooHoo! What a Ride!' "

Good times are had in big and small doses. Yes, shopping in Paris with my daughter Melanie is a treat (big one), but so is spotting a perfect seashell on the sugar-white beach of Gulf Shores...or getting a card in the mail from a friend, just because...or going barefoot in the rain...or that first fizzy sip of Coke®...or finding a dollar in your jeans at the laundry...or licking the frosting off the beaters when you're done icing a cake. Life itself is a treat. Live! Laugh! Love! Enjoy it; eat your dessert first.

This cookie was a favorite at the old LuLu's. We made them the size of saucers, so they were affectionately dubbed "the BIG COOKIE." This is my personal "knock-off" of the famous Neiman Marcus recipe that, as urban legend has it, cost a woman a fortune. Though these cookies are rich as sin, the recipe uses a lot of oatmeal, so I like to consider it a "health food" to make me feel a little better about it.

LuLu's Big Chocolate Chunky Cookie

MAKES 4 DOZEN LARGE COOKIES

2½ cups old-fashioned oatmeal (not quick-cooking oats)

2 cups all-purpose flour

1 teaspoon baking powder

1 teaspoon baking soda

½ teaspoon salt

2 (1.45-ounce) milk chocolate candy bars

1 cup semi-sweet chocolate morsels

1 cup white chocolate morsels

2 sticks unsalted butter, softened

1 cup granulated sugar

1 cup light brown sugar, loosely packed

1 teaspoon pure vanilla extract

2 eggs

1½ cups large pecan pieces

Milk as needed

1. Preheat oven to 375 degrees.
2. Place oatmeal in a food processor and blend to a very fine texture.
3. Combine fine oatmeal, flour, baking powder, baking soda, and salt in a large mixing bowl. Run hands through the dry mixture or stir with a wooden spoon to mix evenly.
4. Chop chocolate bars into ¼-inch chunks and mix with semi-sweet and white chocolate morsels.
5. In a large bowl, beat butter with granulated sugar, brown sugar, and vanilla until light and fluffy and all the sugar has dissolved.
6. Add eggs one at a time, beating well after each addition.
7. Gradually add dry ingredients, about 1 cup at a time, beating thoroughly after each addition.
8. Fold in chocolate pieces and pecans, mixing well. (I actually mix the dough with my hands at this point.) If dough is too thick and hard to handle, add a little milk to make it easier to work with.
9. Roll into 2-inch balls and place, about 2 inches apart, on an ungreased baking sheet.
10. Bake for 9 to 11 minutes; the longer the cookies bake, the crispier they will be. Cool cookies completely before removing from pan.

LuLu Clue: This dough freezes beautifully.

Key Lime Pie with Grand Marnier® Whipped Cream

2 cups finely-crushed graham crackers

1 stick unsalted butter, melted

3 tablespoons sugar

1 teaspoon unflavored gelatin

2 tablespoons cold water

2 egg yolks

½ cup Key lime juice, freshly squeezed if available

1 (14-ounce) can sweetened condensed milk

Grand Marnier® Whipped Cream (recipe on next page)

1 lime, thinly sliced for garnish

1. Preheat oven to 350 degrees.
2. Combine cracker crumbs, melted butter, and sugar in a small mixing bowl.
3. Press evenly into a 9-inch pie pan with hands or the back of a spoon.
4. Bake for 10 minutes or until lightly brown. Set aside to cool.
5. In a small mixing bowl, dissolve gelatin in cold water, stir, and set aside.
6. In a heavy saucepan, combine egg yolks and lime juice and stir over medium-low heat for 10 minutes or until slightly thick and very hot. Be careful not to bring to a full boil.
7. Add softened gelatin to lime juice mixture. Whisk well for 1 minute or until gelatin is dissolved.
8. To quickly cool mixture, place saucepan in a large bowl filled with ice.
9. When completely cool, gradually whisk in condensed milk, stirring until blended well and mixture becomes thick.
10. Spoon into graham cracker crust and spread evenly.
11. Cover filling with plastic wrap and refrigerate.
12. When ready to serve, top pie with fresh Grand Marnier® Whipped Cream and lime slices.

LuLu Clue: This is one of the few recipes for which I would substitute a bottled juice. A good quality Key lime juice is available in most large grocery stores.

CONTINUED

GRAND MARNIER®
WHIPPED CREAM

½ pint heavy cream, well chilled

2 tablespoons sugar

1 tablespoon Grand Marnier®
   liqueur, optional

1. In a stainless steel mixing bowl, combine cream, sugar, and liqueur.

2. Whip with an electric mixer on high until cream holds peaks. Be careful not to over-whip cream or it will separate. Cream is properly whipped when you can drag a finger through it and a trough remains.

LuLu Clue: Chill the stainless steel bowl and beaters before whipping the cream for quicker results.

In the early days of LuLu's, when I was wearing just about every hat an owner can wear, Laureta "Weedy" Daniels helped me stay sane. She had a long history of working in the food and beverage industry in our area. She was retired, but came to "help out" part-time when I needed her. Weedy taught me many things, including how to run a cash register, mother our wayward crew, yank somebody up when necessary, and laugh at the end of another zany night in the surreal subculture of the restaurant business.

Weedy built her dream house in the country where she was surrounded by her husband and children, her beloved beagles, and the apple of her eye, her granddaughter. She was not going to do restaurant work anymore but rather indulge in her passion for gardening. Still, she just couldn't resist when LuLu's was in need of a new dessert. She gave us the recipe for her Margarita Cheesecake, but when the kitchen made it, it just wasn't up to her standards, so she said, "Hell, I'll just do it myself." And that she did for several years. Cheers, Weedy! Thanks for helping me make LuLu's happen.

Weedy's Margarita Cheesecake

MAKES 1 PIE

CRUST
1¼ cups graham cracker crumbs

4 tablespoons unsalted butter, melted

FILLING
24 ounces cream cheese, softened

1¼ cups sour cream

¾ cup plus 2 tablespoons sugar

2½ tablespoons orange liqueur

2½ tablespoons tequila

2½ tablespoons freshly squeezed lime juice

4 eggs

1. Preheat oven to 350 degrees.
2. Spray a 9-inch springform pan with nonstick cooking spray.
3. In a medium mixing bowl, combine graham cracker crumbs and melted butter. Press crumbs evenly into bottom of pan to form a crust. Refrigerate while preparing filling.
4. To make filling, in a large mixing bowl, beat cream cheese until fluffy.
5. Folding in one at a time, add sour cream, sugar, orange liqueur, tequila, lime juice, and eggs.
6. Pour filling into crust.
7. Bake 50 minutes on center rack of oven.
8. Remove from oven and set to the side. Turn off the oven, but keep the door closed so it will remain as hot as possible.

CONTINUED

LuLu Clue: "Springform" and "cheesecake" pans are interchangeable terms for the kind of pan that has a clamp on the side. When clamp is released, the sides of the pan "spring" away from the cake, gently releasing delicate cakes without needing to invert them. There really is no substitute for a springform pan when making a cheesecake.

TOPPING

¾ cup sour cream

1 tablespoon sugar

1 tablespoon lime juice

Thin fresh lime slices and peel for garnish

9. For topping, whisk together sour cream, sugar, and lime juice in a small bowl. Spread topping evenly over cheesecake.
10. Return to the warm oven for 45 minutes to set.
11. Refrigerate cheesecake in pan until well chilled.
12. Run a knife around the edges of pan, release spring clasp, and remove cake.
13. Garnish with thin lime slices and lime peel.

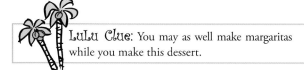

LuLu Clue: You may as well make margaritas while you make this dessert.

LuLu with Weedy's daughter, Shannon Porter

SWEET THINGS

Chocolate Pound Cake with Mocha Glaze

MAKES 1 CAKE

BATTER

½ cup shortening, plus extra to grease pan

3 cups granulated sugar

2 sticks unsalted butter, softened

5 eggs

3 cups all-purpose flour, plus extra to flour pan

½ teaspoon baking powder

½ teaspoon salt

4 heaping teaspoons cocoa powder

1 cup whole milk

1 teaspoon vanilla extract

MOCHA GLAZE

5 tablespoons unsalted butter, softened

1½ cups powdered sugar, sifted

1 tablespoon cocoa powder

1 teaspoon vanilla extract

1-3 tablespoons hot coffee

1. Preheat oven to 325 degrees.
2. Grease and flour a tube or Bundt® cake pan.
3. Beat shortening, sugar, and butter together until light and fluffy.
4. Fold in eggs, one at a time.
5. In a large mixing bowl, combine flour, baking powder, salt, and cocoa powder.
6. Fold dry ingredients, alternately with milk, into creamed mixture until smooth. Stir in vanilla and mix well.
7. Pour batter into prepared cake pan. Bake for 1 hour, 15 minutes or until a toothpick inserted in center comes out clean.
8. Prepare Mocha Glaze while cake is baking. In a mixing bowl, combine butter, powdered sugar, and cocoa powder. Stir in vanilla. Gradually add enough coffee to reach desired consistency.
9. Allow cake to cool for about 30 minutes.
10. Run a sharp knife around the edges of the pan to loosen cake. Invert onto a serving plate.
11. Drizzle glaze over top while cake is still warm.

Homemade Banana Puddin' with Nilla® Wafers

MAKES 6 TO 8 SERVINGS

2½ cups whole milk

¾ cup sugar, divided

4 eggs, separated

½ cup all-purpose flour

¼ teaspoon salt

1½ teaspoons vanilla extract, divided

1 tablespoon butter

1 (12-ounce) box Nabisco Nilla® wafers

4-5 ripe (but still firm) bananas, sliced

½ teaspoon cream of tartar

1. Preheat oven to 350 degrees.
2. In a heavy saucepan, slowly heat milk and ½ cup sugar until sugar dissolves.
3. Using a whisk, gradually add egg yolks, flour, and salt. Reduce heat to low, if necessary, being careful not to scorch the milk or overcook the eggs. If too hot, you might end up with something resembling scrambled eggs rather than a creamy custard.
4. Cook on low, uncovered and stirring constantly for 10 to 15 minutes or until thickened to a custard consistency.
5. Remove from heat. Add vanilla and butter and stir well.
6. Cool for ½ to 1 hour in the refrigerator.
7. In a 2-quart baking dish, arrange a layer of wafers, a layer of banana slices, and one-third of custard. Repeat twice to make 3 layers.
8. Beat egg whites with an electric mixer on high speed until stiff peaks form.
9. Gradually fold in remaining ¼ cup sugar and cream of tartar. Continue beating until stiff.
10. Spoon meringue on top of pudding, spreading evenly to the edge of the pan.
11. To create soft peaks, take the back of a spoon, lightly touch meringue, and gently lift up. Repeat over surface of pudding.
13. Bake for 15 to 20 minutes or until meringue is lightly browned. Remove from oven and serve when cool.

LuLu Clue: I like to serve my 'nana puddin' before refrigerating, when it's still warm and creamy and a visually lovely dish. My family, on the other hand, all agree it's better the next morning (literally for breakfast), chilled in the fridge overnight, when all the flavors have melded and set.

For years, my dear friend Suzanne Cleveland arrived at every pier-party, holiday get-together, or general shin-dig with her trademark lemon squares, usually burned. The children would wait impatiently for her to arrive with a tray of tasty treats, powdered sugar all over their faces and fingers within minutes. This dessert is inspired by her recipe, with a tart little Key lime twist.

Key Lime Squares

MAKES 10 TO 12 SQUARES

CRUST

¼ cup slivered blanched almonds

2 sticks unsalted butter, softened

2 cups all-purpose flour

1 tablespoon powdered sugar

¼ teaspoon almond extract

KEY LIME FILLING

5 eggs

2 cups granulated sugar

Pinch of salt

¾ cup Key lime juice

½ teaspoon orange zest

¼ cup powdered sugar
   for topping

1. Preheat oven to 350 degrees.
2. Using a mini-food-processor, chop almonds into a fine meal.
3. In a large mixing bowl or food processor, combine almonds, butter, flour, powdered sugar, and almond extract. Blend into a thick pastry and pat into the bottom of a well-greased 8x12-inch baking dish.
4. Bake crust for 15 minutes. Remove from oven and reduce oven temperature to 325 degrees.
5. To prepare filling, beat eggs. Add granulated sugar, salt, lime juice, and orange zest. Mix thoroughly.
6. Pour filling over partially baked crust and return to the oven.
7. Bake 20 to 30 minutes or until filling is set.
8. Remove from oven and cool.
9. Sift powdered sugar over top and cut into squares.

LuLu Clue: As in the Key Lime Pie, I might substitute a bottled juice. A good quality Key lime juice is available in most large grocery stores.

195

In 1852, Sam German developed a sweet baking bar for Baker's Chocolate Co. In 1957, a Dallas newspaper ran the first published recipe for a "German's" chocolate cake, submitted by a Texas homemaker. The Baker's Company quickly began printing the recipe on the back of the box. To this day, I've seen many versions of this recipe but basically they're the same since there was really no improving on this classic.

The person who made it famous in our household and at the old LuLu's was our parents' dear friend and, later in life, caretaker, Elease Molony. She was a consummate "country" cook, a hilarious character, an exquisite baker and a beautiful woman. She used to make German chocolate cakes for the old LuLu's that were so popular that we had a customer who would actually drive from Birmingham for the weekend to buy an entire cake.

We like to think that Elease and her husband, Dan, are sipping a few cold ones with Peets and J.D. on the stern of a celestial sailing vessel at eternal sunset just as they used to do together in Key West.

German Chocolate Cake with Coconut-Pecan Frosting

MAKES 1 CAKE

BATTER

2 cups all-purpose flour

1 teaspoon baking soda

¼ teaspoon salt

½ cup water

1 (4-ounce) package German's® Sweet Chocolate, chopped

2 sticks unsalted butter, softened

2 cups sugar

4 eggs, separated

1 teaspoon vanilla

1 cup buttermilk

1. Preheat oven to 350 degrees.
2. Grease and line three 9-inch round cake pans with waxed paper.
3. Mix flour, baking soda, and salt in a bowl. Set aside.
4. Heat water and chocolate in a small heavy saucepan over low heat, stirring constantly until chocolate is completely melted. Remove from heat and cool completely.
5. In a large mixing bowl, beat butter and sugar until light and fluffy.
6. Fold in egg yolks one at a time, beating well between additions.
7. Add melted chocolate and vanilla.
8. Alternately fold dry ingredients and buttermilk into creamed mixture until smooth.
9. In another bowl, beat egg whites with an electric mixer on high until stiff peaks form. Gently fold into batter.
10. Pour batter evenly into prepared pans.
11. Bake for 30 minutes or until cake springs back when lightly touched in the center.
12. Remove from oven and cool on racks.

CONTINUED

COCONUT-PECAN FROSTING

1 (12-ounce) can evaporated milk

1½ cups sugar

1½ sticks butter

4 egg yolks, lightly beaten

1 teaspoon vanilla

1 (7-ounce) package sweetened coconut flakes

1½ cups chopped pecans

13. While cake cools, prepare frosting. In a large saucepan, heat milk, sugar, butter, egg yolks, and vanilla over medium heat for 12 minutes or until thickened. Remove from heat, stir in coconut and pecans. Continue stirring until cool and frosting is of spreading consistency.

14. To remove cooled cake from pans, run a knife around edge of each pan. Invert one layer onto a serving plate. Remove waxed paper and spread frosting over top. Invert second layer on top of first cake, frost top and repeat with remaining layer.

General Manager Johnny Fisher

  SWEET THINGS

Josie's Red Velvet Cake with Cream Cheese Frosting

MAKES 1 CAKE

BATTER

1½ cups sugar

2 sticks butter, softened

2 eggs

2 ounces red food coloring

2¼ cups sifted cake flour, plus a small amount to flour pans

2 tablespoons cocoa powder

1 teaspoon salt

1 teaspoon baking soda

1 cup buttermilk

1 teaspoon white vinegar

1 teaspoon vanilla

CREAM CHEESE FROSTING

1 stick butter, softened

8 ounces cream cheese, softened

1 teaspoon vanilla

1 pound powdered sugar

1 tablespoon milk

1 cup chopped pecans

1. Preheat oven to 350 degrees.
2. Beat sugar and butter together until light and fluffy.
3. Fold in eggs one at a time, beating for 1 minute after each addition.
4. Carefully fold in food coloring. (I do mean carefully...otherwise your kitchen will look like a crime scene!)
5. In a mixing bowl, combine flour, cocoa powder, salt, and baking soda.
6. In a separate bowl, combine buttermilk, vinegar, and vanilla.
7. Alternate folding dry ingredients and buttermilk mixture into creamed mixture. Beat on medium speed until well mixed.
8. Pour batter into two 9-inch greased and floured cake pans.
9. Bake for 35 to 40 minutes or until a toothpick inserted in the center comes out clean.
10. While cake is baking, prepare frosting. In a mixing bowl, combine butter and cream cheese. Add vanilla and powdered sugar. Beat until creamy. Add milk and stir in pecans.
11. Allow cake to cool completely. Run a sharp knife around the edges of each pan to loosen. Invert one cake onto a serving plate.
12. Spread frosting over top of first cake.
13. Invert second cake on top of first. Frost entire cake.

Red Velvet Girlfriend

Jo Ann Glasscock might be the most loyal human being on the planet. Once she names you "friend," woe be unto the fool who tries to cross or hurt you! She is the epitome of the Southern idiom "steel magnolia," for beyond her iron will and proven mettle, she is simply the gentlest soul you'd care to meet. A child of the smelt and ore of Birmingham, Jo Ann created a career in the gritty man's world of coal and established herself as a presence not to be trifled with. Swimming with the sharks of that industry finally convinced Jo Ann to relax somewhere with less dangerous fins. And, lo, we were blessed to have her become part of the fabric of L.A.

She defines Lucy as a "true friend"...a term Lucy reciprocates. Jo Ann can be counted on for a laugh, can be counted on for a shoulder, can be counted on to tell the truth when the gumbo's not up to par, can be counted on to join the fray at a moment's notice...can be counted on. She is that rare creature that we seek to find in life — a constant, unconditionally loving friend.

Lucy's daughter Mara brokered the deal, introducing them in the neo-natal days of LuLu's. Jo Ann was curious about the raves she'd heard about this incredible gumbo and beat a path to Lucy's "high-class dive." The gumbo was as good as advertised, but Mara insisted that Jo Ann mustn't leave without meeting her mom. Suffice to say that the meeting that day of two iron-jawed angels sealed the deal. Jo Ann officially "had Lucy's back." It is a marvelous thing when you ask, "What's your favorite thing about LuLu's?" to have Jo Ann respond, "That it makes my friend so happy." Though Jo Ann sometimes misses the camaraderie of the small family of regulars that peopled the original LuLu's, she dismisses that loss as part of the grander scheme of life...there is no constant but change. Ah, but that can't be right...there's always Jo Ann.

Jo Ann is a salve, a cool drink on a hot day, a dolce. Indulge in her delicious Red Velvet Cake and taste in it the everlasting texture of friendship.

~Diva

LITTLE CHICKENS' TASTY POT PIE

CHICKEN AND YUM DUMPLINGS

WEE BURGERS

CHUNKY CHEESY PASTA SALAD

TOAD-N-A-HOLE EGGS

GO FISHIN' YELLOW GRITS

SUNDAY MORNING DRIVE-THROUGHS

CINNAMON SUGAR TOAST

FRESH BLACKBERRY COBBLER

SUMMER STRAWBERRY THUMBPRINT COOKIES

FOUNTAINS FOR YOUTH

LuLu's has grown-up to become a fully evolved family-friendly restaurant. I had intended to have a dive bar, serve some cheeseburgers, and chill out with the flip-flop-wearing "River Rats." Well, we do serve cheeseburgers and everybody wears flip-flops, but the "dive bar" part of the equation got lost along the way. Clearly parents want a place to go where their children can play while they can enjoy a little downtime. Evidently a sandy beach is a premier babysitter. Throw some white sand down where children can play in clear view of the parents' tables and everyone's happy; happy customers come back for more. I learned this lesson quickly at the old LuLu's and welcomed the sand-mountain climbing children with open arms. Now the beach is massive, and my imaginative staff has developed plenty of great activities and events to provide children with fun, playtime opportunities. Be sure to check out the adorable "Fountain of/for Youth," constructed of brightly painted galvanized pails!

It might be the best service LuLu's can provide: giving parents a chance to enjoy one another's company without having to worry whether their youngsters are having a good time. This way, everyone gets to have a good time. And if everyone's laughing and smiling, I'm happy.

I know how difficult it can be to balance parenting and playing. Rearing my daughters, Mara and Melanie, has been my most important, most challenging job. They were creative and intelligent children who have grown into lovely, independent young women. We had some very interesting times as they grew up...um, that's an understatement. I just hope they wait until I shuffle off this mortal coil before they publish their tell-all memoirs! We had a lot of fun together, and they had a lot of fun spending time at their grandparents' (my parents') home on Mobile Bay, "Homeport." I like to think they inherited a healthy sense of living life to its fullest. They learned to cook at my knee, so I asked them to comment on some childhood favorite recipes to include in this book. I'm proud that they rose to the challenge, citing some funny memories and recalling some easy-but-yummy dishes. My hope is that some of the many parents who enjoy LuLu's will enjoy time cooking together with their children as much I did with mine.

One cold rainy Saturday,

Mom was in the mood for some family fun. Always up for a challenge in the kitchen, she orchestrated a contest. She had a friend over, and the two of them were to make homemade chicken pot pies. Mara and I were the judges. After all, what little kid doesn't love chicken pot pie?

Mom whipped up this artisan pot pie, seasoning the chicken and pulling it in shreds. Her filling was a delicate broth of chicken stock and herbes de Provence. She used a variety of colorful Baldwin county produce and the whole pot was lightly sweetened with fresh-picked Silver Queen corn kernels. The flaky phyllo crust was the "icing on the cake."

Her friend did not lose sight of the judges and whipped up a thick filling of cream and butter, big chunks of boiled chicken, frozen peas, and lots of salt and pepper. She threw it all into a frozen pie crust.

Okay, so maybe little kids shouldn't be the judges in such important culinary competitions. Mom was always a winner in our hearts.

~Mel

Little Chickens' Tasty Pot Pie

MAKES 4 SERVINGS

1 small potato

1 small sweet potato

3 tablespoons unsalted butter

3 tablespoons all-purpose flour

2 cups chicken broth

2 cups cubed cooked chicken, white or dark meat

1½ cups frozen mixed vegetables (peas, carrots, green beans, corn, etc.)

1 teaspoon salt

1½ cups Bisquick® baking mix

¾ cup milk

1 egg

1. Preheat oven to 400 degrees.
2. Peel and dice both potatoes. Cook in boiling water until just barely tender. Drain and set aside.
3. Melt butter in a large saucepan.
4. Add flour and cook over medium heat for about 5 minutes.
5. Add chicken broth and heat until mixture just begins to boil.
6. Reduce heat. Add chicken, potatoes, mixed vegetables, and salt. Cook until heated through.
7. Pour into a greased 2-quart casserole dish.
8. Combine Bisquick®, milk, and egg and mix well; pour over chicken mixture.
9. Bake for 30 minutes or until golden brown.

This is one of the easiest and most delicious recipes in the world! It has only five elements: chicken, salt, pepper, Bisquick®, and milk. But it just might be the most blissful, divine, and uncomplicated combination of those ingredients ever conjured this side of heaven. It has very powerful healing properties, too. A bowl of chicken n' dumplings is the ultimate feel-good food. It can cure everything from a bad head cold to a sad heartbreak, guaranteed — take it from one who knows. I was taught to make this dish in my grandmother's kitchen when I was a little girl. It's a very kid-friendly dish to make. It's fun to roll out the dough, even though it is just a little messy. You can show your child how to cut the dumplings using a blunt butter knife. Always make sure the chicken is thoroughly cooled before pulling the meat from the bones to avoid burning little fingers. My favorite childhood memories will forever include delightful visions of standing on a stool at the counter, rolling pin in hand, covered from head-to-toe in flour, giggling, singing, and dancing while we cooked. I still make a big pot of this every year as soon as the very first hint of Fall chills the air or anytime a loved-one is under the weather, feeling gloomy, over-the-moon, or just plain hungry. It's a consistently amazing dish.

~Mara

Chicken and Yum Dumplings

MAKES 6 TO 8 SERVINGS

1 (3-pound) chicken

8 cups water, or enough to cover chicken

Salt and pepper to taste

2 tablespoons unsalted butter

6 cups Bisquick® baking mix, plus extra for sprinkling, divided

2 cups cold milk, divided

Rolling pin (a clean, empty wine bottle works great!)

1. Remove neck and gizzards from inside chicken cavity and discard. Rinse the chicken thoroughly under cold water and pat dry.
2. Place chicken on a plate and sprinkle with salt and pepper. Rub seasonings into the skin. This should be all the seasoning this dish requires. Be careful not to over-season the chicken. More salt can be added later.
3. Place chicken in a large pot and add enough water to cover the entire chicken by at least 3 to 4 inches.
4. Bring to a boil. Cover, reduce heat, and simmer for 1½ hours or until tender.
5. When the chicken is done and the meat almost falls from the bone, use durable tongs to remove the chicken from the broth. Set aside to cool.
6. Skim any bits of fat and foam from the broth that may have accumulated during cooking. Continue to simmer broth.

CONTINUED

7. To make the dumplings, in a mixing bowl combine 2 cups Bisquick® with ⅔ cup cold milk and mix well. Repeat 2 times until you have 3 large, round balls of dough. Set aside for 5 to 10 minutes to let the dough expand and rise a bit. This makes for fluffier dumplings.

8. On a large, flat surface, sprinkle a little Bisquick® flour and spread with hands to cover surface evenly. Place round ball of dough on surface and roll flat to about ¼-inch thick, with a rolling pin. Dumplings should not be too thick or they will not cook well in the broth and will stay somewhat doughy. Likewise, rolling them too thin will result in stringy dumplings that will not hold their shape.

9. Run a knife as many times as necessary the length of the rolled dough to form long strips. Then run the knife horizontally across the strips creating little squares.

10. Bring broth back to a boil. Drop dough squares/dumplings, a few pieces at a time, into boiling broth, carefully stirring after each addition to separate dumplings. They will immediately blow up and bubble on the top; as they cook they will drop to the bottom of the soup. Keep stirring as you drop new dumplings into the broth to keep the bottom dumplings from sticking together.

11. Reduce heat to medium-low, stirring frequently.

12. Meanwhile, remove skin from cooled chicken and pull meat from the bone. Cut the chicken into bite-sized pieces. Return meat to broth.

13. Cook 8 to 10 minutes or until chicken is reheated and broth has reached desired thickness.

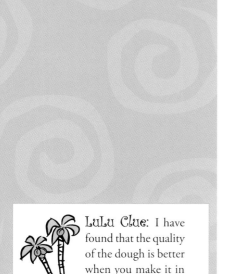

LuLu Clue: I have found that the quality of the dough is better when you make it in three separate batches instead of dividing one batch of dough in thirds.

CHILD'S PLAY

Wee Burgers

BURGERS

1 pound ground beef sirloin

¼ teaspoon salt

¼ teaspoon freshly ground black pepper

1 egg yolk, lightly beaten

2 tablespoons steak sauce or Worcestershire sauce

2-3 tablespoons olive oil

12 mini burger buns or standard dinner rolls

1. In a medium mixing bowl, break up ground beef by hand and season with salt and pepper.

2. Whisk together egg yolk and steak sauce and add to ground beef. Continue mixing everything by hand.

3. Using about 2 tablespoons of ground beef for each, roll beef gently into 12 equal balls and gently press down to make ½-inch-thick patties. Make a thumb-indentation in the middle of each patty.

4. Place all toppings on a serving platter and refrigerate until burgers are cooked.

5. Heat olive oil in a heavy skillet over medium-hot heat. Cook burgers about 3 minutes on each side. Add cheese squares once done. Melt cheese a little and remove from heat to stand for a few minutes.

LuLu Clue: For homemade baby-buns, use Pillsbury® refrigerated French bread dough. Cut into equal parts, roll into balls, dip into sesame seeds and bake according to package directions. One package will make 12 buns.

CONTINUED

CHILD'S PLAY

TOPPINGS, OPTIONAL

Cherry tomatoes, cut in small rounds

Green leaf lettuce, torn in tiny pieces

3 slices cheese, each cut into 4 equal squares

Small pickle slices

Ketchup, mustard, or mayonnaise

6. For crispy, warm buns, place cut-side down on the skillet to lightly brown.

7. Build your mini burgers, adding a dollop of ketchup, mustard, or mayonnaise on bottom half of bun. Layer mini patty, tomato, lettuce, pickle and the top half of bun. You might want to use a decorative toothpick through each mini burger to help hold them together until you serve.

Chunky Cheesy Pasta Salad

MAKES 12 CUPS

1 pound wagon wheel pasta

2 tablespoons salt

1 cup broccoli florets, cut into bite-sized pieces

1 cup asparagus, trimmed and cut into bite-sized lengths

1 cup frozen green peas, thawed

1 carrot, cut into ¼-inch coins

1 cup cherry tomatoes, quartered and lightly salted

1 cup finely chopped green or purple onion, optional

½ cup each red, orange, and yellow bell peppers, cut into bite-sized chunks

2 cups mixed mild cheeses, such as mozzarella, Cheddar, Swiss, or Monterey Jack, cut into ½-inch cubes

8 ounces bacon, fried, crumbled, and cooled

1-2 cups zesty Italian dressing

½ cup finely chopped fresh parsley

Salt and pepper to taste

1. Cook pasta in a gallon of boiling water seasoned with 2 tablespoons salt (that's right, 2 tablespoons!) until just tender. Drain, but do not rinse the pasta. Cool to room temperature, then chill in the refrigerator while preparing remaining ingredients.

2. Steam or boil broccoli, asparagus, and green peas until just barely cooked, but still crisp and very green. Set aside and let cool.

3. In a large mixing bowl mix chilled pasta, broccoli, asparagus, green peas, carrots, tomatoes, onions, all bell peppers, cheese, and meat. Stir until all ingredients are well mixed.

4. Add Italian dressing.

5. Add parsley; season with salt and pepper to taste and mix well.

6. Serve chilled.

CHILD'S PLAY

Much to my partying

parents' dismay, I did not like Saturday morning cartoons, and I always woke up hungry (still do). So on Saturday mornings, Mom had to rely on breakfast to keep me entertained, and making a Toad-n-a-Hole was fun.

I loved pressing the hole out of the soft white bread. Finding appropriate glassware was part of the adventure. It had to be thin to cut the bread and a good circumference to fit an egg just right. The little left-over medallions of bread made dreamy miniature peanut butter and jelly sandwiches for dessert. How the egg fit just perfectly in the hole seemed scientific and amazing, and I had to try hard not to think about frogs while eating my Toad-n-a-Hole!

Remember the rule, "Don't play with your food"? Crumbling crispy bacon into my grits and then fishing out all those little pieces felt rebellious and exciting. Who needed superheroes when there was so much action to be had in the kitchen?

~Mel

Toad-n-a-Hole Eggs

MAKES 4 SERVINGS

2 tablespoons butter, softened

4 slices bread of choice

4 eggs

1. Lightly butter both sides of bread slices.
2. With a cookie cutter or upside down small glass, cut a circular hole in the center of each bread slice.
3. Heat a non-stick skillet over medium heat. Place bread in skillet and crack the egg gently into the center hole. When bread is lightly browned, flip and cook to desired doneness.

LuLu Clue: I like to fry the cut-out circle of bread along with the rest to dip in a slightly runny center or spread with jam or preserves.

Go Fishin' Yellow Grits

MAKES 4 SERVINGS

8 slices bacon

2 cups water

1 cup whole milk

1 cup stone-ground yellow grits
(I use Bob's Red Mill® organic
yellow corn grits, found in
health food stores and some
supermarkets)

1 teaspoon salt or more to taste

Black pepper to taste

4 tablespoons butter, divided

1. Cook bacon in a large, heavy skillet over medium-low heat, turning with a fork to keep bacon from curling up. (The secret to good, crispy bacon is cooking it slowly over a medium-low heat for 2-3 minutes on each side.) When bacon is crispy, transfer to a plate lined with paper towels to drain.

2. In medium saucepan, bring water to a boil. Add milk and allow to warm up a bit.

3. Stir in grits, salt, and pepper. Stir well, cover tightly, and cook over low heat for 4 to 5 minutes or until grits are creamy.

4. Stir in 2 tablespoons butter until melted. (Reserve remaining butter for garnish, if your taste buds need it.)

5. Spoon grits into individual serving bowls. Add butter, salt, and pepper as desired.

6. Crumble 2 slices of bacon on the top of each bowl of grits.

7. The grits are the pond and the bacon bits are the little fishies... each time you dip your spoon in the pond, you're "goin' fishin'."

 LuLu Clue: Grits are not always easy to find in the supermarket unless you live in the South. Sometimes all you may find are the quick-cooking or instant-style grits. These are OK to use in this recipe, plus they make the cooking time almost nil, which is helpful if you're feeling extra lazy or stressed for time.

These little breakfast sandwiches are called "Sunday Morning Drive-Throughs" because every weekend I would ask my mom if we could go to one of my favorite fast food places for breakfast. Her typical response was usually a coy, "Well...maybe." Then she would whip up these perfect imitations of what I was craving. For anyone familiar with the hilarious Eddie Murphy skit about the kid who always wants to eat what the famous clown serves, we all know that for kids the cheeseburger CANNOT be replicated...but those tasty breakfast sandwiches CAN be with this recipe.

~Mara

Sunday Morning Drive-Throughs

MAKES 1 EGG SANDWICH

1 egg, beaten
1 teaspoon water
1 teaspoon milk
Pinch of salt and pepper
½ tablespoon butter
1 English muffin
1-2 slices precooked Canadian bacon or sausage patty
1 slice American or Cheddar cheese

1. In a small bowl, beat egg with water, milk, and salt and pepper. Set aside.
2. Spray the inside of an empty, well-cleaned tuna tin with nonstick cooking spray.
3. Heat tuna tin in the center of a small skillet with a lid (it is very important it has a lid) over medium-high heat. Melt butter in tin.
4. Pour egg into tuna tin.
5. Immediately pour an inch of water into the bottom of the hot skillet. The water will bubble and steam. Quickly cover skillet and let the heat and steam cook egg for 3 to 4 minutes. Remove tin from skillet with tongs.
6. Warm precooked Canadian bacon or sausage patty in hot skillet or microwave.
7. Cut an English muffin in half and toast in toaster.
8. Invert tuna tin over a plate to remove egg; the egg comes out looking just like the "real thing."
9. Assemble the cheese, egg, and meat on toasted English muffin.
10. For fun, wrap the sandwich in a piece of waxed paper and microwave for 10 seconds... it's warm and steamy, and it tastes exactly like what the clown serves at the drive-through window!

Cinnamon Sugar Toast

MAKES 4 SERVINGS

¼ cup sugar

1-2 tablespoons cinnamon

4 slices bread, white is the classic, but I love wheat and even raisin bread

1 tablespoon butter, softened

1. Preheat broiler.
2. In a small bowl, mix sugar and cinnamon together.
3. Arrange bread on a baking sheet and spread butter on one side of each slice.
4. Sprinkle generously with cinnamon sugar...the more the better.
5. Broil for about 1 minute, watching carefully to prevent browning.

GUMBO PREP 101: KITCHEN KIDS

Our mom was constantly in the kitchen, so naturally that's where Mara and I always wanted to be — holding on to her apron strings. (I think she's still trying to cut those things!) "Half the job of cooking is cleaning up," she would say. One of my earliest memories was begging her to let me do the dishes. It seemed like such a fun, sudsy activity. Always encouraging fun, she pulled a chair up to the sink and let me make more of a mess of the dishes than there was to clean up. Maybe it was belting out "Chucky's in Love" while doing menial tasks that made it seem so wonderful. (Perhaps I should try that tonight.)

Gumbo preparation is my first memory of actually helping to make a dish. Unlike most kids who started out reading Dr. Seuss and Babar, we cut our teeth reading jars of herbs and spices. Mom would "hole-up" in the kitchen for hours on end and so would we, just to be near her. Being 5 and 6 meant we were able-bodied and could be put to work.

Sometimes "playing hospital" meant Mom nursing a hangover. Other times it was Mom playing "Kitchen Doctor." Mara and I were tiny little attending nurses during a life-saving operation; the bubbling pot on the stove was our critical care patient. She would call out for her surgical instruments: "Slotted-Spoon!" "Coriander!" "Salt!" When the roux burned, it always felt like we had "a man down." This rarely happened, but when it did, we swung into full life-saving mode. A new roux was made, and the Gumbo was saved! It was that intense. Her success rate is still 100%.

~Mel

Our childhood home

was appropriately named "Homeport" by our grandfather, J.D. Buffett. It was meant to be a special place where a family scattered from Key West to Montana could always find each other and, when needed, a refuge to find ourselves.

Nestled on a tiny bluff at the northeast corner of Mobile Bay, the beach at Homeport was a natural kids' paradise. The creeks were full of schooling minnows. The air was thick with the fragrance of honeysuckle. Vines of it hung from every tree on the beach. Also growing wild were thickets of blackberries. Our grandmother, Peetsy, often sent us down with a pail to collect berries for a summer cobbler, and J.D. carefully showed us how to pick them without getting caught in the stickers.

With fingers, faces, and clothes stained indigo, we would scramble back up the bluff and deliver our buckets full of blackberries to Peetsy. These were our first lessons in "fruits of thy labor" — work hard, earn fresh-baked cobbler.

~Mel & Mara

Fresh Blackberry Cobbler

MAKES 8 TO 10 SERVINGS

1 stick unsalted butter

2 tablespoons cornstarch

¼ cup cold water

3½ cups blackberries, picked through, rinsed, and drained

3 cups sugar, divided

2 cups self-rising flour

½ teaspoon salt

2 teaspoons baking powder

2 cups whole milk

1. Preheat oven to 350 degrees.
2. Cut butter into several thick chunks and place in a 9x13-inch baking dish. Place baking dish in preheated oven to melt butter.
3. In a large bowl, combine cornstarch and cold water. Add blackberries and 1 cup sugar. Let stand about 20 minutes or until a natural syrup forms.
4. In a separate bowl, mix together remaining 2 cups sugar, flour, salt, baking powder, and milk; the batter will be slightly lumpy.
5. Pour batter on top of melted butter in baking pan. Do not mix butter and batter together.
6. Spoon blackberries and syrup into batter. If more crust is desired, use fewer blackberries.
7. Bake 45 to 50 minutes or until dough rises and is golden. Serve warm with vanilla ice cream.

Summer Strawberry Thumbprint Cookies

MAKES 2 DOZEN COOKIES

1 stick unsalted butter, softened

½ cup shortening

½ cup light brown sugar

2 eggs, separated

1 teaspoon vanilla

2 cups all-purpose flour

¼ teaspoon baking soda

½ teaspoon salt

1 cup pecans, finely chopped

½ cup strawberry jam

1 cup fresh strawberries, halved or quartered, depending on size of berries

1. Preheat oven to 350 degrees.
2. In a mixing bowl, cream together butter, shortening, and brown sugar until light and fluffy.
3. Beat in egg yolks and vanilla.
4. Stir in flour, baking soda, and salt.
5. Shape the dough into 1-inch balls.
6. Lightly beat egg whites.
7. Dip balls into egg whites and roll in pecans. Place balls about 1-inch apart on a nonstick baking sheet.
8. Press thumb deeply into center of each ball.
9. Place a small dollop of strawberry jam into each thumbprint.
10. Press one strawberry piece gently into each.
11. Bake 10 minutes or until light brown.
12. Immediately remove from baking sheet and cool thoroughly.

LuLu Clue: Sometimes I like to use chocolate kisses instead of the fresh strawberries. If I do, I add jam in the thumbprint *before* baking and the kisses *after* baking.

CHILD'S PLAY

ROSEMARY ANDOUILLE BAKED GRITS

GRITS AND GRILLADES

LUMP CRAB À LA LULU OVER GARLIC CHEESE GRITS

HOT DAMN GOUDA GRITS CAKES

SUNDAY BRUNCH CRABMEAT OMELET
WITH PEPPER JACK GRITS

THE ULTIMATE SOUTHERN COMFORT FOOD

We served breakfast at LuLu's for a blink of time; actually, we served it out of the adjoining bait shop. That's right, live (and recently deceased) shrimp, crickets, fishing tackle, and bologna omelets! It was a short menu, but of course it included grits. You won't find too many breakfast joints south of the Mason-Dixon line that don't serve grits. It is essential that they're served piping hot; cold grits are simply inedible.

Grits are easy to make and easy to screw up, especially if you're unfamiliar with them. You want a creamy dish, not spackling compound. The trick is to keep the proportion of water to grits just right and keep on stirring!

I enjoy grits simply prepared with salt and butter, but also as the basis for any number of other toppings and mix-ins. Serve gumbo over grits instead of rice or slather some Sloppy Shrimp (see recipe page 108) over a bowl of grits. I love mixing Crazy Cheesy Queso Dip (see recipe page 112) into my grits.

In the Creole South, certainly in the booted heel of Louisiana, count yourself lucky to be treated to the sumptuous delight that is grits and grillades. It's even fun to say it. "Gree-ahds." From the hard-times of the backwater swamps to the elegant courtyards of the New Orleans Garden District, Creoles and Cajuns have been making delicious food out of available resources for ages. So I suggest you don't waste any time worrying about whether the grillades are Angus beef, wild rabbit, milk-fed veal, or freshly-skinned squirrel; just have faith, and you'll never have a bad meal in the bayou. This delicious dish is standard fare for brunch in New Orleans, but I'll serve it as a special treat for any meal.

In the debutante coastal South, prized local blue crabmeat is a delicious variation. I feel like my very own blood turns blue when I indulge in succulent sautéed lump crabmeat with my grits, especially if I've been able to catch the bright blue lovelies off the end of a pier. Just for those who might not know, a blue crab's shell is a beautiful blue in the water but turns bright orange in the boiling pot; the juicy meat is no particular color whatsoever really, ranging from pale-grey to pinkish-white. The best, jumbo lump, is practically a pearl white.

Grits are comfort food. They are the front porch swing and gentlemen carrying handkerchiefs. They are nostalgia and home. I love them best with garlic and Cheddar cheese. But sometimes I like to stir up a memory and serve grits alongside a favorite handed-down recipe for a meal of comfort. It's hard to be in a bad mood with a belly full of warm grits.

LuLu's stint as a breakfast place was fairly short-lived; you'd think that the aroma of live bait would keep customers away, but it was well received by the local fishermen and early-birds who enjoyed visiting over a cup of coffee, stretching "morning" as far as it could go. I think the demise of the bait-shop-breakfast had more to do with rounding up enough employees to stumble, zombie-like, into work that early in the morning!

The Original "River Rats" Bait Shop Breakfast

I accidentally-on-purpose made this for breakfast one morning for my husband, using my trusty method of tossing together whatever I had in the fridge. It was a hit, and we had a new recipe for the book!

Rosemary Andouille Baked Grits

MAKES 8 TO 10 SERVINGS

2 tablespoons unsalted butter

4 cloves garlic, finely chopped

½ cup finely chopped yellow onions

¾ cup thinly sliced mushrooms

1 jalapeño pepper, seeded and finely chopped

1 pound andouille sausage, chopped into quarter-sized rounds (about 1½ cups)

½ cup hot coffee

3 tomatoes, peeled and coarsely chopped

2 teaspoons salt, divided

1 teaspoon white pepper

½ teaspoon sugar

1 teaspoon LuLu's Crazy Creola Seasoning™ (page 50)

2 tablespoons finely chopped fresh rosemary, plus a sprinkle for garnish

6 cups water

2 cups heavy cream

2 cups grits

1-2 cups shredded Gruyère cheese

1. Preheat oven to 350 degrees.
2. In a heavy skillet, melt butter over medium heat. Add garlic and cook 1 minute.
3. Add onions and cook for 2 minutes.
4. Add mushrooms and jalapeños. Cover, reduce heat to medium-low, and cook for 2 to 3 minutes. Remove from heat.
5. Lightly spray cooking oil in a cast iron skillet. Sauté sausage over medium-high heat until very browned and pieces of sausage are sticking to the pan. Remove sausage from pan and drain on paper towels.
6. Add coffee to deglaze skillet and continue cooking to reduce liquid by about half.
7. Add tomatoes, sautéed vegetables, and sausage and continue cooking, covered, for 1 to 2 minutes. Uncover and simmer for a few more minutes until almost no liquid remains.
8. Add 1½ teaspoons salt, white pepper, sugar, Creole seasoning, and rosemary. Cook for 1 to 2 minutes longer. Remove from heat.
9. In a large saucepan, combine water, cream, and remaining ½ teaspoon salt and bring to a boil over medium-high heat.

LuLu Clue: To ease the peeling process, drop tomatoes in boiling water for 1 minute. Cool for a minute and the skins will peel right off.

10. Whisk grits into boiling liquid. Reduce heat to low, whisking often. Cook until grits thicken.
11. Add sausage mixture and mix well.
12. Grease a 2-quart baking dish with cooking oil. Pour grits mixture into dish.
13. Top with cheese and garnish with a sprinkle of rosemary.
14. Bake for 30 minutes.
15. Broil for 3 minutes or until top is browned.
16. Allow to cool for at least 15 minutes before serving. When you first remove dish from the oven, it'll be as hot as a heat tile on the space shuttle, and unless you really want to injure your guests, it's best to wait a few minutes before serving.

LuLu Clue: I use hot coffee, because it's usually breakfast time when I'm making grits, but it doesn't matter whether it's hot or not.

LuLu's Rosemary Andouille Baked Grits

At our test kitchen

brunch, this dish was clearly the favorite, even for our rogue Yankee friend who slipped in attesting to "hating" grits. We quickly forgave his breach when he reached for a second... then a third helping. This rich, sumptuous dish is best when allowed to cook down and really tenderize the meat. You can use veal, as some recipes call for, but I used tenderloin of beef and was very pleased with the results.

Grits and Grillades

MAKES 10 TO 12 SERVINGS

GRILLADES

4 pounds beef tenderloin

1 tablespoon salt

½ teaspoon black pepper

1 teaspoon cayenne pepper

1 teaspoon garlic powder

½ cup all-purpose flour

4 tablespoons extra virgin olive oil

2 cups chopped onions

1 cup chopped celery

1 cup chopped green bell peppers

3 cups whole canned tomatoes, crushed with juice

2 cups beef broth

2 bay leaves

1 tablespoon oregano

1 tablespoon basil

LuLu's Perfect Pepper Hot Sauce™ to taste

2 tablespoons minced fresh garlic

1 cup thinly sliced green onions

½ cup freshly chopped parsley, plus extra for garnish

Baked Cheese Grits (next page)

1. Remove and discard any fat from tenderloin. Pound meat between waxed paper or plastic wrap until slightly flattened to about ½-inch thick. Cut into 2-inch squares.
2. In a small bowl, combine salt, black pepper, cayenne pepper, and garlic powder.
3. Sprinkle beef with seasoning mixture and toss to coat evenly.
4. Once meat is thoroughly seasoned, sprinkle with flour and toss to coat evenly.
5. In a heavy stockpot or Dutch oven, heat olive oil over medium heat. Add sirloin and brown on all sides. Do this in batches, if needed, being careful not to overcrowd the pieces. Remove seared meat to a platter.
6. In the same pan, add chopped onions and cook for 2 minutes.
7. Add celery and bell peppers and cook for another 5 minutes.
8. Add tomatoes, beef broth, bay leaves, oregano, and basil. Bring to a boil.
9. Add seared meat and cook, uncovered, on low heat for 1½ hours or until meat is fork tender. If gravy becomes too thick while cooking, add a little more water or beef broth.
10. Five minutes before serving, add minced garlic, green onions, parsley, and hot sauce to taste.
11. Serve over Baked Cheese Grits and garnish with extra parsley.

CONTINUED

BAKED CHEESE GRITS

6 cups hot cooked grits (prepared according to package directions)

3 cups shredded cheese, divided, such as sharp Cheddar, Gruyère, or smoked Gouda

4 tablespoons unsalted butter

½ cup whole milk

3 eggs, beaten

½ teaspoon salt

¼ teaspoon black pepper

1-2 dashes LuLu's Perfect Pepper Hot Sauce™

1. Preheat oven to 350 degrees.
2. Add 2 cups cheese and butter to hot grits and stir well until cheese melts.
3. Beat together milk and eggs.
4. Whisk a small portion of hot grits into milk mixture. Return to pot of grits and stir well.
5. Season with salt, pepper, and hot sauce.
6. Pour grits into a 2-quart greased baking dish.
7. Bake for 30 minutes, top with remaining cheese, and bake for another 15 minutes or until grits are golden brown.
8. Remove from oven and cool for at least 15 minutes before serving.

Lump Crab à la LuLu over Garlic Cheese Grits

MAKES 4 SERVINGS

1 stick unsalted butter

1 large leek, including green part, cut in ¼-inch slices

½ cup coarsely chopped green bell peppers

½ cup coarsely chopped yellow bell peppers

½ cup sliced mushrooms

1 large tomato, peeled and chopped

¾ cup good white wine

1½ teaspoons kosher salt

1 teaspoon black pepper

1 pound jumbo lump crabmeat

Large handful of fresh basil leaves, cut into ribbons

1 cup shredded Parmesan cheese

Garlic Cheese Grits (next page)

1. In a large heavy sauté pan, melt butter over medium heat. Just as butter begins to sizzle, add leeks and cook 5 minutes or until tender.
2. Add all bell peppers and continue to cook for 2 minutes.
3. Add mushrooms and cook for 2 minutes longer or until mushrooms are softened and mixture is juicy.
4. Add tomato and continue cooking for 2 minutes.
5. Add wine, salt, and pepper and mix well. Cover.
6. When liquid is bubbling, gently add crabmeat. Shake the pan instead of stirring so as not to break apart the large lumps of crab. Cover and cook for 1 minute or until crab is heated through and mixture is back to bubbling.
7. Add basil to crab and top with Parmesan cheese. Do not stir. Cover and reduce heat to low. Cook for 1 minute. Adjust seasonings. Serve immediately over Garlic Cheese Grits.

 LuLu Clue: The fancy name for cutting basil into ribbons is "chiffonade." The easy way to do this is place several leaves on top of each other, roll up like a cigar, and slice thinly into long shreds.

LuLu's management team

CONTINUED

GARLIC CHEESE GRITS
MAKES 4 SERVINGS

2 tablespoons unsalted butter

6 cloves garlic, minced, or more to taste

4 cups water

½ cup heavy cream

1 cup uncooked regular grits

½ teaspoon salt

2 cups shredded sharp white Cheddar cheese

Salt and pepper to taste

LuLu's Perfect Pepper Hot Sauce™ to taste

1. In a small skillet, melt butter. Add garlic and sauté until garlic is barely soft, being careful not to burn. Set aside.

2. In a heavy saucepan, heat water and cream but do not boil.

3. Slowly add grits and salt, stirring constantly to avoid clumping.

4. Reduce heat to medium-low and simmer, stirring often, for 15 to 20 minutes or until thick and creamy.

5. Add cheese and sautéed garlic and cook until cheese melts. Season with salt and pepper and hot sauce. Serve immediately.

Hot Damn Gouda Grits Cakes

MAKES 6 SERVINGS

5 cups water

½ teaspoon salt

1 stick butter

1⅓ cups uncooked grits

2 tablespoons finely chopped fresh garlic

1 cup shredded smoked Gouda cheese

2 jalapeño peppers, seeded and finely chopped

6 cups peanut or vegetable oil, or enough to fill frying pan about 2 inches deep

LuLu's Crazy Frying Flour (page 52)

2 cups whole milk

1. In a heavy saucepan, bring water, salt, and butter to a boil.

2. Add grits and cook over medium-low heat until liquid has evaporated and grits are smooth and creamy.

3. Add garlic, cheese, and jalapeños. Stir well and cook until cheese melts.

4. Pour grits into a greased casserole dish and refrigerate overnight.

5. Just before serving, cut grits into any desired shape. I like to cut mine like big brownies and then into triangles.

6. In a cast iron or heavy skillet, heat oil to 355 degrees over medium-high heat. (Use a candy or fry thermometer for accuracy or heat until a little flour flicked into the oil sizzles.)

7. Dredge grits cakes through frying flour, dip in milk, then dredge through flour again.

8. Gently drop into hot oil. Fry 2 minutes on each side until golden brown or until they float to the top. Drain on paper towels and serve immediately.

 LuLu Clue: These cakes are divine when served with Sloppy Shrimp (page 108) or gumbo instead of rice.

There was a great old restaurant in Mobile, Alabama called Constantine's. It was a favorite of my father's, and he would always order the crabmeat omelet and top it with ketchup. This version is made like pancakes instead of flipped in an omelet pan. They are thin and light with the egg mixture ladled in small amounts onto a hot griddle or into a very large fry pan. The end result almost resembles crêpes. I like to serve these with Chunky Cherry Tomato Salsa.

Sunday Brunch Crabmeat Omelet with Pepper Jack Grits

MAKES 6 SERVINGS

8 eggs

½ cup heavy cream

¼ teaspoon dry mustard

½ teaspoon salt

¼ teaspoon black pepper

½ teaspoon LuLu's Perfect Pepper Hot Sauce™ or any medium hot sauce

½ cup finely chopped green onions

1 cup lump crabmeat

1 tablespoon butter, or more if needed

Pepper Jack Cheese Grits (next page)

Chunky Cherry Tomato Salsa (page 177)

1. Preheat oven to 200 degrees.
2. In a large bowl, combine eggs with heavy cream, dry mustard, salt, black pepper, and hot sauce. Beat until mixture is light and fluffy.
3. Add green onions and crabmeat and stir once gently, being careful not to break up the jumbo lumps.
4. In a large heavy frying pan or on a flat-top griddle, melt 1 tablespoon butter over medium heat until it is just about to sizzle, but not browned.
5. Scooping from the bottom to evenly distribute crabmeat, ladle ¼ cup of egg mixture onto the hot frying pan in order to make a thin, crêpe-like omelet about 4 inches in diameter. If the pan is large enough, make 2 omelets at a time.
6. After eggs have set and are slightly brown on the bottom, use a thin metal spatula and quickly flip each omelet over onto itself, forming half-moons. Continue to cook 1 to 2 minutes on each side or until eggs have set and are no longer runny.
7. Repeat until all egg mixture is cooked, using more butter as necessary. (You may want to wipe the pan with a paper towel, removing the browned butter before adding new butter.) Place cooked omelets in oven to keep warm.
8. Serve immediately with Pepper Jack Grits and Chunky Cherry Tomato Salsa.

CONTINUED

PEPPER JACK GRITS

MAKES 6 SERVINGS

6 cups water

½ cup milk or heavy cream

1⅓ cups uncooked regular grits

2 tablespoons unsalted butter

½ teaspoon salt

2 cups cubed Velveeta® Pepper Jack cheese

Black pepper to taste

LuLu's Perfect Pepper Hot Sauce™ to taste

1. In a heavy saucepan, heat water and milk, but do not boil.
2. Slowly add grits, stirring constantly to avoid clumping.
3. Add butter and salt.
4. Reduce heat to medium-low and simmer, stirring often, for 15 to 20 minutes or until thick and creamy.
5. Add cheese and cook until cheese melts. Season to taste with salt, pepper, and hot sauce.

☼ LIFE IS GOOD GRITS

Favorite Dinner Party Menus

SOUTHERN SUMMER DINNER PARTY

PARADISE ISLAND LUNCHEON

TRADITIONAL UNCHRISTMAS DINNER

MAMA'S 80TH BIRTHDAY

NEW ORLEANS JAZZ FEST THURSDAY
DINNER PARTY

MONTANA RODEO PICNIC

DEEP SOUTH SUNDAY DINNER

ICE CHEST AND PICNIC BASICS

Breakin' Bread with Loved Ones

It happens at least once a week at our home — a dinner party. Having a handful of folks over for an impromptu meal or entertaining hundreds comes as naturally for me as making my bed. Sometimes it is a planned occasion with a carefully designed menu implemented after weeks of preparation. More often it's a spontaneous gathering of a boat-load of neighbors stopping by for a beer or a pit-stop at our pool pavilion.

Dinner parties are more a part of my personal life than my LuLu's life, although we've hosted our fair share of large, themed parties at the restaurant. But since this cookbook is all about cuisine and conversation, I wanted to share a few of my successful party menus here to keep the banter going. Unless you're into board games or cards, usually the activities of a dinner party are dining and talking. That's the fun of breaking bread with loved ones and new friends, sharing hilarious stories and learning more about each other.

I come by the gift of gab honestly; my mother was a great conversationalist, and you may have heard some of my brother's stories told in song. I love to visit and chat and I've found that a little libation loosens lips; pretty soon all manner of great gossip is being dished. You can learn a lot over a dinner table!

I like breaking out the fancy china and crystal and really getting swanky for my dinner parties, but these days I've simplified my life and found that what I'm serving and to whom is far more important than Bernardaud and Waterford. Lively conversation and tasty food can be served on plain white dishes and be just as enjoyable. I do like to throw some color on the table with a big bowl of fresh fruit or vase of cut flowers from the garden, but often the most colorful things at the table are the guests themselves and their crazy tales.

There are many different occasions and reasons for throwing a dinner party, and I've included some memorable favorites here, but I've found that often the best reason is none at all. Bring your friends and family close to your heart, and you can't go wrong no matter the menu.

BOB MERIWETHER-
A PhD In Party and Lifestyle

When my children were tiny, as soon as they awoke they would run up the stairs to get in bed with me. This happened every day except when there was no room. Why? Because my bed was covered with open cookbooks and magazines filled with recipes of dishes I had never heard of. On those days I'd instruct them to go play, and they'd dive into the treasured costume box. I would continue to pore over the recipes and pictures of exotic dishes, planning my next party. I had developed a daring habit of inviting friends over for dinner and cooking some complicated meal that I had never prepared before. Crazy? Of course, but being an experiential learner, that's how I earned my chef's coat.

I have never been satisfied with "normal," a condition I attribute to genetics, and one important factor that nurtured my intrigue for the unusual was the time I spent apprenticing in the art-of-entertaining with my dear friend, Bob Meriwether. I had my daughters at a very young age and wasn't able to finish college, but I received my PhD in lifestyle from Bob, an interior designer who lived in the graceful Oakleigh Garden District in Mobile. His eclectic style was impeccable, but his charming personality was deliciously dangerous. He had everyone he knew eating out of the palm of his hand and sometimes paying him to do it.

Bob collected people like he collected antiques — for his pleasure and delight. Even though he was born in Pensacola, he had spent his early years in Hollywood and had discovered his God-given talent for inspiring the dramatic in others. He wrote the recipe for having a good time: a beautiful home, plenty of libations, musical entertainment, and delectable food. The last ingredient is why I was recruited and allowed to be his friend. With Bob you had to earn your keep, contributing to his amusement, but he gave back as good as he got. He opened up a whole new world of finery, fashion, and culture to me.

Bob's Washington Square home was a showpiece, meticulously thought out. Each piece of furniture, wallpaper, drapery, art, or tchotchke had some purpose or significance. It was the epitome of style, often featured in design and architectural

magazines, and was regularly part of national and local historic tours. From the outside, it appeared to be a palace of respectability, at least to the innocent observer. The gaiety and ruthless hilarity that went on inside defies description; at least that is my story, and I'm sticking to it.

The "group" that gravitated to Bob was a stellar example of diversity, especially as far as occupations go: actor, musician, handyman, paralegal, Southern belle, shady lawyer, Elvis impersonator, artist, professor, hotelier, carpenter, heiress, insurance salesman, longshoreman, doctor, real estate magnate, writer, white collar criminal, wannabe decorators, produce shippers, and the occasional runaway. As the cook, I had the perfect vantage point into the lives of the lost souls that wandered through the revolving door of his life. We found camaraderie with each other because we shared the Southern "craziness" so well documented by writers of the ages.

On any random night of the week, the players would begin to gather around dusk. Ice would tinkle in crystal, corks would pop out of bottles of wine, and I would be sizzling in the kitchen. Bob paid for the ingredients and created my own little test kitchen, allowing me to try out the latest recipe that had struck my fancy. Sometimes it was a beef Stroganoff served on heirloom Spode china. Other times it was quick chicken spaghetti on paper plates. I knew it was time to serve dinner when the laughter in the living room had escalated to hooting and the decibel level reached a resounding "OH, MY GAWD!" We were all partners in crime barreling down the highway of escapism looking for a little rest from a hard day's work.

It never failed that the evening would end in the "play" room. Three of the walls were murals of vivid green tropical foliage that a set decorator friend of Bob's from Los Angeles had painted. The remaining wall was completely mirrored, showcasing a snow-white baby-grand piano! The performances that happened around that piano were nothing short of Broadway. We would gather in a cluster while our friend Fred played everything from Bach to Elton John. We sang ourselves hoarse and howled until our sides ached. Just when we thought we couldn't take another moment of fun, Bob would skip into the room, humming in full costume, and deliver his spot-on imitation of Prissy in *Gone With The Wind*. It always brought down the house!

Under Bob's tutelage, I learned how to live life well. I will always be grateful that he taught me to use humor and irreverence in the face of pain and sorrow. When he was diagnosed with Lou Gehrig's disease, he responded, "And I've never even played baseball." I'm sure he's rearranging the furniture in Heaven's living room and having gin and tonics with my mama every afternoon.

Southern Summer Dinner Party

SCREAMING EASY WILD SHRIMP WASABI

SWEET TOMATO PIE

SILVER QUEEN SUCCOTASH

LULU'S LEMON MOUSSE WITH RASPBERRY FILLING

MINT JULEP

SPICY SUMMER SHRIMP MEETS
HUMBLE TOMATO PIE —
A MARRIAGE MADE IN SILVER QUEEN HEAVEN

Summer might be the best time for a Southern dinner party. Deep South cooking in summertime is all about using wonderful seasonal fruits and vegetables from local farmers and their markets. Here in Baldwin County we have a bounty of fresh produce available, especially the super-sweet deliciousness of Silver Queen corn. I swear you can eat it raw, it's so good. The dream of having my own farmer's market at LuLu's still tickles around my head sometimes. Mac and I enjoy our garden of tomatoes, vegetables, herbs, and roses, the product of which lightens and brightens our summertime meals.

And, generally speaking, if you're in Baldwin County, you're usually only a few minutes away from a mess of fresh shrimp. Bon Secour is home to several fresh fish markets, their wharves lined up with graceful, bedraggled shrimp boats — I can pretty much guarantee the boats will be there if you go; it's nigh unto impossible to get up any earlier than a shrimper finishes his day's work. I've grown up around shrimping, and let me tell you, that's a very tough gig. Over on the other side of the Bay, the best place to find fresh shrimp is Bayou la Batre, which took a terrible beating during Hurricane Katrina. The local shrimping industry has been hit hard by global trade and repeated hurricanes.

I created the Screamin' Easy Wild Shrimp Wasabi to cook at the Great American Seafood Cook-off in New Orleans in 2005. I was promoting the Eat Alabama Wild Shrimp campaign, for which I was a spokesperson.

At the cook-off, I knew I would be competing against some very highfalutin chefs, so I wanted to make something that anyone could cook. This dish is soooo easy, it is almost a crime. I didn't win, but the judges cleaned their plates, and I think my beloved Alabama shrimpers would have been proud of how I represented them in true LuLu style.

Between the sweltering temperatures and my hot flashes, I'm not terribly inclined to turn on the oven right now, but I could probably be convinced if it meant I got to have some Sweet Tomato Pie. I have some ripe tomatoes on my sill...I might just crank the AC down to brrrr, mix up a batch of mint juleps, and catch up on some Court TV and gossip rags while the pie bakes...hmmm, or invite some friends over for a dinner of shrimp, corn, and tomatoes, topped off with a cool lemon mousse. Yum. I'd better get moving...

Screaming Easy Wild Shrimp Wasabi

MAKES 4 TO 6 SERVINGS

1 tablespoon wasabi powder

¼ cup beer (I use Landshark® beer and drink the rest while cooking)

1 tablespoon prepared horseradish

2 pounds large headless shrimp

1 tablespoon coarse sea salt

2 tablespoons unsalted butter

1 tablespoon finely chopped fresh cilantro

Lime slices for garnish

1. Combine wasabi powder, beer, and horseradish. Set aside.
2. Peel and devein shrimp, leaving tails intact.
3. Place a cast iron skillet over high heat. When it begins to smoke, add shrimp. Shake skillet and toss or stir shrimp for 15 seconds or until they just begin to turn pink.
4. Add salt, wasabi mixture, and butter. Stir quickly, turning shrimp for another 15 seconds, then cover tightly and remove from heat. Let shrimp rest for 5 minutes.
5. Add cilantro, stir once, and cover again. Wait another 5 minutes.
6. Garnish with lime slices and serve immediately.

LuLu Clue: This dish can also be prepared leaving the shrimp in their shells. It's messy, fun food.

The maritime industry in Alabama has a proud heritage of families valuing hard-work, a legacy passed down for generations. Please visit the website (http://www.eatalabamawildshrimp.com/) and help preserve this legacy. Buy, sell, and serve Alabama Wild Shrimp!

Successful baking depends on precision.

Since I tend to improvise when cooking, I'm not a very good baker, which is why I use a ready-made pastry. I've found Pillsbury® to be the closest to homemade. Look for the kind sold in the box in the dairy case. Just unroll the dough and press it into a pie pan. If you're an avid baker or proficient pastry chef, by all means use your favorite pie crust recipe. However, make sure it is not sweet dough; between the caramelized onions and the tomatoes, this dish is already plenty sweet.

Sweet Tomato Pie

MAKES 6 TO 8 SERVINGS

2 tablespoons all-purpose flour

1 Pillsbury® refrigerated pie crust

2 tablespoons unsalted butter

1 tablespoon extra virgin olive oil

1 large onion, thinly sliced

1 tablespoon sugar

4 cloves garlic, thinly sliced

4 ounces cream cheese, softened

½ cup mayonnaise

2 tablespoons heavy cream

1 tablespoon sour cream

1 tablespoon honey mustard

1 cup shredded Parmesan cheese

4 green onions, cut into 2-inch
　　pieces, including green part

4 large red tomatoes, sliced into
　　¼-inch slices, preferably
　　homegrown

½ teaspoon kosher salt

½ teaspoon coarsely ground
　　pepper

½ cup fresh basil, cut in ribbons

2 cups shredded Gruyère or Swiss
　　cheese

1. Preheat oven to 450 degrees.
2. Sprinkle flour over counter or pastry marble and roll pie crust dough to fit a 7x11-inch rectangular baking dish, making sure dough comes up the sides of the dish. Poke bottom of crust with a fork in several places. Bake for 9 to 10 minutes or until crust is lightly browned.
3. Remove from oven to cool. Reduce oven temperature to 400 degrees.
4. In a cast iron or heavy skillet, heat butter and olive oil over medium heat until it begins to sizzle. Add onions and sugar. Sauté until onions are very brown and caramelized.
5. Add garlic and stir constantly for another 1 to 2 minutes or until garlic is cooked through and tender. Remove onions and garlic from skillet and set aside to cool.
6. In the bowl of a food processor, combine cream cheese, mayonnaise, heavy cream, sour cream, honey mustard, Parmesan cheese, and green onions. Process until well mixed. Transfer to small mixing bowl; set aside.
7. In the cooled pie crust, layer half of the following ingredients: sautéed onions, cream cheese mixture, sliced tomatoes, salt, black pepper, basil, and Gruyère cheese. Repeat layering using remaining ingredients.
8. Bake 35 minutes or until pie is bubbling and top is browned.
9. Remove from oven and cool for 15 to 20 minutes before slicing.

Silver Queen Succotash

2 slices bacon, cut into 2-inch pieces

1 tablespoon extra virgin olive oil

1 medium onion, coarsely chopped

4 ears fresh Silver Queen corn, shucked

4 cups fresh green butter beans, or 1 pound frozen

1 (10-ounce) can Rotel® Original diced tomatoes and green chilies

3 cups hot water

2 teaspoons kosher salt

½ teaspoon ground black pepper

1 teaspoon ground thyme

4 cups fresh sliced okra, or 1 pound frozen

LuLu's Perfect Pepper Hot Sauce™, optional

1. In a heavy Dutch oven, fry bacon over medium-low heat until almost crisp.
2. Add olive oil and onions.
3. While onions are cooking, cut corn kernels off cobs and set aside.
4. When onions are translucent, add butter beans, tomatoes, water, salt, pepper, and thyme.
5. Increase heat and bring to a boil.
6. Reduce heat to medium-low and cook, uncovered, for 30 minutes.
7. Add okra and cover. Reduce heat to low and cook for 15 minutes.
8. Add corn and cover. Cook for 5 minutes longer.
9. Add hot sauce and adjust seasonings.

LuLu with her "rock" Margaret Daniels

LuLu's Lemon Mousse with Raspberry Filling

MAKES 8 TO 10 SERVINGS

RASPBERRY FILLING

1 (15-ounce) package frozen raspberries with juice, thawed

2 tablespoons freshly squeezed lemon juice

½ cup sugar

2 teaspoons cornstarch

¼ cup raspberry liqueur

MOUSSE

1 (¼-ounce) package unflavored gelatin

1 cup lemon juice

6 eggs, separated

1 cup plus 4 tablespoons sugar, divided

Zest of 1 lemon

3 cups heavy cream, divided

1 tablespoon Grand Marnier®

Fresh raspberries for garnish

1. For filling, place raspberries and lemon juice in a blender. Blend until smooth.
2. Strain mixture into a saucepan to remove all seeds.
3. Add sugar. Bring to a boil over medium-high heat. Simmer for 15 minutes. Remove from heat.
4. Dissolve cornstarch in liqueur and stir into raspberry mixture. Cool completely.
5. To prepare mousse, dissolve gelatin in lemon juice in a small heavy saucepan. Place over low heat to melt. Remove from heat and cool completely.
6. Beat egg yolks with 1 cup sugar until sugar is dissolved.
7. Fold cooled gelatin mixture and zest into beaten yolks.
8. In a separate bowl, beat egg whites with an electric mixer on high until stiff peaks form, gradually adding 2 tablespoons sugar while beating.
9. Fold beaten whites into lemon-egg mixture very carefully until completely mixed.
10. Whip 2 cups cream with an electric mixer until fluffy peaks hold. Carefully fold into lemon-egg mixture until thoroughly blended.
11. Pour half of mousse into a glass trifle dish. Refrigerate for 15 minutes.
12. Spread filling over mousse. Pour remaining mousse over filling.
13. Whip remaining 1 cup cream, gradually adding remaining 2 tablespoons sugar and Grand Marnier®, on high speed until stiff peaks form. Spread whipped cream evenly over mousse.
14. Garnish with fresh raspberries. Refrigerate for at least 1 hour before serving.

PARTY FAVORS

Mint Julep

MAKES 10 TO 12 SERVINGS

2 cups sugar

2 cups water

6 sprigs fresh mint, plus some for garnish

2 cups bourbon whiskey

1. Make a simple syrup by dissolving sugar in water and bring to a low boil. Once sugar is completely dissolved and mixture is piping hot, remove from heat.
2. Pluck mint leaves from stems and add to syrup.
3. Cool completely.
4. Pour syrup into a serving pitcher and add bourbon. Stir to mix well.
5. Fill a high-ball glass with ice and a sprig of mint.
6. Cover ice with bourbon mixture and serve.

LuLu Clue: Allow mint syrup to steep as long as possible before serving. This refreshing beverage is meant to be sipped, as you would a martini "on the rocks."

SOUTHERN SUMMER DINNER PARTY

Paradise Island Luncheon

MO-BAY SHRIMP CREOLE

BAHAMIAN PIGEON PEAS AND COCONUT RICE

MANGO-AVOCADO SALSA

KEY LIME SQUARES

BETTY BRUCE'S CAYO HUESO HIGHBALL

FOR THE SUN, THE WATER, AND THE PEOPLE

I love the island lifestyle of the Caribbean, especially the Bahamas. In fact, Mac and I ran off to Crooked Island to marry. Instead of flowers for my wedding, the Bahamian people who became our attendants for the spur-of-the-moment ceremony made me bouquets of ribbons and bows in the colors of the Bahamian flag: yellow (for the sun), blue (for the water), and black (for the people). These kind and generous people joyfully became our wedding party as we wed in swimsuits and flip-flops.

The "no worries" way of life in the tropics has always been the way I've spent my happiest days, toes in the sandy beaches of crystalline waters. Some of my favorite stories come from the chapters of my life spent in the Bahamas, Belize, Jamaica and our own Caribbean country — the Conch Republic (Key West) — stories too numerous to mention or perhaps unmentionable in proper company! Suffice to say, everybody seems to be able to chill out a little easier to the tunes of reggae and junkanoo with a frosty, cool umbrella-drink.

I came home from my trip to Jamaica inspired by the cuisine there, having fallen in love with the unique, subtle spiciness. So this menu is a Caribbean-destination tasting menu, highlighting fresh seafood and fruits, as well as pigeon peas and rice, all staples of island dining. Finish it all off with a refreshing visit to Key West with a Key Lime Square and Betty Bruce's Caya Hueso Highball. My dear friend Dink is a 5th generation Conch (native of Key West), and he very graciously allowed me to publish his mama's favorite highball in my cookbook. Thanks, Dink!

Dink Bruce,
Louie's Backyard, Key West

Mo-Bay Shrimp Creole

MO-BAY MARINADE

⅓ cup coconut milk

¼ cup extra virgin olive oil

¼ cup freshly squeezed lime juice
(about 2 limes)

2 teaspoons salt

2 teaspoons black pepper

2 tablespoons freshly minced garlic

1 tablespoon finely chopped fresh
cilantro

3 pounds large shrimp, peeled
and deveined

1. Combine all marinade ingredients except shrimp in a plastic container or stainless steel bowl.

2. Add shrimp. Toss well to make sure shrimp are well coated. Cover and refrigerate while preparing sauce.

CONTINUED

LuLu & Diva, dishin'

MO-BAY SAUCE

2 tablespoons extra virgin olive oil

4 tablespoons finely chopped fresh garlic, divided

2 cups coarsely chopped yellow onions

1 cup coarsely chopped green bell peppers

6 ribs celery, coarsely chopped

1 Scotch bonnet pepper or fresh jalapeño pepper, seeded and finely chopped

2 (28-ounce) cans crushed tomatoes with juice

3 tablespoons tomato paste

4 cups Shrimp Stock (page 57)

2 bay leaves

1 tablespoon thyme

4 tablespoons ground coriander, divided

4 tablespoons finely chopped fresh cilantro, divided

1 tablespoon salt

½ tablespoon black pepper

2 tablespoons sugar

1 bunch green onions, chopped

½ cup coconut milk

2 tablespoons Pickapeppa® sauce

3. For sauce, heat olive oil in large Dutch oven over medium heat. Add 2 tablespoons garlic and sauté for 30 seconds.

4. Add onions and sauté for 3 to 5 minutes or until translucent.

5. Add bell peppers and celery and sauté for 2 minutes or until softened.

6. Add Scotch bonnet pepper, tomatoes, tomato paste, and Shrimp Stock.

7. Season with bay leaves, thyme, 2 tablespoons ground coriander, 2 tablespoons cilantro, salt, black pepper, and sugar.

8. Bring to boil. Reduce heat and simmer, uncovered, for 1 hour, or until vegetables have cooked down and liquid has reduced to create a thick sauce.

9. Add green onions, coconut milk, Pickapeppa® sauce, remaining 2 tablespoons coriander, and remaining 2 tablespoons garlic. Add shrimp with marinade. Cover and cook for 5 minutes or until shrimp are pink and firm.

10. Just before serving, add remaining 2 tablespoons cilantro and stir thoroughly.

Bahamian Pigeon Peas and Coconut Rice

MAKES 10 TO 12 SERVINGS

4 slices bacon, cut into 2-inch pieces

1 cup chopped yellow onions

½ cup diced green bell peppers

1 stalk celery, chopped

1 teaspoon dried thyme

1 teaspoon coriander

3 tablespoons tomato paste

2 cups cooked pigeon peas

1½ cups coconut milk

1½ cups chicken broth

½ teaspoon salt

¼ teaspoon black pepper

2 cups Uncle Ben's® white rice, uncooked

¼ cup finely chopped parsley

½ cup finely chopped green onions

1. In a large saucepan, fry bacon over medium heat until almost crisp.
2. Add chopped onions and cook 2 to 3 minutes or until soft and translucent.
3. Add bell pepper, celery, thyme, coriander, and tomato paste. Sauté for 2 minutes.
4. Add pigeon peas and cook until just heated through. Transfer mixture to a bowl.
5. In the same saucepan, combine coconut milk, chicken broth, salt, and pepper. Bring to a boil.
6. Add uncooked rice and return to a boil. Reduce heat to low and add peas and vegetables. Cover and cook for 25 to 30 minutes or until liquid is absorbed.
7. Just before serving, add parsley and green onions and fluff with a fork.

LuLu Clue: Fresh or canned black-eyed peas can be substituted for the pigeon peas.

Mango-Avocado Salsa

MAKES 4 TO 6 SERVINGS

2 ripe mangoes, peeled and diced

¾ cup finely chopped red onions

¾ cup finely chopped red bell peppers

¾ cup finely chopped green bell peppers

2 tablespoons extra virgin olive oil

2 tablespoons finely chopped fresh cilantro

2 teaspoons finely chopped fresh chives

1 large ripe avocado, pitted, peeled, and diced

3 tablespoons freshly squeezed lime juice

Salt and pepper to taste

1. In a medium bowl, combine mangoes, red onions, all bell peppers, olive oil, cilantro, and chives.
2. Toss avocado with lime juice.
3. Gently add avocado with juice to mango mixture, stirring to combine all the flavors.
4. Season with salt and pepper.

LuLu Clue: Make sure the avocado you use is not overripe or mushy.

Key Lime Squares

MAKES 10 TO 12 SQUARES

CRUST
¼ cup slivered blanched almonds
2 sticks unsalted butter, softened
2 cups all-purpose flour
1 tablespoon powdered sugar
¼ teaspoon almond extract

KEY LIME FILLING
5 eggs
2 cups granulated sugar
Pinch of salt
¾ cup Key lime juice
½ teaspoon orange zest
¼ cup powdered sugar for topping

1. Preheat oven to 350 degrees.
2. Using a mini-food processor, chop almonds into a fine meal.
3. In a large mixing bowl or food processor, combine almonds, butter, flour, powdered sugar, and almond extract. Blend into a thick pastry and pat into the bottom of a well-greased 8x12-inch baking dish.
4. Bake crust for 15 minutes. Remove from oven and reduce oven temperature to 325 degrees.
5. To prepare filling, beat eggs. Add granulated sugar, salt, lime juice, and orange zest. Mix thoroughly.
6. Pour filling over partially baked crust and return to the oven.
7. Bake 20 to 30 minutes or until filling is set.
8. Remove from oven and cool.
9. Sift powdered sugar over top and cut into squares.

LuLu Clue: As in the Key Lime Pie, I might substitute a bottled juice. A good quality Key lime juice is available in most large grocery stores.

Betty Bruce's Cayo Hueso Highball

MAKES 1 DRINK

Juice of ½ fresh Key lime
1½-2 ounces good Cuban (gold) rum
4-6 ounces ginger ale
Fresh mint to garnish

1. Fill a glass with cracked ice.
2. Add lime juice.
3. Add rum.
4. Top off with ginger ale.
5. Stir with love and garnish with mint sprig.

LuLu Clue: To make a bigger batch for a dinner party, mix the juice of 12 Key limes, a fifth of rum, one liter of ginger ale, mint leaves, and crushed ice in a punch bowl and call it Cayo Hueso Punch.

  PARADISE ISLAND LUNCHEON

Traditional UnChristmas Dinner

PASCAGOULA OYSTERS ROCK-A-FELLA

MAINE LOBSTER

POTATO HORSERADISH GRATIN

GRILLED ASPARAGUS

KRISPY KREME® UNCHRISTMAS PUDDING

PINK CHAMPAGNE

A Holly-Jolly-Bottle-O-Bubbly

Christmastime can be a drag… so many expectations, so much craziness, so little "real" time. What a huge drama it's become. My head starts spinning when I think of all the people I "should" have on my gift list. Then, I want to tear my hair out thinking of all the things I "should" be doing. I'm over it. My husband and I started a tradition with our blended family for Christmas — get the hell out of Dodge! Then sometime near the big day, Mac and I throw a big ol' river rats party to Not Celebrate Christmas. No gifts permitted, or you will be thrown out. Just bring a bottle of fancy French pink champagne and an appetite for scrumptious food. We toast our redneck roots with Pascagoula Oysters Rock-A-Fella and feast on fresh lobster. We cook the "bugs" in an extra-large pot with a boiling basket over a propane burner outdoors on the deck overlooking Fish River, even in the dead of winter. I top our picnic tables with old newspaper, lobster crackers, bowls of melted butter, lemon wedges, and several rolls of paper towels, and we dig in. It is messy, but loads of fun digging out the succulent meat while swigging swanky champagne from paper cups. (You can take the girl out of the country, but you can't take the low country boil out of the girl.) Grilled asparagus is very easy and goes well with the lobster, as does the Potato Horseradish Gratin. Warning: the Potato Horseradish Gratin is so good that you should put a moratorium on kitchen-sampling or you won't have any left to serve! The highlight of the meal might just be the Krispy Kreme® UnChristmas Pudding. It is ridiculous how sweet it is, and so good. Almost as good as a "Hot Now" Krispy Kreme® doughnut…almost.

Pascagoula Oysters Rock-A-Fella

MAKES 6 TO 8 SERVINGS

4 tablespoons unsalted butter, divided

12 slices bacon, finely chopped

½ cup chopped yellow onion

½ cup finely chopped green onion

3 tablespoons finely chopped garlic

3 cups finely chopped celery

2 (10-ounce) packages frozen spinach, thawed

3 tablespoons finely chopped parsley

Pinch of dried thyme

Pinch of cayenne pepper

3-4 tablespoons Pernod® or Herbsaint® liqueur

Salt and pepper to taste

LuLu's Perfect Pepper Hot Sauce™ to taste

½ cup fine breadcrumbs

6 (8-inch) metal pie plates

1 (4-pound) box rock salt

3 dozen fresh oysters, freshly shucked on the half shell

6 lemon wedges to garnish

1. In a heavy saucepan, melt 2 tablespoons butter. Add bacon and cook over medium heat until bacon is crispy.
2. Add yellow and green onions, garlic, and celery. Sauté 5 to 6 minutes or until vegetables begin to soften.
3. Drain spinach of all excess liquid. Add to vegetables and cook 5 minutes longer.
4. Stir in parsley, thyme, and cayenne pepper.
5. Drizzle in liqueur. Reduce heat and simmer for 2 minutes or until liqueur evaporates. Season with salt and pepper and hot sauce.
6. In a food processor, purée half the vegetable mixture with breadcrumbs. If mixture is too dry, melt remaining 2 tablespoons butter and add to mixture.
7. Combine puréed mixture with other half of vegetable mixture and cool to room temperature.
8. Preheat broiler.
9. Fill each pie plate with at least a ½-inch rock salt to cover bottom. Position 6 oyster shells on each plate. The rock salt keeps them in place while cooking.
10. Top each oyster with a big spoonful of the spinach mixture.
11. Gently place pie plates in the oven and broil 5 minutes or until the spinach mixture is just brown and bubbly and the edges of the oysters curl slightly. Watch carefully! After all that work, you don't want it to burn! Serve immediately with lemon wedges.

LuLu Clue: I usually use day-old French bread to make my breadcrumbs for this dish.

Maine Lobster

MAKES 8 SERVINGS

2 pounds salted butter
8 lemons, halved
8 live lobsters
1 cup rock salt

1. Fill a very large lobster pot about one-third full of water. Insert boiling basket. Add salt. Place over a propane burner outdoors and bring to a rolling boil.

2. While water is coming to a boil, slowly melt butter in a heavy saucepan. When melted, divide between 8 individual ramekins or small bowls. Place on the tables with 2 lemon halves beside each bowl.

3. Thank the lobsters for volunteering to be dinner and carefully drop them, head first, into boiling water. Caution: make sure there is enough space for lobsters so as not to create a dangerous over-boil.

4. Cook for 15 to 20 minutes or until lobsters are bright red and their tails are tightly curled under. Turn off burner.

5. Remove boiling basket and drain. Place lobsters, using tongs, on newspaper.

6. To get meat from the lobsters, first break off claws. Using metal lobster claw crackers, crack open claws and pick out meat with a fork. Next, break off head from tail. Cut underbelly spine with kitchen shears toward the tip of tail. Bend shells apart and remove tail meat.

LuLu Clue: I order my lobster online from thelobsternet.com. It is a family-owned business that understands the importance of caring customer service. Their products are of the finest quality, providing the freshest possible taste and the convenience of having them delivered directly to your front door. Those tragic creatures swimming around the fishmonger's tank at the local grocery have been there way too long for my taste!

LuLu Clue: Each year I save all the lobster heads and shells and freeze them for Lobster Day. My friend Joni and I have a ritual. We get together after the first of the year and spend an entire day making lobster stock.

LuLu Clue: For clarified or drawn butter, skim foam from top of melted butter. Continue to cook until butter becomes clear and milk solids have fallen to the bottom of the pan. Remove from heat. Ladle clarified butter into ramekins.

Potato Horseradish Gratin

MAKES 8 TO 10 SERVINGS

6 medium potatoes, peeled and finely chopped (about 6 cups)

1 tablespoon plus ½ teaspoon salt, divided

6 tablespoons unsalted butter, softened, divided

½ cup finely chopped green bell peppers

¾ cup finely chopped green onions

6 tablespoons all-purpose flour

2 cups whole milk

4 cups coarsely shredded Gruyère cheese

4 cloves garlic, finely chopped

½ teaspoon black pepper

⅔ cup heavy cream, chilled

2 tablespoons prepared horseradish, drained

1. Preheat oven to 375 degrees.
2. Place potatoes in a heavy stockpot and cover with water. Add 1 tablespoon salt. Bring to a boil and cook until slightly tender; drain. Place potatoes in a greased casserole dish, or greased individual gratin dishes arranged on a baking sheet.
3. In a heavy skillet, melt 2 tablespoons butter. Add bell peppers, green onions, and ¼ teaspoon salt and sauté until just barely soft. Set aside.
4. In a heavy saucepan, melt remaining 4 tablespoons butter over medium-low heat. Just as it begins to sizzle, gradually whisk in flour. Cook, stirring continuously, for about 2 minutes. (You do not want this to brown.)
5. Gradually add milk, continuing to whisk or stir until sauce begins to thicken.
6. Add sautéed vegetables and stir.
7. Add cheese, garlic, and pepper, continuing to stir until cheese is melted. Pour mixture over potatoes.
8. Bake for 30 minutes or until warmed through.
9. Remove from oven and preheat broiler.
10. While potatoes are cooling, beat cream with an electric mixer until it holds soft peaks.
11. Add horseradish and remaining ¼ teaspoon salt to cream and mix well. Spread over potatoes.
12. Place under broiler for a few minutes or until browned; watch carefully to prevent burning. Serve immediately.

PARTY FAVORS

Grilled Asparagus

SERVES 8

2 bunches asparagus, trimmed
¼ cup olive oil
½ teaspoon salt
¼ teaspoon pepper

1. Drizzle olive oil over asparagus and season with salt and pepper. Coat well.
2. Place across a hot grill. Grill about 2 minutes. Roll them to the other side and grill for another 2 minutes.
3. Remove and serve immediately.

LuLu Clue: Some folks like to trim asparagus at its natural breaking point. I like the aesthetic of uniform size, so I simply chop off the ends instead.

Krispy Kreme® UnChristmas Pudding with Vanilla Custard Sauce

MAKES 10 TO 12 SERVINGS

2 tablespoons unsalted butter, divided

2 cups heavy cream

2 cups milk

6 egg yolks

2 eggs

½ cup sweetened condensed milk

1½ teaspoons pure vanilla extract

1¼ teaspoons ground nutmeg

1¼ teaspoons cinnamon

½ cup praline liqueur (can substitute Frangelico®)

2 dozen Krispy Kreme® glazed doughnuts, broken into 2-inch chunks

1 cup chopped pecans

Vanilla Custard Sauce (recipe below)

1. Preheat oven to 350 degrees.
2. Melt 1 tablespoon butter in a 13x9-inch baking dish, being careful not to burn butter. Brush butter up along sides of dish and set aside.
3. In a large bowl, beat together cream, milk, egg yolks, eggs, condensed milk, vanilla, nutmeg, cinnamon, and liqueur.
4. Place doughnuts in baking dish. Pour cream mixture over the top until all doughnuts are covered, smushing them down.
5. Sprinkle pecans over top. Cut remaining tablespoon of butter into small pieces and sprinkle over pecans.
6. Bake for 1 hour or until center is set and top is browned.
7. Serve with Vanilla Custard Sauce spooned over each serving.

VANILLA CUSTARD SAUCE

1½ cups milk

1½ cups heavy cream

¾ cup sugar, divided

6 egg yolks

2 teaspoons pure vanilla extract

1. In a saucepan, combine milk, cream, and ½ cup sugar. Heat thoroughly but do not boil.
2. In a separate bowl, beat together egg yolks and remaining ¼ cup sugar until smooth.
3. Add a small amount of hot milk mixture into egg mixture to temper. (If you add it all at once, the heat from the milk will make something resembling scrambled eggs.) Gradually whisk remaining hot milk mixture into the egg mixture, blending until smooth.
4. Return mixture to saucepan, add vanilla, and cook over low heat, stirring constantly, until sauce coats the spoon. (This is when curdling can occur; be careful not to let the mixture boil!)
5. Ladle 2 to 3 tablespoons over plated bread pudding just before serving.

HONOR THY MOTHER WITH PINK CHAMPAGNE
By Melanie Buffett Ingraffia

Long before the pop star of the same name and hair color made it trendy, Mom has been obsessed with all things pink. Currently, she carries a pink laptop and briefcase, jams to a pink iPod, and sports pink cowboy boots and dazzling pink sapphire earrings. What color is her restaurant painted? PINK!

In our family, bloodlines are strong, so it's no surprise that I inherited the same answer to the age-old question, "What's your favorite color?" Obviously, pink...as it was in the beginning, is now, and ever shall be.

But why? How did she come to this obsession? Many Buffett family behaviors border on the obsessive, but I wanted to know. I (obsessively) needed to get to the root of this one.

Initial theories included Mom's love of music. Maybe it was from her 70's jam-band days listening to The Band's *Music from Big Pink*. Perhaps it was my uncle's *A White Sport Coat and a Pink Crustacean* album. Aretha Franklin's *Pink Cadillac* might be the culprit. She is a big Aretha fan, but I suspect that the origins of Pink Love began earlier than that song was recorded. Okay, she also loves television and movies. Could it have been Fonzie's infinitely cool girlfriend Pinky Tuscadero and her powder pink motorcycle from *Happy Days*? Or better yet, maybe it was the bad-ass chick clique "The Pink Ladies" from the classic movie *Grease*. Their pledge rings in my head: "To act cool, to look cool, and to beeeee cool. 'Til death do us part. Think Pink." This is "so" Mom.

As strong an influence as pop culture may be, I wasn't convinced. I looked to the life of my grandmother, Peets. She was an old-fashioned Southern lady, quick-witted and drawn to elegant things. One of her favorite activities was Royal Tea at Le Salon in the Windsor Court Hotel in New Orleans. She always ordered pink champagne before tea. Sometimes tea was skipped altogether. One of the best pink bubblies is La Grande Dame Rosé, her favorite. I have dream-like memories of eating petit fours in the beautiful tea room on the delicate china while the ladies sipped pretty pink champagne.

One afternoon, not long after my grandmother's passing, Mom visited me in New Orleans. I met her at the hotel; she was staying at the Windsor Court. It was tea time and there was the usual hustle and bustle of ladies in hats and gentleman *gaily* enjoying tea and crumpets. We hadn't planned on tea, but I wasn't surprised to see Mom sitting alone at an elegant table for two sipping on bubbling pink. I knew she was channeling my grandmother, so I rushed over so as not to miss one pink second of it. The setting hadn't changed since I was a little girl, except that now I too had a champagne flute. Right then I realized the love of pink dates way back in "Buffett Woman Lore" to Peetsy, who sparked the Grande Dame in us all.

Mama's 80th Birthday Party

WEST INDIES SALAD

TENDERLOIN OF BEEF WITH WHITE HORSERADISH SAUCE

SLICED HOMEGROWN TOMATOES

SUMMER GRILLED VEGETABLES

WEDDING CAKE WITH
WHITE CHOCOLATE CREAM CHEESE FROSTING
AND FRESH SLICED PEACHES

KEY LIME TANQUERAY® AND TONIC

A Tribute to Mary Loraine Peets Buffett

For the last ten years of my mother Peets' life, she was confined to a wheelchair after suffering a debilitating stroke. This did not prevent her from taking me to Paris for my 40th birthday because I was the only one of her children who had never been to Europe. She insisted that since we were so close to Normandy, we rent a van and visit the American Cemetery. With the help of our dear family friend, Bobbo Jetmundsen, we did just that. It was a remarkable and humbling experience. The natural Southern stoicism with which Peets greeted each day and her determination to live a quality life despite her handicap continues to inspire her family and many friends.

Instead of retreating into self-pity, my mother became a social butterfly. She enlisted me in joining her weekly discussion group at which we would all giggle along with her as I attempted to interpret her sometimes hilarious speech. Most times, it was like playing charades. Mama was so clever, she figured out a way to tell us what she was trying to say by pointing to objects or to the newspapers and magazines constantly cluttered around her.

One of the many things that pleased Peets was going to "school," as she called it, three times a week. "School" was actually speech and occupational therapy. As happened everywhere she went, she won admirers and friends immediately, simply for being who she was — a smart, funny woman who loved life, adored her family, and valued her friends. "School" was no exception. Her therapists marveled at her graciousness and love of learning. Bear in mind, this was a woman who worked for 30 years at the Mobile shipyard, and after her retirement at 65, went back to college to earn her

LaLa, Mama & LuLu, circa 1981

bachelor's degree in English. She had beautiful penmanship prior to her stroke and was determined to learn to write again, even if it was in the primitive scratch of a four-year-old. One day her therapists put Mama at a computer and were amazed at how quickly she was able to peck the keys to spell words easily. She had, after all, learned to type as a teenager and had a lifetime career as a secretary. Mama was delighted and felt she had a new lease on life. Peets began writing short stories for her children and grandchildren that are now family treasures.

Peets never missed seeing Jimmy perform if he was anywhere within a couple of hundred miles. The last time she saw him in Atlanta, we chartered an air-ambulance because the six-hour drive would have been too demanding. My daughter, Melanie, was living with my mother, helping care for her. Someone in the lobby of the small private airport saw Mel getting Peets ready to board the plane and hurried out to offer some comfort, assuming that Mama had taken a turn for the worse. Melanie burst out laughing and explained, "Oh no, she's fine! We're just going to a rock concert."

After I opened LuLu's, Peets came to eat at least three or four times a week. Two booths on the screened porch were deliberately cut to a 45° angle to accommodate her wheelchair. It was well known those were Peets' tables; tourists and locals alike checked to see if she happened to be enjoying an oyster loaf or crab melt, her favorites. And of course, the staff would immediately bring her a Tanqueray® gin and tonic before she ever ordered her meal.

As her 80th birthday approached, there was no question that the celebration would be held at LuLu's; we needed plenty of room for her extensive guest list. Mama's birthday fell in mid-August, so I planned a cold summer buffet. We filled a small sailboat with a flavored-vodka-shot bar and served margaritas galore and plenty of pink champagne. One of her favorite moments was realizing that for her birthday cake, I had ordered a classic wedding cake from The Little Cake Shop in Spanish Fort. If my mother had any addiction over which she was powerless, it was wedding cake. She was notorious for stashing several pieces in her purse whenever she was invited to a reception!

The whole staff rallied to make this event, while still LuLu's-casual, fancier than our usual fare. Hundreds of her friends, from twenty-somethings to fellow octogenarians, partied to the tunes of Frank Sinatra and Jimmy Buffett, her favorites, and enjoyed a magical Southern night under the stars that truly manifested her philosophy of living well. Here's to you, Mama!

LuLu's West Indies Salad

MAKES 4-6 SERVINGS

1 pound fresh jumbo lump blue crabmeat

Salt to taste (about ½ teaspoon)

Freshly ground black pepper to taste (about ¼ teaspoon)

½ medium Vidalia® (or sweet) onion, sliced paper thin, in half moon shape

⅓ cup vegetable oil

⅓ cup white vinegar

⅓ cup ice water (with 4-5 ice cubes)

1. Place half the crabmeat gently on the bottom of a glass bowl or plastic container, gently picking out any shells. Sprinkle with just a smidgen of salt and pepper.
2. Cover crab with a layer of onion.
3. Repeat steps with remaining crab, salt, pepper, and onion.
4. Pour oil and vinegar over layers.
5. Place ice cubes in a liquid measuring cup. Fill with water until volume reaches ⅓ cup and pour over crab.
6. Cover and marinate for at least 2 hours before serving.
7. When ready to serve, shake bowl gently, or if using a leak-proof plastic container, turn upside down and back upright to gently mix salad.
8. Serve in a shallow bowl with juice.

 LuLu Clue: It really is this easy and the ice cubes are crucial. Don't ask me why, but when I haven't included them, the dish just doesn't taste the same.

LuLu Clue: Jumbo lump is expensive because there are only two pieces of the meat yielded from a single crab, but it's worth it. You can use regular lump crab, but you must carefully and delicately pick through it for shells.

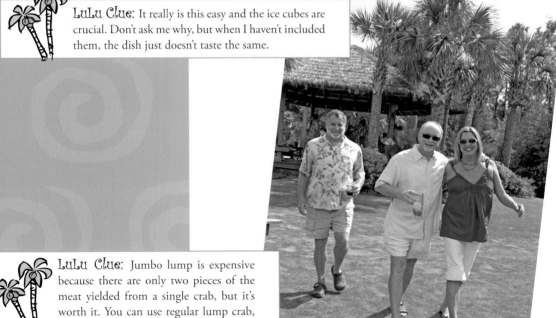

Tenderloin of Beef with White Horseradish Sauce

MAKES 8 SERVINGS

1 (10-pound) beef tenderloin

Coarsely ground black pepper

2 cups One Heart Marinade (page 48)

White Horseradish Sauce (page 174)

1. Trim tenderloin (see LuLu Clue below).
2. Rub beef generously with pepper.
3. Place beef in shallow dish, cover with marinade. Let sit for 1 hour, turn and marinate another hour.
4. Heat grill to 350 degrees.
5. Place tenderloin on grill directly over heat for 7 minutes to sear, basting once with marinade.
6. Turn tenderloin and grill for 24 minutes, basting once.
7. Turn off heat under thinner end of tenderloin. Reduce heat to low under thicker end of tenderloin and continue to cook until you reach desired degree of doneness. (145 degrees for rare, 160 degrees for medium rare — anything beyond that and you should not be buying this quality of meat in the first place.)
8. Let meat rest for 10 minutes prior to slicing; this allows the juices to flow throughout the tenderloin before being pierced.
9. Cut into ¼- to ½-inch rounds and arrange on a platter with a bowl of White Horseradish Sauce in the center.

LuLu Clue: Depending on how trimmed your tenderloin is when you buy it, you may need to trim it further before cooking. Follow these basic steps:

Pull away the outer layer of fat to expose the fatty "chain" of meat.

Pull the chain of fat away from the meat, cut it off, and discard.

Scrape the silver skin at the creases in the thick end to expose the lobes.

Trim away the silver skin by slicing under it and cutting upward.

Turn the tenderloin over and remove the fat from the underside.

In Fairhope, Alabama, you should buy your vine-ripened, homegrown tomatoes from "The Tomato Lady" (Barbara), who can be found each day in growing season at the corner of Fairhope Avenue and Church Street.

Sliced Homegrown Tomatoes

MAKES 8 SERVINGS

4 large tomatoes, thickly sliced

¼ cup fresh basil, chiffonade (cut into ribbons)

½ Vidalia® onion, sliced into paper-thin rings

½ cup crumbled bleu cheese

2 tablespoons balsamic vinegar

2 tablespoons olive oil

Salt and pepper to taste

1. On a beautiful serving platter, arrange tomato slices.
2. Sprinkle basil over platter.
3. Arrange a thin layer of onion rings over tomatoes.
4. Crumble bleu cheese across platter.
5. Drizzle vinegar and oil over all.
6. Finish with a liberal sprinkling of salt and pepper.
7. Refrigerate for at least 1 hour before serving.

 LuLu Clue: Make sure you use a non-reactive glass or ceramic platter for tomatoes.

Summary Grilled Vegetables

MAKES 8 SERVINGS

2 zucchini

2 yellow squash

1 red bell pepper

1 orange bell pepper

1 yellow bell pepper

1 green bell pepper

1 red onion

½ cup olive oil

1 tablespoon finely chopped fresh rosemary, optional

1 tablespoon salt

2 tablespoons black pepper

1. Heat grill to 375 degrees.
2. Cut zucchini and squash in half lengthwise, then again in half lengthwise.
3. Cut all bell peppers in half lengthwise, then in thirds lengthwise.
4. Cut onion into 3 thick slices.
5. In a large bowl, toss vegetables with olive oil, rosemary, salt, and pepper, coating thoroughly.
6. Arrange vegetables on hot grill, preferably skin-side down for the first cooking side. Turn only once, after 10 minutes.
7. Grill on second side for 7 minutes longer.
8. Remove from heat and keep warm in oven as needed prior to serving.

LuLu Clue: You need to cook vegetables directly on grill to achieve the proper markings and slight caramelization. If you prefer, use a grilling basket, but the veggies won't have as strong a grilled flavor.

LuLu Clue: Use good judgment when grilling anything; take some time to get to know your grill and learn its hot spots. Vegetables have varying degrees of density and moisture content, so you'll need to adjust cooking time and placement on the grill accordingly.

Wedding Cake with White Chocolate Cream Cheese Frosting and Fresh Sliced Peaches

MAKES 10 TO 12 SERVINGS

BATTER

2 sticks butter

2 cups plus 1 tablespoon sugar, divided

½ cup milk

¾ cup chopped white chocolate or white chocolate morsels

Zest of 1 orange

1 teaspoon grated fresh gingerroot

1 cup Grand Marnier®

2 eggs

1¾ cups all-purpose flour, sifted

½ cup self-rising flour

8 fresh peaches, peeled, pitted and sliced

2 tablespoons lemon juice

WHITE CHOCOLATE CREAM CHEESE FROSTING

½ cup chopped white chocolate or white chocolate morsels

8 ounces cream cheese

½ teaspoon pure vanilla extract

2 tablespoons heavy cream

3 cups powdered sugar

1. Preheat oven to 350 degrees.
2. In a heavy saucepan, whisk together butter, 2 cups sugar, milk, and white chocolate over medium heat until butter is melted and sugar is dissolved. Transfer mixture to a large bowl and cool slightly.
3. Add orange zest, ginger, Grand Marnier®, eggs, and all flour to butter mixture. Mix well. Pour into a greased 9x13-inch cake pan.
4. Bake 30 minutes or until a toothpick inserted in the center comes out clean.
5. Run a sharp knife around the edges of the pan to loosen and invert cake onto wire rack to cool completely before frosting.
6. Toss sliced peaches with remaining 1 tablespoon sugar and lemon juice. Refrigerate.
7. To prepare frosting, melt white chocolate over low heat, stirring continuously.
8. In the bowl of an electric mixer, combine cream cheese and melted chocolate.
9. Add vanilla and heavy cream to mixture. Beat well at low speed.
10. Gradually add powdered sugar, scraping sides often, until mixture reaches a frosting consistency.
11. Spread frosting over cake. Serve with chilled peach slices.

Key Lime Tanqueray® and Tonic

MAKES 1 DRINK

1 fresh Key lime
Ice cubes
2 ounces Tanqueray® gin
4 ounces tonic
Key lime slice to garnish

1. Cut a Key lime into quarters. Squeeze 2 quarters into a tall glass, making sure to get out all the oil and juice. Place squeezed limes at the bottom of the glass.
2. Fill glass to the top with ice cubes.
3. Squeeze remaining 2 lime quarters on top of ice.
4. Fill one-third of the glass with gin (or more…if you'd like).
5. Fill the rest of glass with tonic.
6. Gently stir the mixture with the knife used to cut the lime.
7. Garnish with a Key lime slice.

New Orleans
Jazz Fest Thursday
Dinner Party

MARGARITA-GLAZED CORNISH HEN

BRIDGET'S CRAWFISH ENCHILADA

BOUDREAUX'S NEW ORLEANS JAZZ FEST GUACAMOLE

CUBAN BLACK BEANS WITH YELLOW RICE

BARQ'S® ROOT BEER CHOCOLATE CAKE

PIMM'S® NO. 1 CUP À LA NAPOLEON HOUSE

Laissez Le Bon Temps Olé!

If Mardi Gras in New Orleans is known for the pageant of decadence and frivolity, then the New Orleans Jazz & Heritage Festival is the celebration of that unique city's music, food, and culture. I've been going since twenty-something had some meaning to me. Just suffice it to say, it has been a long, long time. The festival itself unfolds on numerous stages and in tents at the race track in Mid-City and is held for two consecutive weekends in the spring. The assortment of exceptional music performed includes not only jazz, but also gospel, blues, world funk, and good ol' rock and roll. Hundreds of food tents serve up regional specialties like vats of steaming jambalaya, red beans and rice, crawfish cooked in every imaginable way, fried soft-shell crabs, cochon de lait po-boys, enormous pans of bread pudding, and Louisiana strawberries with shortcake, to name just a few. Artisans sell their wares in blocks and blocks of booths. Indians — both the Mardi Gras and Native American varieties — parade in full native dress around the fairgrounds, mingling with the hundreds of thousands of folks who attend each year. There are literally acres and acres of sensory stimulation. It's truly impossible to describe. It simply must be experienced.

As exciting as the festival is, what goes on around the city is equally exhilarating. Hotels and restaurants are full. The streets are brimming with festival-goers who continue their reverent tribute to the fête by hauling their tired, sweaty bodies into nightclubs blaring even more fabulous music and dancing into the wee hours of morning. At the same time, parties are being held in homes bursting at the seams with out-of-town friends. It's sort of reminiscent of a slumber party or a college dorm. A CEO and a carpenter, who see each other once a year because they share a love of music, will also share a bathroom down the hall. Everyone pitches in and does the dishes or runs to the corner store for more ice. Jazz Fest is for the real people; it's not about the VIP.

Such is the scenario each year at the gracious French Quarter home of my friend, Bob Edmunson. I am one of his Jazz Fest "squatters" and share the top floor of his guest quarters with our mutual gal pal, Bridget Balentine and her husband Rick. Bridget and I also used to live around the corner from each other in the French Quarter and were partners in crime in many pursuits, but mainly we love to cook together.

Every year all of us host a dinner party that, like the Jazz Fest itself, started with humble beginnings. Now it's a 300-person event and one of the social stops on the circuit. It all started when I decided to make a pot of black beans and some salsa to have for dinner after a long day at the fairgrounds and as a thank you to Bob for his hospitality. Bridget whipped up a crawfish enchilada, and Bob decided he would make frozen margaritas and his "own" guacamole. The girls were appalled when he added hard-boiled eggs to the dish and were equally astonished to discover how good it made the guac. We fed it to all of the out-of-towners and local friends — thus was a tradition born.

The menu has evolved over the years, and we've enlisted help so that we can enjoy the party instead of "work it." Since I opened LuLu's, however, I've had to skip a couple of years because the restaurant biz "ain't no joke" (as my girlfriends in L.A. used to say). The years that I've missed, I wasn't even missed. When asked where I was, Bob or Bridget would respond that I was in the kitchen or on the patio. Besides, I'm always there in spirit.

LuLu and Bridget
"We've lost Boudreaux…again!!!"

Margarita-Glazed Cornish Hens

SERVES 8

MARGARITA MARINADE

½ cup tequila

2 tablespoons triple sec

½ cup freshly squeezed lime juice

½ cup orange juice

¼ cup extra virgin olive oil

1 teaspoon salt

1 teaspoon sugar

10 cloves garlic, peeled and halved

1 jalapeño pepper, seeded and
    finely chopped

8 Cornish hens

Salt and pepper to taste

Paprika to taste

½ cup tequila

3 tablespoons triple sec

3 tablespoons Rose's® lime juice

3 cups chicken broth

¼ cup coarsely chopped cilantro

1. Combine all marinade ingredients in a jar and shake well. Set aside for several hours before using.
2. Divide hens between 2 (1-gallon) zip-top bags. Pour marinade into each bag. Seal bags, making sure they are closed tightly. Refrigerate hens for 2 hours.
3. Preheat oven to 400 degrees.
4. Place hens and marinade in a large roasting pan and sprinkle generously with salt and pepper and paprika.
5. Basting hens every 15 minutes, roast for 1 hour or until birds are beautifully browned. Turn off the oven.
6. Remove hens from pan and place on a serving tray. Return to oven to keep warm.
7. Place roasting pan with drippings on stovetop over medium heat.
8. Add tequila, triple sec, lime juice, and chicken broth. Stirring constantly and scraping the bottom of the pan, cook until sauce is reduced to about 2 cups.
9. Drizzle sauce over hens, sprinkle with cilantro, and serve immediately.

LuLu with head chef, Dylan Feenker

I asked my dear friend Bridget to let me use her spicy, sassy enchilada recipe, only to discover that her "version" is essentially K-Paul's with her own brand of sexy blended in. The secret, she says, is in the amount of cleavage revealed while cooking! "Leaning over the shredded cheese and thinking about all the spicy things in life makes it all the mo' better," declares Bridget. "Basically, it's just 'tails, trinity, cheese, butter, and cream, wrapped in a warm tortilla hug!" And don't forget to dress in high heels to cook; show off those great legs.

Bridget's Crawfish Enchilada

MAKES 8 TO 10 SERVINGS

2 sticks unsalted butter, divided

1 cup finely chopped sweet yellow onions

1 cup chopped canned green chilies, drained

¾ cup finely chopped green bell peppers

1 teaspoon finely chopped garlic

2½ teaspoons salt, divided

2½ teaspoons white pepper, divided

1½ teaspoons LuLu's Chipotle Taco Seasoning (page 49), divided

3 cups heavy cream

1 cup sour cream

8 cups shredded Monterey Jack cheese, divided

2 pounds crawfish tails, peeled

⅔ cup finely chopped green onions

¾ teaspoon oregano

20 (6-inch) corn tortillas

1. Preheat oven to 350 degrees.
2. In a large skillet, melt 1 stick of butter. Sauté yellow onions, green chilies, bell peppers, garlic, 1¼ teaspoons salt, 1¼ teaspoons pepper, and ¾ teaspoon seasoning over medium heat for about 10 minutes until vegetables are tender and onions are translucent.
3. Stir in heavy cream and bring mixture to a rapid boil. Reduce heat and simmer, uncovered, for 10 minutes, stirring constantly.
4. Add sour cream and stir continuously for about 3 minutes. Add 3 cups cheese and stir until melted. Set cheese sauce to the side.
5. In a large saucepan, melt remaining stick of butter. Add crawfish tails, green onions, oregano, remaining 1¼ teaspoons salt, remaining 1¼ teaspoons pepper, and remaining ¾ teaspoon seasoning. Sauté over medium heat for 5 to 6 minutes.
6. Add half of the cheese sauce to crawfish mixture and stir well. Simmer for about 10 minutes, stirring occasionally.
7. Spoon about ⅓ cup crawfish mixture over each tortilla. Roll up tortilla and place, seam-side down, in a deep baking pan, lining enchiladas up until pan is filled.
8. Cover enchiladas with remaining cheese sauce. Sprinkle the top with remaining 5 cups shredded cheese.
9. Bake until cheese is fully melted and golden brown.

LuLu Clue: I like cheese in almost any form, but some of the yummiest is the browned, slightly burnt cheese that you get when you run a dish like this under a broiler for a couple minutes. It makes the dish look beautiful and, if possible, even tastier.

Boudreaux plays fast

and loose with the "rules" of recipe-making with this dish; it isn't intended to be exact or precise. It depends largely on your own willingness to experiment, much like the very jazz whose heritage we celebrate every year in New Orleans. Other than the avocados, olive oil, oregano, jalapeño, and green peppers, all other ingredients can be added "to taste," which of course leads to the recommendation that you sample as you go (one of the great joys of the whole process). Add ingredients to the mix slowly, tasting as you go, to create the flavor you like the best, especially as you add the hot sauce. There is a delicate balance to maintain here — hot sauce adds a lovely flavor, but can overpower the avocado if you put in too much.

Boudreaux's New Orleans Jazz Fest Guacamole
(As translated to English by Bob Edmundson)

MAKES ABOUT 1 QUART

20 ripe avocados, peeled and pitted (reserve pits)

1 teaspoon extra virgin olive oil

2 tablespoons freshly squeezed lemon juice

3-4 tablespoons freshly squeezed lime juice

½ cup finely chopped Vidalia® or sweet onions

¼ cup finely chopped green onions

¼ cup finely chopped green bell peppers

½ tablespoon finely chopped fresh jalapeño peppers

3 tablespoons finely chopped fresh cilantro

Pinch of oregano

1½-2 hard-boiled eggs, finely chopped

1 tablespoon LuLu's Perfect Pepper Hot Sauce™, or to taste

Sea salt and pepper to taste

1 fresh tomato, blanched, peeled, seeded and finely chopped, optional

Blue and yellow tortilla chips

1. Chop avocado into medium-large chunks.
2. In large mixing bowl, lightly toss avocados with olive oil, lemon juice, and lime juice.
3. Gently mix in all onions, bell peppers, jalapeño peppers, cilantro, and oregano.
4. Add boiled eggs, hot sauce, and salt and pepper. Mix gently to preferred consistency, adding tomatoes at end.
5. Add several fresh avocado pits to keep the guacamole from turning brown. Cover and chill at least 3 to 4 hours prior to serving to allow the flavors to develop.
6. Remove from refrigerator 30 to 45 minutes before serving. Serve with tortilla chips.

 Boudreaux Note: Unless you are always the lucky produce shopper with impeccable timing, Boudreaux suggests that you buy the avocados in advance while still green and ripen them yourself using the old "box-in-the-closet" or brown paper bag trick. Allow about 4 to 5 days for them to ripen.

 Boudreaux Caution: Simultaneous tequila consumption during preparation can affect your taste buds. Therefore, it is essential that you do not prepare or serve this guacamole with cheap tequila or poorly made margaritas. Good guacamole requires a loving partner to reach its full culinary potential, and we all know cheap tequila has never and will never be a loving culinary partner. There is absolutely no need to even have the brain cell debacle discussion here.

Cuban Black Beans with Yellow Rice

MAKES 8 TO 10 SERVINGS

1 pound dry black beans

7 cups water

2 tablespoons extra virgin olive oil

1 cup diced ham

1 medium onion, chopped

1 green pepper, chopped

2 ribs celery, chopped

1 whole jalapeño, optional

1½ teaspoons salt, divided

1 teaspoon pepper, divided

2 bay leaves

2 teaspoons cumin

1 teaspoon coriander

½ teaspoon oregano

¼-½ cup LuLu's Clearly Crazy Hot Sauce™ or white vinegar

1 (10-ounce) package saffron yellow rice

1. Pick through beans for debris. Soak beans overnight and drain. Rinse well.

2. In a Dutch oven, cover beans with 7 cups water and boil over medium-high heat.

3. In a heavy sauté pan, heat olive oil. Add ham, onions, bell peppers, celery, and whole jalapeño and sauté until slightly tender. Season with 1 teaspoon salt and ½ teaspoon pepper. Add mixture to beans.

4. Add bay leaves, cumin, coriander, and oregano. Stir in remaining ½ teaspoon salt and remaining ½ teaspoon pepper.

5. Cook at a slow boil for at least 1½ hours. Stir beans often, making sure they don't stick to the bottom of the pot. As the beans cook down, add a little more water if necessary.

6. Just before serving, remove jalapeño and add pepper sauce or vinegar. Stir well.

7. Prepare yellow rice according to package instructions. Serve rice with beans.

Barq's® Root Beer Chocolate Cake

MAKES 1 CAKE

BATTER

1 (18-ounce) box chocolate cake mix

1 cup root beer, room temperature

½ cup vegetable oil

¼ cup water

3 eggs

CHOCOLATE CREAM CHEESE FROSTING

4 cups powdered sugar, sifted

⅓ cup cocoa powder

½ teaspoon cinnamon

8 ounces cream cheese, softened

1 stick butter, softened

1 teaspoon pure vanilla extract

1. Preheat oven to 350 degrees.
2. In a large mixing bowl, combine cake mix, root beer, oil, water, and eggs.
3. Mix well and beat with an electric mixer on medium speed for 2 minutes.
4. Pour batter into a lightly greased 9x13-inch cake pan and tap pan lightly on countertop to release air bubbles.
5. Bake 30 to 35 minutes or until a toothpick inserted in the center comes out clean. Cool completely on a wire rack.
6. To prepare frosting, combine powdered sugar, cocoa, and cinnamon in a large bowl; set aside.
7. Beat cream cheese, butter, and vanilla together until smooth.
8. Gradually fold dry ingredients into cream cheese mixture until well blended.
9. Spread frosting over cooled cake.

Pimm's® No.1 Cup à la Napoleon House

MAKES 1 DRINK

1¼ ounces Pimm's® No. 1

3 ounces lemonade

Splash of lemon-lime soda

Cucumber wedge

Mint leaves

Orange slice

1. Fill a tall 12-ounce glass with ice.
2. Add Pimm's® and lemonade.
3. Top off with lemon-lime soda.
4. Garnish with a cucumber wedge, mint leaves, and an orange slice.

Montana Rodeo Picnic

SHRIMP, ANDOUILLE AND CHICKEN JAMBALAYA

GIDDYUP LAYERED SALAD

GARLIC BREAD

CHOCOLATE CHESS PIE

WASHTUB FULL OF COLD BEER

Cowboys Love Shrimp

My husband Tom and I share a love of cutting horses and Alabama seafood. So it was fitting that we would hold an annual gumbo party, with LuLu as the chef, in conjunction with hosting a cutting horse circuit on our ranch in Montana.

Every year we anxiously anticipated LuLu's arrival at the airport, praying the hundreds of pounds of shrimp and crabmeat would arrive on the same plane with her. Usually, after one of these parties, LuLu and I would say, "never again." It became a running joke as we named each party, "The Last Annual Gumbo Party." However, the demand was too high amongst the cowboys and cowgirls. They all knew LuLu and wanted to visit with her every summer and enjoy the fabulous food. We did this for more than fifteen years!

One party in particular is most memorable. It was blazing hot. LuLu had been prepping in the kitchen all day as the competition was rolling along in our barn. Three hundred people were expected at the party after the show. I was sitting on my horse preparing to compete when LuLu walked up to me and whispered, "It's gone bad."

"What's gone bad?" I asked. Then I realized that the roux preparation had spoiled. "Oh god, what do we do?" "Open the bar early, and I'll figure something out," she said.

Luckily, the seafood had not been added to the roux. LuLu put out an S.O.S. She had cowboys driving twenty miles to town for peppers, celery, and okra. She had Norma, our aide de camp, and many friends stirring the re-made roux to perfect consistency. The party was a bit late. No one cared. The gumbo was exceptional.

By the end of the evening, we had runaway housewives, and runaway cowboys, some ending up in Canada and some in Wyoming, along with runaway cattle, which turned our newly-sodded lawn into a landscaper's nightmare. It was all good.

Thank you, my dear sister, for the memories.

Laurie Buffett
McGuane
McLeod,
Montana

Laurie "LaLa" and
Tom McGuane, Montana

Shrimp, Andouille, and Chicken Jambalaya

SERVES 12

1 whole chicken (about 2 pounds cooked meat)

6 bay leaves, divided

1 pound andouille sausage, cut into ¼-inch rounds

1 stick butter

2 tablespoons finely chopped garlic

3 cups chopped sweet yellow onions

1 cup chopped green onions

1 cup chopped green bell peppers

1 cup chopped celery

3 cups Uncle Ben's® white rice

1 (28-ounce) can whole tomatoes, coarsely chopped, with liquid

5 cups chicken broth

1 tablespoon Worcestershire sauce

3 tablespoons LuLu's Crazy Creola Seasoning™ (page 50)

¼ teaspoon cayenne pepper

1 tablespoon thyme

1 teaspoon oregano

1 tablespoon salt

1 teaspoon black pepper

1 pound large shrimp, peeled and deveined

¼ cup chopped parsley

1. Preheat oven to 375 degrees.
2. Place whole chicken in a large stockpot. Cover with water, add 2 bay leaves, and boil chicken until tender. Remove from broth and cool.
3. Remove and discard chicken skin and bones. Chop chicken into large bite-sized pieces. Set aside.
4. Cook sausage in a cast iron or heavy skillet over medium heat until browned. Drain on paper towels.
5. In a large, heavy sauté pan, heat butter over low heat.
6. Add garlic and sauté for about 1 minute; do not allow garlic to brown.
7. Add yellow and green onions and cook for 2 minutes.
8. Add bell peppers and celery. Stir well. Cook for 5 minutes.
9. Place rice in a greased 4-quart baking dish. Mix in chicken, sausage, vegetables, and tomatoes.
10. Add broth, Worcestershire, remaining 4 bay leaves, Creole seasoning, cayenne pepper, thyme, oregano, salt, and black pepper. Mix well.
11. Add shrimp. Mix well and press down to make sure rice is wet with broth.
12. Top with parsley. Tightly cover with aluminum foil.
13. Bake for 45 minutes.

Giddyup Layered Salad

MAKES 8 TO 10 SERVINGS

1 cup frozen shelled edamame
(soybeans) or frozen green
peas

1½ teaspoons salt, divided

1 cup mayonnaise

½ teaspoon sugar

¼ teaspoon white pepper

½ cup shredded Parmesan cheese

1 tablespoon finely chopped fresh
basil, optional

1 head red-leaf lettuce, chopped

½ cup coarsely grated carrots

1½ cups cherry tomatoes,
quartered

¾ cup radishes, thinly sliced in
half-moons

1 cup yellow bell peppers, thinly
sliced in 2-inch strips

¼-½ cup red onion, quartered and
thinly sliced

1. Place edamame in 3 cups boiling water. Add 1 teaspoon salt. Cook, uncovered, over medium heat for about 5 minutes or until tender. Drain and cool completely; set aside.

2. Combine mayonnaise, sugar, white pepper, Parmesan, basil, and remaining ½ teaspoon salt. Mix thoroughly and set aside.

3. In a deep glass bowl, layer the following in order listed: lettuce, carrots, tomatoes, edamame, radishes, bell peppers, and onions.

4. Spread mayonnaise mixture evenly over entire salad, sealing edges. Cover with plastic wrap and refrigerate at least 6 hours or preferably overnight.

5. Serve using tongs and make sure each serving includes all salad layers.

LuLu Clue: Be sure to use a glass bowl; this salad is as pretty as it is tasty.

LaLa in her element

Okay, the truth is

I almost always burn the bread at least once. Sort of like I can never get out of the house on the first try without coming back for something I've forgotten. Garlic bread is so easy that if I could, I'd make it every night. But as my body settles into its 2nd half-century, it's best to serve it just at parties or special dinners. If I was marooned on a desert island and had to choose what I would have to eat for the rest of my life, bread and cheese would definitely be at the top of my list.

Garlic Bread

1 loaf French bread

1 stick unsalted butter, softened

4 cloves garlic, put through garlic press or finely chopped

1-2 tablespoons finely chopped fresh parsley

1 tablespoon LuLu's Crazy Creola Seasoning™ (page 50)

½ cup shredded Parmesan cheese

1. Preheat oven to 350 degrees.
2. Slice bread horizontally.
3. Combine butter, garlic, and parsley. Mix well and spread over cut side of bread halves.
4. Sprinkle with Creole seasoning. Place bread halves back together and wrap in aluminum foil.
5. Bake for 15 minutes. Remove bread and turn oven to broil.
6. Carefully open bread and place open-faced on a broiler pan.
7. Sprinkle Parmesan cheese over bread and run under broiler until bread is brown and toasted. Remove and cut into 1-inch pieces. Serve immediately.

 LuLu Clue: Depending on what I'm serving for dinner, I sometimes use chopped basil or rosemary as a substitution for the parsley. If you like your bread soft instead of toasted, simply skip broiling it.

Chocolate Chess Pie

MAKES 6 TO 8 SERVINGS

2 (1-ounce) semi-sweet chocolate squares, melted

2 eggs

1½ cups granulated sugar

1 (5-ounce) can evaporated milk

4 tablespoons butter, softened

1 teaspoon vanilla

1 (9-inch) pie shell, unbaked

1. Preheat oven to 350 degrees.
2. In a small saucepan, melt chocolate over medium-low heat. Set aside and cool slightly.
3. In a large bowl, beat eggs. Add sugar and beat well. Beat in evaporated milk. Add chocolate, butter, and vanilla and mix well.
4. Pour filling into an unbaked pie shell.
5. Bake for 40 to 45 minutes. Cool for 15 to 20 minutes before serving.

LuLu and LaLa

A LOVE LETTER FROM DIDI

A day with my best friend Lucy (we lucky creatures know her as "Crazy Sista"): We saddle up our horses and head out for our daily ride. (Need I mention that they are the smartest and most beautiful horses on this Earth? I'm talking to you, Banjo!) Usually it's four of us: Lucy, Jan, Paco or Banjo, and me. Sometimes other girlfriends ride along, but normally it's just us.

Once we return to the barn, the real fun begins. We crank up some music and Crazy Sista becomes Chef Lucy. She uncorks some bubbly and gets busy in the kitchen whipping up something she's been thinking about for a while. Lucy's signature dishes are usually accompanied with hours of visiting, eating and sipping wine late into the evening.

What fun to have a best friend that you love to ride, laugh and even cry with... one who'll cook for you to heal your soul. That's my friend Lucy.

I love you Sista,
Dilana

LuLu and friend Dilana Norman

Deep South Sunday Dinner

GRILLLED PORK TENDERLOIN MEDALLIONS

TURNIP GREENS

FRESH FIELD PEAS

J.D.'S BLACK-SKILLET OKRA

JOSIE'S MAC AND CHEESE

HOT WATER CORNBREAD

SOUTHERN STYLE PEACH COBBLER
WITH HOMEMADE VANILLA ICE CREAM

FEED YOUR SOUL

Sundays in the South are all about family and food. Specifically, comfort food. It is the day for slow-cooking and apron strings, rocking chairs and front porches, breaking out the "good" dishes and good "dishing." We talk a lot; it's too hot most times to do much else, and a dinner table laden with food is the perfect place for lively banter.

As I learned at the knee of my grandmother Hilda "Mom" Buffett, who cooked each and every Sunday just like this, some things are just simply a given when it comes to Sunday "dinner." First of all, it isn't served at night (that's "supper"), but just after y'all get home from church. Not only must you serve turnip greens, you must serve them with pepper sauce and cornbread for "sopping." Bacon is the basis for *all* skillet-cooking. If you aren't serving fried chicken, then you serve a roasted meat. Okra — period. You'll definitely have a big pot of butter beans or field peas simmering in seasoning. And what tastes more like comfort than homemade mac-n-cheese? And finally, sweet tea. For those of you outside the Bible Belt, we serve two kinds of tea here: sweet and unsweet, both iced. Sweet tea is not, as some foolish restaurateurs would have you think, unsweet tea with packages of powdery confection stirred in after the fact. It is made sweet while the tea is still piping hot from steeping, then diluted and poured over ice. (Created by Jazzercise® and yuppies, unsweet tea is an abomination we are forced to serve, grudgingly and against better judgment.) Mom Buffett expected us for dinner in Pascagoula at least once a month and served a classic meal for the whole family, divided, of course into grown-ups table and kids' table.

The cornbread on this menu won't taste anything like store-bought cornbread mixes. It is seriously old-school, with roots traced to slave cuisine, an influence that inspires Southern cooking indelibly. It is also known as "scald meal" and it is unique to the Deep South. You make up a mess of small patties; this isn't a pan of baked cornbread. The cakes become gold and crispy and are supposed to be dense in the middle.

Cousin Tricia, LaLa, Bubba, & LuLu, circa 1954

Grilled Pork Tenderloin Medallions

MAKES 8 TO 10 SERVINGS

2 (¾-pound) pork tenderloins

Salt and pepper to taste

1 cup One Heart Marinade
(page 48)

1 tablespoon Dijon mustard

1 tablespoon loosely packed dark
brown sugar

1. Season all sides of tenderloins generously with salt and pepper; set aside.
2. Combine marinade, mustard, and brown sugar.
3. Place seasoned tenderloins in a glass or plastic bowl and cover with marinade mixture. Let stand for at least 30 minutes.
4. Preheat a gas grill to high heat, or prepare a charcoal grill.
5. Sear tenderloins on each side, about 4 minutes per side.
6. Move pork loins to indirect heat and cook with lid closed for 6 minutes on each side. Pork should be crispy on the outside and still a little pink on the inside...not rare, just a little pink... trust me.
7. Remove pork loins from the grill and let rest for 10 minutes.
8. Slice into ½-inch thick medallions.

LuLu Clue: Grilling is a proud science to every man I know. Mac's son, Joe, made this pork tenderloin for me. Perhaps because he is a boat captain, he likes to be aware of all the variables that might affect his grilling. Joe makes sure to check the wind speed and direction along with the barometric pressure before stepping up to the grill. Perhaps it's this attention to detail that makes all of his grilled food perfect.

LuLu Clue: I prefer to use fresh field peas, but dried peas are fine too. If using dried peas, make sure you wash them well and soak overnight. Also, dried peas will take a little longer to cook.

Fresh Field Peas

MAKES 8 TO 10 SERVINGS

2 slices bacon, cut into 2-inch pieces

1 tablespoon extra virgin olive oil

1 sweet yellow onion, chopped

½ teaspoon sugar

¼ cup chicken broth

4 cups fresh field peas

2-3 cups water

1 clove garlic, minced

1 teaspoon salt

½ teaspoon freshly ground black pepper

1. In a large saucepan, fry bacon pieces over a medium-high heat until bacon is almost crispy.
2. Add olive oil and heat through, until just about to sizzle.
3. Add onions and sugar and cook with the bacon until onions are soft and translucent.
4. Add chicken broth to deglaze the pan.
5. Add peas and just enough water to cover the peas. Bring to a boil.
6. Lower heat and cover. Cook peas for 30 minutes or until peas start to soften.
7. Add garlic, salt, and pepper and cook 5 minutes longer.

LuLu Clue: Taste and add salt if needed. You may need more liquid or water as peas cook down. Adding chicken broth gives the peas a heartier flavor.

LuLu Clue: Deglazing is done to collect all the tasty bits that may have become stuck to the bottom of the pan while cooking. You can use any liquid, such as broth or wine. Using a straight-edge wooden spatula, scrape all the little bits of food from the bottom and sides of the pan. The flavors dissolve and melt into the peas while cooking.

LuLu Clue: It's essential to clean turnip greens well prior to cooking. They can be very gritty and dirty, and it will ruin your meal to find mud in your mouth. They should be washed at least three times. My dear friend Nida's mama used to clean hers in a pillowcase in the washing machine.

Turnip Greens

MAKES 8-10 SERVINGS

**5 pounds fresh turnip greens
(about 3 large bunches)**

4 tablespoons butter

1 cup chopped cured ham

1 cup chopped sweet yellow onions

¼ teaspoon dried red pepper flakes

2 cups water

1 teaspoon sugar

1 teaspoon salt

½ teaspoon black pepper

**2-3 turnip roots, peeled and cut
into ½-inch cubes**

**LuLu's Clearly Crazy Hot Sauce™
or pepper vinegar**

1. Prepare turnip greens by cutting off tough stems and any discolored leaves. Wash greens thoroughly.
2. In an 8-quart stock pot, melt butter over medium heat.
3. Add ham and cook for 1 minute.
4. Add onions and sauté for 3 minutes or until onions are soft.
5. Add turnips greens, pepper flakes, water, sugar, salt, and black pepper.
6. Bring to a boil. Reduce heat to low. Cover and simmer for 50 to 60 minutes or until turnips greens are tender.
7. Add turnip roots and cook, stirring occasionally, for 15 minutes or until roots are tender.
8. Serve with pepper vinegar.

LuLu Clue: Turnip greens freeze well, don't be afraid of making too much!

LuLu Clue: The liquid or juice that slowly cooks down with the greens is lovingly referred to as "pot liquor." Heaven, around here, is known as hot water cornbread soaked in pot liquor.

*Red Velvet Girlfriend
& Mac and Cheese Maestro,
Jo Ann Glasscock*

J.D.'s Black Skillet Okra

MAKES 8 TO 10 SIDE DISH SERVINGS

2 slices bacon, cut into 2-inch pieces

1 yellow onion, finely chopped

½ tablespoon sugar

4 cups fresh okra, sliced ½-inch thick

1 teaspoon salt

¼ teaspoon black pepper

1. In a heavy skillet, fry bacon pieces over medium heat until bacon is almost crisp.
2. Add onion and sugar and sauté until onion begins to brown and caramelize.
3. Add okra, salt, and pepper. Reduce heat to low and cover with lid to allow steam to cook the okra down, about 10 minutes.
4. Remove lid and continue to stir occasionally until okra browns.

Josie's Mac and Cheese

MAKES 8 TO 10 SERVINGS

4 cups water

1 (8-ounce) package elbow macaroni

2 eggs, well beaten

2 cups whole milk

7 cups coarsely shredded New York sharp cheese, divided

Salt and pepper to taste

1. Preheat oven to 300 degrees.
2. In a medium saucepan, bring water to a boil. Add macaroni and cook for 20 minutes or until macaroni is tender; drain.
3. In a large mixing bowl, combine drained macaroni, eggs, whole milk, and 6 cups cheese. Season with salt and pepper.
4. Pour mixture into a greased 8x11-inch casserole dish. Spread remaining 1 cup cheese evenly on top.
5. Bake for 30 minutes or until well set. Increase oven temperature to 400 degrees.
6. Bake 10 to 15 minutes longer or until top is brown.

Hot Water Cornbread

MAKES 10 SERVINGS

4 cups white self-rising cornmeal

2 tablespoons LuLu's Crazy Creola Seasoning™ (page 50)

4-5 cups boiling water

Oil for frying

1. Mix together cornmeal and Creole seasoning.
2. Slowly pour in boiling water just until wet enough to form patties. Wait until cool enough to handle.
3. Scoop up by spoonfuls and shape into patties. You can make them round and push them into flatter patties.
4. Drop patties into 3 to 4 inches hot oil and fry until golden brown.
5. Remove from oil and place on a plate lined with paper towels to absorb excess oil.

Southern Style Peach Cobbler with Homemade Vanilla Ice Cream

MAKES 8 TO 10 SERVINGS

4 tablespoons butter

6 cups peeled and sliced peaches

½ cup light brown sugar

½ teaspoon ground cinnamon

¼ teaspoon ground nutmeg

2 teaspoons freshly squeezed lemon juice

1 tablespoon finely chopped gingerroot

2 cups Bisquick® baking mix

½ cup sugar

1½ cups milk

1. Preheat oven to 375 degrees.
2. Melt butter in a 3-quart baking dish, being careful not to burn the butter.
3. Combine peaches, brown sugar, cinnamon, nutmeg, lemon juice, and ginger. Toss to coat evenly and set aside.
4. In a large bowl, combine Bisquick®, sugar, and milk.
5. Pour dough over melted butter, but do not stir the butter and dough together. Use your hands to press the dough to the edges of the pan.
6. Pour fruit mixture on top of the dough. The dough will bake up and over the fruit.
7. Bake 45 to 50 minutes or until the fruit is slightly brown and bubbly.
8. Serve with Homemade Vanilla Ice Cream (recipe below).

HOMEMADE VANILLA ICE CREAM

5 eggs

2 cups sugar

2 quarts whole milk

2 (14-ounce) cans sweetened condensed milk

2 cups heavy cream

4 tablespoons pure vanilla extract

Crushed ice

Rock salt

1. Beat together eggs and sugar. Add whole milk and stir well.
2. Transfer mixture to a heavy saucepan and cook slowly over medium-low heat, stirring constantly, until mixture coats the spoon. Remove from heat and cool thoroughly.
3. Add condensed milk, heavy cream, and vanilla.
4. Pour mixture into the metal canister of an electric ice cream freezer, filling only three-fourths of the way to the top.
5. Insert paddle and return canister to barrel of freezer.
6. Surround canister with 4 inches of ice. Add a layer of rock salt. Repeat ice and salt layers until you reach the level just below the canister lid.
7. Freeze as directed by freezer manufacturer.

LuLu Clue: Prepare ice cream outside or in a sink to avoid making a huge mess. Or if this is all just way too hard, pick up a pint of Häagen Dazs® Vanilla Ice Cream and call it church.

Ice Chest and Picnic Basics

WEST INDIES SALAD

PIMENTO CHEESE TEA SANDWICHES

CHILLED PEEL AND EAT SHRIMP

CHERRY TOMATOES

WATERMELON CHUNKS

COLD FRIED CHICKEN

DEVILED EGGS

MOTHER'S MILK

VODKA AND PINK GRAPEFRUIT JUICE

COLD BEER ~ BOTTLED WATER

We spend a lot of time boating around our neighborhood: Weeks Bay, Fish River, Magnolia River, Mobile Bay, Bon Secour River, Terry Cove, Cotton Bayou, Oyster Bay, Wolf Bay, Perdido Bay, Ole River, the Gulf of Mexico, and let's not forget LuLu's front yard — the Intracoastal Waterway. My husband is a boat designer with a successful, innovative line of new boats; our friends are boaters; and, of course, I come from a long line of sailors and boat lovers. With all of that, I guess it goes without saying that we've learned how to pack a cooler for a day of fun in the sun. Here are some tried-and-true boat-ride favorites:

Boat Food ~ Ice Chest and Picnic Basics

West Indies Salad (page 99) — Make sure you pack plenty of saltine crackers and a roll of paper towels (works better than loose napkins).

Pimento Party Cheese Tea Sandwiches (page 119) — Keep these wrapped in waxed paper in a zip-top bag to prevent them from getting soggy.

Chilled Peel and Eat Shrimp (page 95) — Bring along some Red Horseradish Sauce (page 174) and lemons in small containers. Peel the shrimp over the side of the boat and use the lemons to clean your hands.

Cherry Tomatoes — If my husband was stranded on a deserted island and had to eat the same food for the rest of his life, it would be tomatoes, preferably sliced homegrown German Johnson tomatoes that he grows in his garden. We have tomatoes at almost every meal! When tomatoes are not in season, I always use cherry tomatoes, especially when we picnic on the boat, because they are easy to pop in your mouth with no mess or fuss.

Watermelon Chunks — Sure, you can drag a whole watermelon on board and carve it up right there, but if your captain's a stickler for keeping the sole of the boat clean, it's probably best to go ahead and cut the melon up into chunks ahead of time and pack them in a zip-top bag. When you have been out in the boat all day and you are feeling salty and parched, there is nothing quite as refreshing as eating ice cold chunks of sweet watermelon.

Cold Fried Chicken — This is a standard ice-chest staple, just as delicious cold as hot — perfect for a long haul to the perfect green waters of Destin. Make a run to your best local fried chicken joint the day before your trip and refrigerate overnight.

Mac's boat

Deviled Eggs — This is such old-school picnic food, but every time I serve them, they are scooped up well before the fancier fare. I just love them, and they remind me of the summertime cocktail parties that my parents took me to when we stayed "over the Bay" in Point Clear, Alabama.

Mother's Milk (page 87) — Sid, owner of Sloppy Joe's in Key West, informed us once, "Of course you can drink rum all day...but you can't drink Coca-Cola® all day." So his solution is "Mother's Milk," a not-too-sweet rum, such as Mount Gay® or an Anejo rum, topped off with club soda and just a splash of Coke®.

Vodka and Freshly-Squeezed Pink Grapefruit Juice — My all-time favorite cocktail: bring along a thermos of freshly-squeezed pink grapefruit juice (it is imperative that it be fresh - there is no substitute) and give your vodka a bit of color.

Ice Cold Beer and Bottled Water — The beer is to toast the first fish you catch, even it is 7:30 a.m. The water is to ease your conscience for drinking beer before noon and a necessary item in case you run out of gas or have engine problems. Even if you ordinarily drink beer from a bottle, it's best to pack canned beer. You'll drastically reduce the risk of injury, and just in case some fool litters, you can race back and pick up a floating can.

 LuLu Clue: Use separate coolers for drink-ice and food. You'll go into your drink-ice cooler far more often and you want the food to stay as cool as possible. If your cooler's large enough, block ice is a good idea for the food. And pack plenty of ice — more than you think you'll need. Worst case scenario is that it will melt. Big deal. It's not expensive, and you'll wish you had some when you run out on a hot August day miles away from the nearest marina!

Note: Page numbers in *italics* refer to photographs.

Recipe Index

A Very Special Acknowledgement:

Deep gratitude and enduring love to my Nutty Professor, Mac McAleer. Your tireless passion, persistence, and out-of-the-box thinking elevated LuLu's (and me) to another level.

ACKNOWLEDGEMENTS

Writing is a solitary adventure, but publishing a cookbook requires the "multitudes." Having many cooks did not spoil this broth. A lot of people helped make this book a savory and spicy gumbo of recipes and stories.

First, thank you to everyone at Wimmer Cookbooks, especially Kimberly Eller and Ardith Bradshaw, for making this first-time publishing experience exceptionally easy and rewarding. I would also like to mention Doug McNeill, Melanie Thompson, Jim Hall, and Maureen Fortune for going the extra mile.

The reason this cookbook even exists is because of LuLu's, my little dive that could, did, and continues to do so, thanks to our patrons, old-friend locals, and new-friend visitors.

I am deeply grateful to my crew at LuLu's for providing the most professional restaurant experience on the Gulf Coast. I especially want to thank Johnny Fisher, who takes the helm every day making it possible for me to guide from a distance. In your hands, LuLu's has truly flourished. Hooray for the team, especially Nancy Van Wynen and Shannon Porter, who have been with me since the beginning of LuLu-time.

Somebody's got to be the crab-claw-counter. Brenda Lake is ours and more. She reigns as LuLu's "mother superior," a loving and sage voice of reason. You are my rock. Helping Brenda with the impossible task of keeping me on the straight and narrow is my CPA and hero Jimmy Crook. You have never steered me wrong, and I am grateful you took me on as a client, even when the coffers were empty.

Some of LuLu's kitchen and bar crew contributed directly to this book: Dylan Feenker, our executive chef, I applaud your talent and the respect you exhibit every day for your galley crew. Additional thanks to Sam Stanczak, Eric Mills, and Lou & Julia Germany for preparing some of the food for our beautiful photos and to Dustin, the Gulf Coast's best bartender, for making the drinks!

It is not easy to shoot photographs in July at LuLu's. Sara Essex and Stephen Savage were warriors in "getting the shot" and produced fantastic images under hot, crowded conditions. Their photographs make the dishes mouth-watering and bring the LuLu's Lifestyle to living color. Thanks to Stephanie Easterling for great style and décor and to Sara Lake for being everywhere all the time for the photo shoots.

Every one of these recipes had to be cooked again and again to get it right. God-dess bless the posse of river-gals who tested for me: Carol Holman, Joni Noletto, Barbara Dee Cramton, and Jo Ann Glasscock, all exquisite cooks in their own right.

I raise a margarita glass to our Key West comrades. Here's to Cindy Thompson, Jed Tenney, and Dink Bruce, who always makes me feel like I've come home, and to Sunshine Smith for sprinkling a little of her guardian angel magic dust on this project. Cheers to Pat Tenney for your taste in fine champagne and always having a table for me at Louie's — thanks for your kind words!

Big kudos to the husbands of all of the women who assisted with this project for remaining invaluably supportive despite being abandoned to fend for yourselves. Special nods to Kevin, with Sushi and Baci; Mike, for the love of Diva; and of course, my own sweet Mac.

There are two women who help me keep my many plates spinning. Their fingerprints are all over this book. Debra Bigge-Holloran tackles every project I fling her way with fierce determination and elegant aplomb. Margaret Daniels is my lifeline, keeping my world behind-the-scenes quietly intact, with her delightful laugh and gentle heart. Ladies, I thank you for putting up with my crazy ninety-to-nothing life-style. At least life's never boring in the world of LuLu!

Some of my dearest friends and partners-in-crime contributed their love and their words to this book. Suffice to say, we've all had some very large times together involving food and drink, and at one time or another, each of these people has saved my life at least once: Bobbo "Baaabbbbyyyy" Jetmundsen, Bob "Boudreaux" Edmundson, Bridget Balentine, and Dilana Norman with her "baby Jesus lost and found." Thanks y'all, for always having my back.

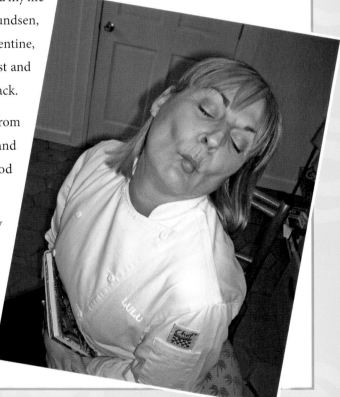

Special thanks to Chappy Hardy, the man from H.U.N.G.E.R., not only a fine food critic and gourmand, but a great cook. Getting a good review from you thrills me.

Producing this cookbook has been a family affair. Thanks to all of the children and grandchildren who comprise our merged "McBuffaleer" tribe for being willing guinea pigs, especially Karen Sipe, galley-queen and Chief Recipe Tester. Karen, you were always prepared to take on a challenge

("Y'all, there's no cheese in this pimento cheese!") and grill-master, Joe McAleer. To Mark Lumpkin, thanks for the shared memory of our Pascagoula grandmother. Very special gumbo love goes out to my wise Yogi-daughter, Melanie Buffett Ingrafia, for the clever, funny, wonderfully "pink" contributions to this book. Thank you for your memories of your grandmother and your childhood.

Tom McGuane, your encouragement and love over the years has helped keep my writing dreams breathing. Laurie "LaLa" Buffett McGuane, camp director and cowgirl extraordinaire, you are steadfast in your unconditional love and support of me. I've always been able to depend on you, and it gives me great joy to be your crazy sista. (But if I'm the crazy one, what are you?)

Jimmy "Bubba" Buffett, what can I say that I haven't said a hundred times? Thanks for having faith in me and taking a chance on LuLu's. Of the many things you've taught me over the years, probably the most important is how to live well. You continue to amaze and inspire millions of people including me. The heavens have been good to you, and you have always paid it forward by being good to family. Bravo, my brother!

Quite simply, I'd still be on page one if it weren't for these two women: Mara Buffett and Anastasia Arnold. You both wore many hats and kept the momentum going, always purring softly in the background so as not to overwhelm me. Your love and devotion quite simply pulled me through and I am humbly in your debt.

Mara, my firstborn, you've taken such good care of my words, and in the process, my health and my heart. Your star is shining brightly! Having your help on this project makes realizing this dream so much sweeter. Thank you especially for sharing Huckleberry, "tiny muse/tiny genius," with me.

Oh, Anastasia, how far we have come! You are simply the Diva, not only of words, but of life. My beloved Libra soul-sista, in your hands, my homespun stories have been transformed from home cooking to gourmet delicacies. Though I may never play Scrabble with you again, I will be eternally grateful to you for being my editor, co-author, sounding board, and political ally, but mainly for being my treasured friend.

Lucy Buffett
Fish River
October 2007

Huckleberry "Tiny Muse"

AUTHOR PROFILES

Lucy Anne Buffett enjoys "living large" from Baldwin County, Alabama, to Key West, Florida; from anyplace in the Caribbean to L.A. and Montana, with side-trips to NYC and Paris. Inspired by her horses, she writes primarily at her Point Clear barn. Inspired by love, she cooks primarily at the Fish River home she shares with her husband, Mac McAleer. Lucy is a busy girl.

It's been said of freelance writer and editor, Anastasia Arnold, aka Diva, that she is "a great group of girls." Her husband, Michael Ferrell, has his hands full and wouldn't have it any other way. They live a very happy life on the banks of Fish River in Lower Alabama sunning with their cats, Axle and Zelda, and generally being up to no good. They can usually be found on a boat at sunset.

Together, Lucy and Anastasia, the Sistas Edamame, share a healthy love of movies, *Vanity Fair* magazine, bookstores, celebrity gossip rags, Mexican food, and a rather unhealthy love of expensive red wines. ("The good news is I've got Stag's Leap…the bad news is, I've got four bottles!!!!") To say they have a pretty good time is an understatement. As they love to say, "That's just how we roll here in Marlow."

Anastasia and LuLu, Crazy Sistas Forever

CRAZY SISTA *Cooking*
Cuisine & Conversation

Already Done, LLC
200 East 25th Avenue
Gulf Shores, AL 36542
251-967-LULU • www.crazysistacooking.com
www.lulubuffett.com
www.lulusfunfoods.com

Please visit www.crazysistacooking.com
for a listing of Lucy's personal appearances and signings,
LuLu's events, and to order additional copies of
CRAZY SISTA *Cooking*